tagalog
corazon salvacion castle
and
laurence mcgonnell

For over 60 years, more than 50 million people have learnt over 750 subjects the **teach yourself** way, with impressive results.

be where you want to be
with **teach yourself**

About the authors

Corazon Salvacion Castle (MA in TESL/Applied Linguistics) is an author, writer, translator and teacher of English and Tagalog at SOAS. **Laurence McGonnell** MA, MPS is a member of St. Joseph's Missionary Society and lives and works in the Philippines.

For UK order enquiries: please contact Bookpoint Ltd, 130 Milton Park, Abingdon, Oxon OX14 4SB. Telephone: +44 (0) 1235 827720. Fax: +44 (0) 1235 400454. Lines are open 09.00–18.00, Monday to Saturday, with a 24-hour message answering service. Details about our titles and how to order are available at www.teachyourself.co.uk

For USA order enquiries: please contact McGraw-Hill Customer Services, PO Box 545, Blacklick, OH 43004-0545, USA. Telephone: 1-800-722-4726. Fax: 1-614-755-5645.

For Canada order enquiries: please contact McGraw-Hill Ryerson Ltd, 300 Water St, Whitby, Ontario L1N 9B6, Canada. Telephone: 905 430 5000. Fax: 905 430 5020.

Long renowned as the authoritative source for self-guided learning – with more than 40 million copies sold worldwide – the **teach yourself** series includes over 300 titles in the fields of languages, crafts, hobbies, business, computing and education.

British Library Cataloguing in Publication Data: a catalogue record for this title is available from the British Library.

Library of Congress Catalog Card Number: on file.

First published in UK 2000 by Hodder Arnold, 338 Euston Road, London, NW1 3BH.

First published in US 2000 by Contemporary Books, a Division of the McGraw-Hill Companies, 1 Prudential Plaza, 130 East Randolph Street, Chicago, IL 60601 USA.

This edition published 2003.

The **teach yourself** name is a registered trade mark of Hodder Headline Ltd.

Typeset by Transet Limited, Coventry, England.
Printed in Great Britain for Hodder Arnold, a division of Hodder Headline, 338 Euston Road, London NW1 3BH, by Cox & Wyman Ltd, Reading, Berkshire.

Hodder Headline's policy is to use papers that are natural, renewable and recyclable products and made from wood grown in sustainable forests. The logging and manufacturing processes are expected to conform to the environmental regulations of the country of origin.

Impression number	10 9 8
Year	2008 2007 2006

CONTENTS

Acknowledgements

Cora expresses her gratitude to the people who made this book a reality. To Sue
Hart of Hodder and Stoughton for commissioning her to write this book. To Dr
Nigel Philips of the University of London for persuading her to continue with this
project. And most especially to Larry, for agreeing to co-author this book,
contributing valuable cultural tips, and for patiently going through the original
manuscripts. Also to Rebecca Green for her infinite patience, to friends Eric,
Shirley and Arnan, and to Dr Doming Landicho for his helpful advice. Her
heartfelt love and gratitude also go to Roy, her husband, for his endless assistance,
and her special thanks to Louie, Baby, Elian and Divin for their support.

Larry would like to express a word of thanks to Fr. Jose Leslie Andre who kindly
offered advice in the preparation of some of the cultural tips in this book. Thanks
also go to Nenet Penetrante for her behind the scenes assistance and to my family
and colleagues at St. Joseph's College, Mill Hill, for their support. Thanks to Bert
and Leting Tronosco for providing some of the photographs reproduced in this
book. Finally, a word of thanks to Sue Hart and Rebecca Green at Hodder &
Stoughton for their patient assistance throughout this project.

The Publishers would like to thank Roy Castle for the illustrations.

INTRODUCTION

This *Teach Yourself Tagalog* course is intended to supply the beginner with a simple and well-selected stock of words in easy-to-understand lessons.

This book is a fascinating introduction to not only the Tagalog language, but also the Filipino way of life. Here, we will follow the day-to-day 'adventures' of the Cook family: Bill, Louise and Roy. Follow them from the minute they touch down at Ninoy Aquino International Airport, as they check in to their hotel, visit places of interest and attend local festivities while travelling around the country by bus, jeepney and boat. By following them, we will learn much about the ways and customs of the Filipino people, and of course plenty of Tagalog!

The chapters are graded in complexity and each includes a dialogue, a vocabulary box, a comprehensive grammar explanation, drills, practice tests and plenty of cultural tips. Prepare to be informed and entertained: Learn how to haggle at a Sunday market, discover your ability to mix with the locals while enjoying the pleasures of Tagalog learning. *Teach Yourself Tagalog* is a veritable treasure trove of information, activities – and learning.

The phonetic pronunciations in this book are specifically designed for native English speakers and follow standard English pronunciation. They offer the nearest possible approximation of Tagalog sounds, available to the native English speaker. For a highly polished Tagalog pronunciation, listen carefully to native Tagalog speakers.

A list of common words can be found as an appendix for your convenience and interest.

The authors want you to be able to learn Tagalog as painlessly as possible and to develop self-confidence in speaking and writing your new language. So relax and *Teach Yourself Tagalog*!

PRONUNCIATION GUIDE

The Tagalog language is relatively easy to pronounce for the English speaker. It is in fact read or pronounced as written or printed, making it almost phonetic. We can safely say that the pronunciation of Tagalog more or less rests on the five vowels:

a *ah*   **e** *eh*   **i** *ee*   **o** *aw*   **u** *oo*

The consonants are as follows:

b *bah*   **k** *kah*   **d** *dah*   **g** *gah*   **h** *hah*   **l** *lah*   **m** *mah*   **n** *nah*
ng *ngah*   **p** *pah*   **r** *rah*   **s** *sah*   **t** *tah*   **w** *wah*   **y** *yah*

The letters C, F, J, Q, V, X and Z are not strictly part of the Tagalog alphabet though they do appear in the names of people, i.e. Corazon, Josefa, Victoria; places, i.e. Quezon, Luzon, Virac, Zamboanga; and names of things, i.e., Xerox, Kleenex etc.

The letters **b**, **p** and **t** are not aspirated in Tagalog. An easy way to test whether your **b**'s, **p**'s and **t**'s are aspirated is to hold a piece of paper in front of your mouth while pronouncing each letter. The paper should not move whenever these letters are pronounced. Why not try it out? If the paper didn't move then congratulations, you have pronounced them the Tagalog way.

Every syllable in Tagalog is pronounced. Even if a word has two successive vowels, then each vowel is treated as a separate syllable and pronounced. For example, the Tagalog word **Oo** (meaning: yes) is not pronounced as 'ooh' but rather as *aw-aw*. This rule does not however apply to foreign words that have been assimilated into the Tagalog language, for example, Quezon (a personal noun of Spanish origin).

Examples:

Aa	(*ah-ah*)	dirt; filth (*used only when speaking to small children about anything dirty. Also used by children themselves*).
Saan	(*sah-ahn*)	where
Leeg	(*leh-ehg*)	neck
Iniiwan	(*ee-nee-ee-wahn*)	being left (*passive voice*)
Uuwi	(*oo-oo-wee*)	will go home (*active voice*)
Biik	(*bee-eek*)	piglet
Tsaa	(*tsah-ah*)	tea
Maasim	(*mah-ah-seem*)	sour

The more you study and listen to Tagalog, the more foreign words (mainly Spanish and English) you will begin to notice in the vocabulary.

Examples:

Garahe	(*gah-rah-heh*)	garage	(origin: Spanish)
Recibo	(*reh-see-baw*)	receipt	(origin: Spanish)
Kalye	(*kahl-ye*)	street	(origin: Spanish)
Tseke	(*tseh-keh*)	cheque	(origin: English)
Notbuk	(*nawt-book*)	notebook	(origin: English)

In Tagalog, **ch** is pronounced like the '*ch*' in 'cheque' or 'cha cha'. There is no **sh** combination in Tagalog, hence the English word 'shoes' is likely to be pronounced '*syoos*' and the word 'shame' becomes '*syaym*'. The soft **th** as in 'thing' does not exist and so is pronounced as '*teeng*'. The hard **th** as in 'that' is also absent from Tagalog and so the word is pronounced as '*daht*'.

The final **s** is never pronounced as a **z** in Tagalog. Any word ending in **s** is therefore pronounced as an **s**.

The letters **F**, **PH** and **V** are replaced in Tagalog by **P** and **B** respectively.

Examples:

Father	*pronounced 'pah-dehr'*	=	pader
Philip	*pronounced 'Pee-leep'*	=	Pilip
Vanilla	*pronounced 'bah-neel-yah'*	=	banilya
Victory	*pronounced 'beek-taw-ree'*	=	biktori

B, **D** and **G** tend to be voiceless and heard as **P**, **T** and **K**.

When a group of consonants (non-vowels) appear at the beginning of a word, they tend to invite the softening touch of a vowel. These vowels are known as *intrusive vowels*. For example:

School	*becomes*	eskul	*(es-kool)*
Start	*becomes*	istart	*(is-tart)*
Scheme	*becomes*	iskim	*(is-keem)*

The endings of words can sometimes be dropped or changed, and this is most apparent in the pronunciation of words ending in **D** or **T**.

Examples:

Stand	*becomes*	stan	*(stahn)*
Trends	*becomes*	trens	*(trehns)*
Wants	*becomes*	wans	*(wahns)*
Canned	*becomes*	can	*(kahn)*

There are no **WH** sound in Tagalog pronunciation. The straight-forward **W** sound replaces it.

Examples:

What	*becomes*	wat	*(waht)*
When	*becomes*	wen	*(wehn)*
Which	*becomes*	wits	*(weets)*
Why	*becomes*	wahy	*(wigh)*

Tagalog makes no regular distinction between the **I** in 'hit' and the **I** in 'heat', between the **U** in 'tool' and the **U** in 'pull'.

Examples:

Kit	*becomes*	keet	*(keeht)*
Keats	*becomes*	keets	*(keehts)*
Sit	*becomes*	seet	*(seeht)*
Seat	*becomes*	seet	*(seeht)*
Rule	*becomes*	rool	*(roohl)*

Accents have been provided on all words in the Tagalog–English glossary at the back of the book to assist with a more accurate pronunciation.

1 | SA PALIPARAN
At the airport

In this unit you will learn how to

■ introduce yourself and address others
■ greet people at different times of the day
■ form simple sentences

Introducing yourself and addressing others

Dialogue 1

The Cook family has arrived at Ninoy Aquino International Airport (NAIA) in Manila. It is 7.30 in the evening. A friendly customs official approaches them.

Opisyal   Maganda**ng** ga**bi** *po* sa in**yo**. Kumu**sta** ka**yo**? Si Gino**ong Sa**ntos ak**o**. Ano**ng** pan**ga**lan nin**yo**?

Bill   Ma**bu**ti nam**an**, sal**am**at. Bill Cook ang pan**ga**lan ko.

Louise   Ma**bu**ti rin nam**an**. Mar**a**ming sal**a**mat. Louise Cook ang pan**ga**lan ko.

Roy   Ma**bu**ti *po* nam**an**. Sal**a**mat *po*. Roy Cook *po* ang pan**ga**lan ko.

Opisyal   Ikina**ga**gal**a**k ko kay**ong** makil**a**la.

To help build your confidence, we have included two simple pronunciation aids in the Unit Dialogues throughout this book. The **bold** typeface syllables in each word indicate where to add stress, while the *italicised* words indicate a glottal stop.

Talasalitaan	*Vocabulary*
magandang gabi po	*good evening* (polite)
sa inyo	*to you* (plural)
kumusta kayo	*how are you* (polite)
anong pangalan ninyo?	*what's your name?* (formal)
ang pangalan ko	*my name is* _____
mabuti naman	*fine also* (lit.)
maraming salamat	*Thank you very much*
ikinagagalak ko kayong makilala	*I'm pleased to meet you*
mabuti rin naman	*I'm fine too*
mabuti po naman	*I'm fine too* (formal)

Translation

Officer   Good evening to you. How are you? I'm Mr. Santos.

Bill   (I'm) fine. Thank you. My name is Bill Cook.

Louise   I'm fine too. Thank you very much. My name is Louise Cook.

Roy   I'm fine too. My name is Roy Cook. Thank you.

Officer   I'm pleased to meet you.

Did you notice the different ways in which the official and the Cook family introduced themselves? Bill Cook simply said: 'Bill Cook ang pangalan ko', whereas Roy Cook said 'Roy Cook po ang pangalan ko.' Filipinos traditionally place a high value on respect and politeness. They often insert the word '**po**' or '**opo**' into a sentence as an indicator of respect, especially when addressing older people or persons in authority. It is good practice for the visitor to the Philippines to show sensitivity to this cultural value from the outset. By using the more formal '**po**' or '**opo**', you are assured of making a good first impression. Now try using the two different ways of introducing yourself (formal and informal). Write the sentences down, this time using your own name. Why not try recording the new sentences and listening to your own voice and pronunciation. Listen once again to Dialogue 1 and compare your Tagalog pronunciation with that of Bill Cook.

Anong pangalan mo?   *What is your name?*

Did you notice how the official asked Bill Cook for his name? There are different ways in which people may ask your name. Look at the following examples and listen carefully to their pronunciation on the accompanying tape. Tagalog word sounds are quite different from English word sounds. Try to repeat what you hear as closely as you can.

Magandang umaga po.	*Good morning.*
Anong pangalan mo?	*What's your name?*
Joe Bulman.	*(I'm) Joe Bulman*
Sino ka?	*Who are you?*
Si Phil ako.	*I am Phil.*
Sino po kayo?	*Who are you?* (polite)
Si Ginoong John Smith ako.	*I am Mr John Smith*
Sino po kayo?	*Who are you?*
Si Margaret Hough ako.	*I am Margaret Hough.*

Addressing others   *I, you, he/she etc.*

Talasalitaan	*Vocabulary*
anong pangalan mo	*what's your name?*
pangalan mo	*your name*
sino	*who*

In our day-to-day conversations, we do not always use people's names. Sometimes we drop the names in favour of words such as **I**, **he**, **she**, etc. These are known as personal pronouns.

The following table shows both singular (only one person) and plural (more than one) personal pronouns.

Tagalog sometimes uses the plural form (normally reserved for addressing more than one person) to address a single individual. For the Tagalog speaker, this has the same effect as using '**po**' or '**opo**', in that it conveys politeness and respect to the listener. For example, we would normally understand 'kumusta kayo?' to mean, 'how are you (all)?' However, when addressed to a single individual, it can be understood as a very polite way of asking how someone is.

Airport tip

	Singular	**Plural**
1st person (speaker)	**ako** *I*	**kami** *we* (excluding listener)
		tayo *we* (including listener)
2nd person (spoken to)	**ka/ikaw** *you* (informal) **kayo** *you* (formal)	**kayo** *you* (plural)
3rd person (spoken about)	**siya** *he/she*	**sila** *they*

(i) Notice that 'you' (singular) has two forms: **ka** and **ikaw**. The

On arriving in Manila, you may be reluctant to carry any heavy luggage by hand through the airport. You may wish to make use of an airport trolley, but be aware that there is a charge of around 40 pesos. You will need to buy a trolley ticket from the booth clearly marked near the luggage retrieval carousel.

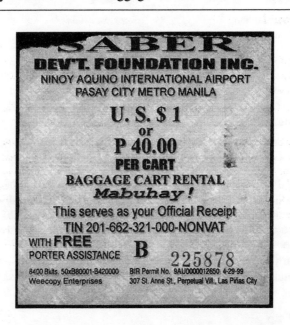

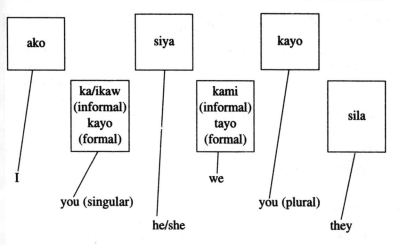

simple difference is that **ka** is *always* used as part of a sentence, 'kumusta **ka**?' (how are you?), whereas **ikaw** can stand alone (without being used in a sentence).

Exercise 1

Listen to the following Tagalog sentences on the tape. Practise reading each sentence aloud. Follow the pronunciation closely until you can repeat each word and sound with confidence.

Tagalog	Literal translation	Translation
Si Mary Smith **ako**	Mary Smith I	*I am Mary Smith*
Si Letty Zapanta **ako**	Letty Zapanta I	*I am Letty Zapanta*
Si Doktor Rivera **kayo**	Doctor Rivera you	*You are Dr Rivera* (formal)
Si Ramon Tenoso **siya**	Ramon Tenoso he/she	*He is Ramon Tenoso*
Pilipino **kami**	Filipinos we	*We are Filipinos*
Estudyante **tayo**	Students we	*We are students*
Amerikano **sila**	Americans they	*They are Americans*

✔ Exercise 2

Underline the correct word.

1. He/ she is a nurse.	Nars (ka, ako, siya).
2. We are Americans.	Amerikano (kami, kayo, sila).
3. I am a tourist.	Turista (tayo, ako, kami).
4. You are a teacher.	Guro (ka, siya, ako).
5. They are priests.	Pari (kayo, tayo, sila).
6. You (plural) are doctors.	Doktor (kami, ka, kayo).
7. We are students.	Estudyante (tayo, ako, sila).
8. You (polite) are British.	British (ka, ikaw, kayo).
9. They are engineers.	Inhinyero (siya, sila, kayo).
10. He/she is a lawyer.	Abogado (kayo, siya, ka).

Greeting people at different times of the day

Exercise 3

Match up the correct sentence with the correct drawing.

1. Magandang umaga   *Good morning*
2. Magandang tanghali   *Good noon* (midday)
3. Magandang hapon   *Good afternoon*
4. Magandang gabi   *Good evening*

Exercise 4

What greeting would you use at the following times of day?

1. 6:00 a.m.   Magandang _____
2. 6:30 p.m.   Magandang _____
3. 12:00 a.m.   Magandang _____
4. 3:00 p.m.   Magandang _____

Saying hello and goodbye

How you say 'hello' in Tagalog depends very much on who you are talking to. Four possible ways of saying hello follow, ranging from the informal '**kumusta**', commonly used with friends and family, to the very formal and polite '**Kumusta po kayo**'. Why not try practicing each of the examples given and think of someone you would use each example with. Saying goodbye in Tagalog is much less complicated than saying 'hello'. Any of the three examples given are acceptable in most circumstances.

Look at the different ways of saying hello and goodbye. All are commonly used. Listen carefully to the pronunciation on the accompanying tape. Try to copy what you hear by repeating each sentence.

Hello, goodbye

1. Kumusta? *Hello/how are you?*
   Mabuti naman *Fine, thank you*
   Paalam na! *Goodbye for now*

2. Kumusta ka? *Hello, how are you?*
   Mabuti naman *Fine, thank you*
   Hanggang sa muli *Till next time*

3. Kumusta kayo? *Hello, how are you?*
   Mabuti po naman *Fine, thank you* (formal)
   O, sige ha? *Until next time*
4. Kumusta po kayo? *Hello, how are you?* (formal)
   Mabuti po naman *Fine, thank you*

Dialogue 2

Using what you have learned so far, translate the following dialogue into English. Use the vocabulary box to help you with words you have not yet met. See how much you have learned in only a few pages!

Jobert meets the Cook family at the airport.

Bill Jobert, kumusta kayo?
Jobert Mabuti po naman, at kayo?
Bill Mabuti naman.
Jobert Kumusta kayo, Ginang Cook?
Louise Mabuti naman.
Jobert Kumusta ka, Roy?
Roy Mabuti rin naman.

Talasalitaan	*Vocabulary*
at kayo	*and you*
Ginang	*Mrs*
rin	*too, also, as well*

Exercise 5:

How would you say hello to the following people? Align the correct answer with the right person.

a.	your mother	1.	Kumusta ka
b.	close friend	2.	Kumusta kayo
c.	doctor	3.	Kumusta po kayo
d.	young shop assistant	4.	Kumusta kayo
e.	the local mayor	5.	Kumusta po kayo
f.	taxi driver	6.	Kumusta

Language Skills

1 Si, Sina

In Tagalog, when using a person's name (including your own) always place the word 'si' before the name, i.e. **si** Cora, **si** Larry (Cora, Larry). When Cora or Larry are with their friends (i.e., more than one person) then '**sina**' is used which is the plural of **si**, i.e., **sina** Cora, **sina** Larry (Cora and her friends, Larry and his friends). In jargon, **si** and **sina** are known as markers.

2 Simple sentence construction

Broadly speaking, a simple English sentence consists of two main elements:

a *subject* (that is, 'who' or 'what' is being talked about) and a *comment* or a word which tells us something about the subject. For example, Bernie (subject) eats (comment), Tina (subject) sings (comment). Of course, there are different types of words and exceptions involved, but we will address each of these as we come to them. Look at the following table and compare the English sentence construction with that of Tagalog.

English				Tagalog	
Manny *subject*	is	an	engineer *comment*	Inhinyero *comment*	si Manny *subject*
You *subject*	are		beautiful *comment*	Maganda *comment*	ka *subject*
This *subject*	is	a	table *comment*	Mesa *comment*	ito *subject*
Bernie *subject*	is		eating *comment*	Kumakain *comment*	si Bernie *subject*

You will notice that the Tagalog is much simpler than its English equivalent.

(i) Cultural tip

> You may have noticed that the Filipino approach to time is quite
> different from a Western approach. Filipinos commonly have a
> more relaxed approach to time. This sometimes irritates
> Westerners. Just relax and be patient! This is normal. A Filipino
> may not consider himself 'late' for an appointment until he is at
> least an hour beyond the arranged time. This is known as 'Filipino
> time'.

3 Formal or informal? Ka, kayo　You

The emphasis on politeness in Filipino culture comes through
clearly in the language of the people. In the Philippines, the
English word '*you*' is represented in two forms: One form is
informal: **ka**, the second is the formal, polite form: **kayo**. At work,
Filipinos address their superiors with **kayo** (you, polite singular)
and use **ka** (you, familiar singular) with their colleagues and
friends. Here is a table showing the differences in use:

Situation	Polite formal	Informal familiar	Plural
Child to parent	kayo		kayo
Parent to child		ka/ikaw	kayo
Friend to friend		ka/ikaw	kayo
Worker to superior	kayo		kayo
Superior to worker		ka/ikaw	kayo
Person to stranger	kayo		kayo
To older people	kayo		kayo
To people in authority	kayo		kayo
Colleague to colleague		ka/ikaw	kayo

Exercise 6

Look at the pictures. Can you decide which is the correct word to use? Is it ka or kayo?

a. A little boy kissing his grandmother's hand

b. A father to a son

c. A husband to wife

d. A child to another child

One-minute phrases

Segunda mano (*seh-goon-daw mah-naw*) Of Spanish origin, meaning *second hand*

Bilugin ang ulo (*bee-loo-geen ahng oo-law*) Literally, *to make the head round*. A common colloquial phrase meaning *to fool someone*

Aywan ko sa iyo (*eh-one-ko-sah-ee-yo*)
Literally, *I don't know with you*. A common Tagalog phrase, used to mean *it's up to you*

Huwag naman (*hoo-wag-nah-man*) This phrase is used as a polite way of saying: *please don't*

Hindi na bale (*hin-dee-nah-bah-lee*) Can be used to mean *not to worry* or *it's not worth worrying about*

(i) **Cultural tip**

Whenever you meet someone for the first time, always use a formal address. Filipinos tend to begin new relationships on this more 'formal' level, progressing to the informal when they feel more comfortable with you. If you appear relaxed and friendly in their company, they will soon feel relaxed and friendly with you, too.

2 | ANONG ORAS ANG ALMUSAL?
What time is breakfast?

In this unit you will learn how to

- check in to your hotel
- ask simple questions
- use the verb 'to be'

Checking in to your hotel

Dialogue 1

Bill Cook and family arrive at their hotel. They will be staying here for five days, before moving on to the Abiva home in White Plains. Try to notice the different sounds of the Tagalog words.

Bill	May kuwarto ba kayo?
Manedyer	Mayroon *po*. Ibig po ba ninyo ng pang-isahan o pandalawahan?
Bill	Ibig namin ng pandalawahan at pang-isahan para sa anak kong si Roy. Magkakano ba ang mga kuwarto?
Manedyer	Ang pandalawahan *po* ay ₱900 isang gabi at ang pang-isahan ay ₱750 isang gabi. Puwede na *po* ba para sa inyo?
Bill	Oo, mabuti, salamat. Saan ako pipirma?
Manedyer	Dito lang *po* sa *ibaba*, sir.

Talasalitaan	Vocabulary
may kuwarto ba kayo	have/has
mayroon	there is / there are
ibig po ba ninyo ng	do you want/like a
pandalawahan	double
at	and
pang-isahan	single
ibig namin	we want/like
para sa anak kong	for my son
magkakano	how much each
ang mga kuwarto	the rooms
isang gabi	per night
puede na po ba	is it alright sir / ma'am?
para sa inyo	for you
oo, mabuti	yes, good
salamat	thank you
saan ako pipirma	where do I sign?
dito lang po sa ibaba	just here below

Translation

Bill   Do you have a room?

Manager   Yes sir, we have. Do you want a single or a double room?

Bill   I need a double room and also a single room for my son, Roy. How much are the rooms?

Manager   The double is ₱900 per night and the single is ₱750. Is that all right, sir?

Bill   Yes, that's fine. Thank you. Where do I sign?

Manager   Just here below, sir.

Asking for a room... or anything else

Did you notice how Bill enquired about the rooms? He asked: 'May kuwarto ba kayo?' It's very easy to make an enquiry in Tagalog. Whether you want to ask about rooms, tee-shirts, sun tan lotion or banana splits, just remember to use the word '**may**' (sounds like *MEH*) before the subject (thing) you want to ask about. Notice the word '**ba**'. This is a simple word which follows the subject and lets the other person know that you are asking a question. Let's look at a few examples:

Tagalog	Literal translation	English
May tsinelas ba kayo?	Have sandals you?	*Do you have any sandals?*
May kuwarto ba kayo?	Have room you?	*Do you have a room?*
May mangga ba kayo?	Have mango you?	*Do you have a mango?*
May panahon ba kayo?	Have time you?	*Do you have time?*

Exercise 1

Here are pictures of some everyday items you might need to ask for in your hotel. Practice asking for them using the formula: 'May (name of item) ba kayo?'

Tuwalya
Towel

Sabon
Soap

Telepono
Telephone

Menu
Menu

Telebisyon
Television

(i) Cultural tip

Hospitality is very important in Filipino culture. Filipinos will warmly welcome a visitor into their home. However, if you wish to avoid drawing a Filipino into an embarrassing situation, try to avoid calling in unexpectedly at mealtimes. Out of politeness, you will be offered food or a place at table. You are not really expected to accept the invitation. Such a situation is potentially very embarrassing for your hosts as they may not have prepared enough food. Refuse politely. If you are offered a second or third time by the same person, then you should eat something, even if it is just a small amount. Filipinos are very sensitive to body language, so try not to grimace, even if you don't really like the taste of what you're eating!

⊙ Language skills

1 Verb 'to be'

Remember the 'comment' we met in Unit 1? A comment tells us something about the subject. When the comment is a verb, then we know that an action is involved. Verbs are 'doing' words which describe an action. For example, Bob (subject) is reading (verb / action word). The dog (subject) is barking (verb / action word). The verb 'to be' is used as a helping verb to form parts of other verbs. For example, we say 'I am working', not 'I working'. The verb 'to be' has eight different forms. They are: be, am, is, are, was, were, being, been.

There is no direct translation of the verb 'to be' in Tagalog. It is usually implied in the construction of the sentence. For example:

Tagalog	Literal translation	English
Guro ako	Teacher I	*I am a teacher*
Doktor kayo	Doctor you	*You are a Doctor*
Nars siya dati	Nurse she formerly	*Formerly she was a nurse*
Nanggaling si Anna sa palengke	Came from Anna the market	*Anna has been to the market*

Look at the Tagalog equivalent of the verb 'to be':

Singular	Tagalog	Plural	Tagalog
I am/was	Ako	We are/were	Kami, tayo
You are/were	Ka, ikaw	You are/were	Kayo
He/she is/was	Siya	They are/were	Sila

(There are more ways in which the verb 'to be' may be used in a sentence. We will look at these in later units.)

Exercise 2

Listen to the following sentences.

Tagalog	Literal translation	English
Turista ako	Tourist I	*I am a tourist*
Amerikano siya	He/she American	*He/she is American*
Pilipino kami	We Filipinos	*We are Filipinos*
Matangkad ka	Tall you	*You are tall*
Doktor tayo	Doctors we	*We are doctors*
Maganda sila	Beautiful they	*They are beautiful*

You will notice that each sentence is spoken slowly. Try to repeat what you hear during the pause after each sentence. Carry on until you become familiar with the words in each sentence.

Exercise 3

Now let's see how well you've mastered what you heard on the tape. Write down a Tagalog sentence to translate the English. The first one has been done for you.

They are doctors.
Doctor sila.

I am a tourist.

_____

They are tall.

_____

She is beautiful.

_____

You are an American.

_____

ⓘ **Cultural Tip**

Avoid giving offence in all things. Western culture tends to be more 'direct' in approaching any problem or difficulty that may arise. Be discreet and you will find that many potential problems will simply evaporate.

Enquiring about meals

Dialogue 2

We join Bill Cook at the reception desk of the hotel. He is asking the receptionist about mealtimes.

Bill	Magan**dang** umaga ma'am. **Ano** ang mga **o**ras ng pag**ka**in **di**to sa hotel?
Receptionist	Aba **o**po. Ang almus**a**l ay **bu**hat sa **a**las sa**i**s y med**ya** hang**gang** a**la**s nu**we**be y med**ya**. Ang tanghal**i**an ay **bu**hat sa **a**las **do**se hang**gang** a**las** dos nang **ha**pon. Ang hap**u**nan ay **bu**hat sa **a**las **sa**is hang**gang** a**las** nu**we**be nang ga**bi**. May room service _po_ sa la**ha**t ng **o**ras.
Bill	May maka**ka**inan bang mala**pi**t **di**to?
Receptionist	Aba, **o**po. Ang 'Lola's Litson' ay may pag**ka**in hang**gang** ha**ti**nggabi.
Bill	Ma**bu**ti kung gano**on**. Hin**di** ba ma**hal**?
Receptionist	Hin**di** _po_. Masa**ra**p ang pag**ka**in at **mu**ra ang hala**ga**.
Bill	Mar**a**ming sa**la**mat.

Talasalitaan	*Vocabulary*
magandang umaga	*good morning*
ano ang mga oras ng	*what are the times of...*
pagkain dito	*food here*
aba opo	*certainly sir*
almusal	*breakfast*
buhat sa	*from*
alas sais y medya	*6.30*
hanggang	*until*
alas nuwebe y medya	*9.30*
tanghalian	*lunch*
alas dose	*12.00 midday*
alas dos nang hapon	*2.00 p.m.*
hapunan	*supper*
alas sais	*6 o'clock*
alas nuwebe nang gabi	*9.00 p.m.*
sa lahat nang oras	*at anytime*
may makakainan bang	*is there any place to eat*
malapit dito	*near here*
may pagkain	*there is food*
hatinggabi	*midnight*
mabuti kung ganoon	*that's good*
hindi ba mahal?	*not expensive (I hope)?*
hindi po	*no sir*
masarap ang pagkain	*the food is delicious/great*
mura ang halaga	*the price is cheap/ right*

Translation

Bill Good morning, Madame. What time are the meals in the hotel?

Receptionist Of course, sir. Breakfast is from 6.30 until 9.30. Lunch is from 12.00 until 2.00pm. Supper is from 6.00 until 9.00pm. Room service is available at anytime sir.

Bill Are there any nice places to eat nearby?

Receptionist Certainly sir. 'Lola's Litson' serves delicious food until midnight.

Bill That's good. Is it very expensive?

Receptionist No sir. The food is good and the price is cheap.

Bill Thank you.

Language skills

2 May, mayroon *Has/have, there/there are* Wala *None (no)*

Remember the word 'may' we met on page 18? **May** always expresses possession of some specific but previously unidentified object or objects. **May** is always followed by the word or phrase expressing the object possessed. Confused? Don't panic! Take a look at these examples:

May problema sila.	*They have a problem*
May sukli ba kayo?	*Do you have change?* (formal)
May taksi na po.	*There is a taxi now* (formal)
May tao pa sa banyo.	*There is still someone in the bathroom* (lit.) or *Someone is still in the bathroom*
May lapis ka ba?	*Do you have a pencil?*

Mayroon (also meaning has / have, there is / there are) is very similar to the word **may**, differing only in that it is used as a form of reply which stands alone. Whereas **may** must always be used in conjunction with a sentence, **mayroon** can be used as a one word reply. Don't be surprised if you often hear people say **meron** instead of **mayroon**. Both words have exactly the same meaning!

Q: May aklat ba si John?	*Has John got a book?*
A: Oo. Mayroon	*Yes he has* (a book)
Q: May problema ba kayo?	*Do you have a problem?*
A: Mayroon	*We have*

Exercise 4 Listening and understanding

Listen to the following example sentences:

1. Q: May guro ka ba?   *Do you have a teacher?*
   A: Oo. Mayroon   *Yes. I have* (a teacher)
2. Q. May barya ka ba?   *Do you have change?*
   A: Oo. Mayroon   *Yes. I have* (change)
3. Q: May lapis ba kayo?   *Do you have a pencil?* (formal)
   A: Oo. Mayroon   *Yes. I have* (a pencil)

4.	Q: May asawa ba kayo?	*Do you have a husband/wife?* (formal)
	A: Oo. Mayroon.	*Yes. I have* (a husband/wife).
5.	Q: May anak ba kayo?	*Do you have any children?* (formal)
	A: Oo. Mayroon.	*Yes. I have* (children)

Repeat each sentence as you hear it, following the sound of the words as closely as possible. Why not try repeating the same exercise, this time without the help of the tape?

Exercise 5

Try constructing five sentences of your own, using the vocabulary provided. Answer all sentences by using **Oo, Mayroon** ('Yes. There is/there are').

Talasalitaan	*Vocabulary*
sasakyan	*vehicle*
payong	*umbrella*
kutsilyo	*knife*
pinggan	*plate*
baso	*drinking glass*
ka	*you* (singular)
kayo	*you* (formal)

1. _____

2. _____

3. _____

4. _____

5. _____

This time practise answering in the negative. The opposite to **may**, **mayroon** (there is, there are, has, have) is **wala** (no, none). This time, answer using **wala** or **wala akong** (I do not have).

Examples:

1. Q: May asawa ba kayo?   *Do you have a wife/husband?*
   A: Wala (Wala akong asawa)   *No* (I don't have a wife/husband)

2. Q: May problema po ba kayo? *Do you have a problem?*
   (formal)
   A: Wala (Wala akong   *No* (I don't have a problem)
   problema)
3. Q: May anak ba kayo?   *Do you have children?*
   A: Wala (Wala akong anak)   *No* (I don't have any children)

☑ Exercise 6

Use the pictures to help you fill in the space with the correct answer (using **may** and **wala**). The first one has already been done for you. The vocabulary box will help you, too.

Talasalitaan	*Vocabulary*
barko	*ship*
dagat	*sea/ocean*
mesa	*table*
kuwarto	*room*
walang kuwarta	*no money*
pitaka	*wallet*
basura	*rubbish*
daan	*road*
sombrero	*hat*
lalaki	*man*
walang pasahero	*no passenger*
taksi	*taxi*
sanggol	*baby*
babae	*woman*

1. May libro si Anna.

2. _____ sa dagat.

3. _____ sa kuwarto.

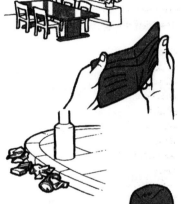

4. _____ ang pitaka.

5. _____ sa daan.

6. _____ ang lalaki.

7. _____ ang taksi.

8. _____ ang babae.

Cultural tip

> Filipino culture is very family oriented. If you want to make a
> good impression with your new Filipino friends, show genuine
> interest in their family. Learning names and nicknames of family
> members as quickly as possible is a good indication of your
> desire to be friendly. Typical Filipino nicknames include Toto,
> Nene, Boboy, Boy, Pinky and Baby.

3 Question words: Sino? ano?, Who? what?

When we want to ask a question we start with words such as who,
what, why, when, whose, where, how etc. Let's take a closer look
at two of these words.

Sino

The Tagalog question word **sino** (meaning 'who' or 'whom') is
used in three different ways:

1. with personal pronouns: ako, ka, siya, kami, tayo, kayo and sila
(I, you, he/she, we, you (pl.), they)

2. with **si** plus a person's name (see Language skills, Unit 1)

3. with **ang** plus a word that tells us something about the subject.

The word which tells us something about the subject is called a
noun; it tells us the name of a person, place or thing. As the
question word we are using is **sino** or 'who?', the noun tells us
something about a person, rather than a place or a thing. Don't
worry if this sounds daunting. Listen to the following examples on
the tape and then repeat them.

Question	Translation	Reply	Translation
Sino po kayo?	*Who are you?* (formal)	**Si Larry** ako	*I am Larry*
Sino siya?	*Who is he?*	**Si Louie** siya	*He is Louie*
Sino ang guro?	*Who is the teacher?*	**Ako** ang guro	*I am the teacher*
Sino ang guro mo?	*Who is your teacher?*	**Si Cora** ang guro ko	*Cora is my teacher*

Sino ang bisita?	*Who is the visitor?*	Ang **babae** ang bisita	*The woman is the visitor*
Sino ang estudyante?	*Who is the student?*	**Ikaw** ang estudyante	*You are the student*

Did you notice how **sino** has been substituted with **si**, followed by the name of a person? Remember that every time you ask a question using **sino** (who?), the reply you receive will either be a person's name, **ang** + a noun, or a personal pronoun. Look at these examples:

Sentence	Translation	Reply	Translation
Sino ang British dito?	*Who is the British (one) here?*	**Siya** ang British dito	*He is the British (one) here?*
Sino ang guro?	*Who is the teacher?*	**Ako** ang guro	*I am the teacher*
Sino ang estudyante?	*Who is the student?*	**Ikaw** ang estudyante.	*You are the student*
Sino ang mga turista?	*Who are the tourists?*	**Kami** ang mga turista	*We are the tourists*

Ano

This is the most versatile of all Tagalog question words and is used to mean 'what?'. It may be used in connection with any of the following:

a noun (a name of a person, place or thing)
an adjective (a word that describes a noun, e.g. big, dirty, small)
a verb (a 'doing' word, e.g. drink, eat, sleep, sing).

Examples:

Sentence	Translation	Reply	Translation
Ano po kayo?	*What are you?* (very formal) (* = what do you do?)	**Guro** ako.	*I am a teacher*
Ano siya?	*What is she?*	**Nars** siya.	*She is a nurse*
Ano ang pangalan mo?	*What is your name?*	John Joseph	*(My name is) John Joseph*
Ano ito?	*What is this?*	**Lapis** iyan	*That is a pencil*

Exercise 7

Let's try using the words **sino** and **ano**. Look at the pictures. Can you ask a simple question using either **sino** or **ano**? Use the examples and the vocabulary box provided to help you.

Talasalitaan	*Vocabulary*
pagod	*tired*
oras	*time*
reyna	*queen*
bandera	*flag*
kulay	*colour*
ng	*of the*
na	*now/already*

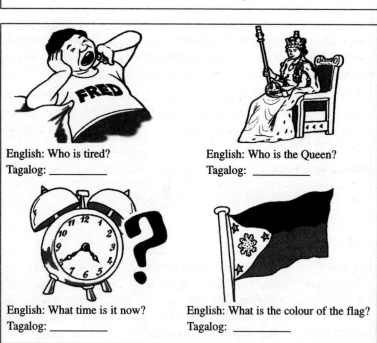

English: Who is tired?
Tagalog: _____

English: Who is the Queen?
Tagalog: _____

English: What time is it now?
Tagalog: _____

English: What is the colour of the flag?
Tagalog: _____

One-minute phrases

Laman ng kalye (*lah-man-nang-kal-yeh*) Literally, *contents of the street*. This phrase is commonly used to refer to a person who seems to spend more time on the streets than at home.

Lutong Makaw (*loo-tong-mah-kao*) Literally, *cooked in the Portuguese colony of Macau*. This phrase is used to refer to something that has been manipulated or 'fixed' behind the scenes in order to ensure a particular outcome (i.e. the results of an election or a beauty contest, etc.)

Pantulak (*pahn-too-lahk*) Literally, *something to push with*. This popular and common Tagalog expression applies to any kind of drink consumed following food. The implication is that it will help the food slide down more easily to the stomach. For example: 'Ako ang bibili ng pansit at tinapay, ikaw ang bahala sa pantulak.' *I'll buy the noodles and bread and you take care of something to wash it down with [drink]*

Kape at gatas (*kah-peh-at-gah-tas*) Literally, *coffee and milk*. This phrase is similar in meaning to the English expression 'chalk and cheese'. It can be used to express notable differences between two people.

Kanang kamay (*kah-nang-kah-my*) Literally, *right hand*. This phrase is almost identical to the English expression 'my right hand'. It denotes a clear level of dependability.

) Cultural tip

A smile will get you everywhere! Many Filipinos are very shy by nature. They may feel nervous when interacting with foreigners, mainly because they are not sure how to behave. A smile frequently offers the reassurance they need and communicates friendliness. If in doubt, try it out!

3 PARA SA INYO ANG REGALONG ITO
This gift is for you

In this unit you will learn how to
■ meet your friend's family
■ say 'thank you'
■ use the definite and indefinite article
■ make a statement negative

Meeting your friend's family

Dialogue 1

Roy Cook goes to the Abiva house to say hello to Jobert's family. He feels a little nervous, but Jobert is at hand to introduce him to everyone.

Jobert Halikayo, ito ang kaibigan ko na taga England.
Roy Magandang hapon sa inyong lahat. Si Roy ako, Roy Cook.
Jobert Ang nanay ko ito, si Teresita.
Teresita Kumusta ka, Roy?
Jobert Ang tatay ko ito, si Juan.
Juan Kumusta ang England?
Jobert At si Pinky at Lovely, ang kapatid ko.
Pinky Maligayang pagdating, Roy.
Jobert At ang Lolo at Lola.
Roy Ikinagagalak ko kayong makilala!

Talasalitaan	*Vocabulary*
halikayo	*come on everyone*
ito	*this*
kaibigan	*friend*
ko	*my*
taga	*from*
magandang hapon	*good afternoon*
sa inyong lahat	*to you all*
nanay	*mother*
tatay	*father*
kapatid	*sister/brother*
lolo	*grandfather*
lola	*grandmother*

Translation

Jobert   Come on everyone, this is my friend from England.
Roy   Good afternoon to you all. I'm Roy, Roy Cook.
Jobert   This is my mother, Teresita.
Teresita   How are you, Roy?
Jobert   This is my father, Juan.
Juan   How is England?
Jobert   And Pinky, my sister.
Pinky   Pleased to meet you, Roy.
Jobert   And finally, grandfather and grandmother.
Roy   I'm pleased to meet you all!

Did you notice how Jobert introduced his family? Study the Tagalog dialogue for a few minutes, reading it aloud. Can you see how easy it was for Jobert to introduce everyone? You can use the same formula for introducing other relatives or friends, too. Take a look at some more examples:

Kapatid ko ito, si Anne.	*This is my sister, Anne.*
Pamangkin ko ito, si Lina.	*This is my niece, Lina.*
Pinsan ko siya.	*He/she is my cousin.*
Bayaw ko si Bob.	*Bob is my brother-in-law.*
Hipag ko ito, si Elizabeth.	*This is my sister-in-law, Elizabeth.*

Pamangkin ko ito, si Paul.	*This is my nephew, Paul.*
Pamangkin ko ito, si Beth.	*This is my niece, Beth.*

Exercise 1

Using Jobert's words as a guide, try to introduce your own family to your Filipino friends. Use the examples just given and the vocabulary box to help you.

English	Tagalog
a. Good Afternoon to you all.	_____
b. This is my grandmother.	_____
c. This is my father,_____.	_____
d. And _____, my brother.	_____
e. This is my grandfather.	_____
f. This is _____, my sister.	_____
g. And finally, my mother.	_____

Exercise 2

The plane journey to the Philippines is very long and tiring. Roy still has a bit of jet-lag and needs your help. Look at the picture gallery of different members of the Cook family. The names and pictures appear to have been mixed up. Can you help Roy place them in the correct order?

a) Nanay

b) Kuya at Ate

c) Pamangkin

d) Lola at Lolo

e) Hipag

f) Tatay

g) Bayaw

Cultural tip

Never be afraid to try out the Tagalog you know, even if you don't feel too confident yet. What you say may not be 'perfect', but it will be highly appreciated by your Filipino friends. You will be surprised just how far a little goes!

Language skills

1 The indefinite article, *a* and *an*

The English words 'a' and 'an' are known as indefinite articles. We use these words when referring to a person or thing about which we do not want to be specific. For example, a house, a car, a doctor, a tree. When the word begins with a vowel (a, e, i, o or u), then the indefinite article becomes 'an', for example, an apple, an aeroplane, an elephant. In Tagalog, there are two basic ways of representing the indefinite article. First, the indefinite article is implied (i.e. estudyante = a student, lapis = a pencil, aeroplano = an aeroplane). Second, both 'a' and 'an' are represented by the word **ng** pronounced (*nang*) when there is an action word (verb) in the sentence followed by an object. For example, 'Domingo has bought a book.' Bumili **ng aklat** si Domingo. 'Mario ate an apple.' Kumain **ng mansanas** si Mario.

Look at these sample sentences:

Tagalog	Literal translation	English
Kumakain si Manny **ng mansanas**	Eating Manny an apple	*Manny is eating an apple*
Arkitekto si Roy	Architect Roy	*Roy is an architect*
Doktor si Jonathan	Doctor Jonathan	*Jonathan is a doctor*
Nagbabasa si Joe **ng aklat**	Reading Joe a book	*Joe is reading a book*
Bumili kami ng mapa	Bought we a map	*We bought a map*

✔ Exercise 3

When you arrive in Manila, you may need to buy a few things before travelling around the country. Complete the sentences below using the sample sentences and the vocabulary box to guide you:

Talasalitaan	*Vocabulary*
kailangan ko	*I need/want*
gusto kong bumili	*I'd like to buy*
payong	*umbrella*
posporo	*a box of matches*
nagtitinda ba kayo	*do you sell*
shampoo	*shampoo*
tee-shirt	*tee-shirt*
street guide	*street guide*
tinapay	*bread*
mapa	*map*

Tagalog	**English**
1. Kailangan ko ng _____ .	I need a map.
2. Gusto kong bumili ng _____ .	I want to buy an umbrella.
3. May _____ ba kayo?	Do you have a box of matches?
4. Nagtitinda ba kayo ng _____?	Do you sell shampoo?

Exercise 4

Translate into Tagalog.

English	Tagalog
1. I need a tee-shirt. (use **ng**)	_____
2. I want to buy a ticket (use **ng**)	_____
3. Do you have a street guide?	_____
4. Do you sell bread? (use **ng**)	_____

Cultural tip

If you don't know the Tagalog word, use the English one. Mixing Tagalog and English is known as *Taglish* and is quite acceptable. It is much more acceptable than just speaking English. If you have a keen ear, you may also have noticed many Spanish words in the Tagalog vocabulary. This is hardly surprising, given that the Spanish occupied the Philippines for more than 300 years. Spanish, however, has not been used as an official language in the Philippines for over 100 years.

2 Ang *the definite article, the*

In English, when we want to be specific about a person or a thing, we use the word 'the'. This word is known as the definite article. In Tagalog, the word 'the' is translated as '**ang**'. For example: masarap **ang** pagkain = the food is delicious; matangkad **ang** estudyante = the student is tall; maganda **ang** dalaga = the girl is beautiful.

Exercise 5

Bill Cook had a little too much to drink last night and is now having trouble with his Tagalog. His sentences are a bit jumbled. Can you help him sort them out? Use the vocabulary box to help you. Don't forget, the correct Tagalog sentence structure should be comment – definite article – subject. The correct English sentence is on the left:

English	Jumbled words	Tagalog
1. The weather is hot.	panahon mainit ang	_____
2. The street is dirty.	ang kalye marumi	_____
3. The car is clean.	kotse ang malinis	_____
4. The house is beautiful.	bahay maganda ang	_____
5. The man is a doctor.	ang lalaki doktor	_____

Bill has now sobered up a little, and some of his sentences are correct. However, he is still making a few mistakes. Can you tell which sentences are correct and which ones are not?

English	Tagalog
1. The room is small.	Maliit ang kuwarto.
2. The Jeepney is colourful.	Jeepney ang makulay.
3. The flower smells fragrant.	Mabango ang bulaklak.
4. The family is happy.	Masaya ang pamilya.
5. The fish is fresh.	Isda ang sariwa.

Talasalitaan	Vocabulary
panahon	weather
mainit	hot
kalsada	street
marumi	dirty
kotse	car
malinis	clean
bahay	house
maganda	beautiful
isda	fish
sariwa	fresh
pamilya	family
masaya	happy
bulaklak	flower
mabango	fragrant
mukulay	colourful
maliit	small

Saying 'thank you'

Dialogue 2

Roy gives a pasalubong (gift) to Jobert's parents.

Roy Para sa inyo ang regalong ito. Magustuhan sana ninyo.

Mrs Abiva Isang kahon ng tsokolate! Mukhang masarap! Maraming salamat, Roy.

Roy *Wala* pong anuman. Para sa inyo naman ito.

Mr Abiva Ang paborito kong tabako buhat sa Inglaterra! Maraming-maraming salamat na *muli*.

Roy *Wala* pong anuman.

Talasalitaan	Vocabulary
para sa inyo	for you
regalong ito	this gift
magustuhan sana ninyo	I hope you'd like it
rin	also
isang kahon	one box
mukhang	looks/appears
ang paborito kong	my favourite
buhat sa	from
muli	again/once more

Translation

Roy This gift is for you. I hope you'll like it.

Mrs Abiva A box of chocolates! They look delicious! Thank you very much, Roy.

Roy You're welcome (polite). And this is for you.

Mr Abiva My favourite cigars from England. Thank you very much again, Roy.

Roy You're welcome (polite).

Expressing gratitude

Filipinos have many different ways of expressing their gratitude. This is part of the cultural stress on politeness. It is a good idea to learn as many different ways of saying 'thank you' as possible.

Here are some commonly used examples:

Salamat	*Thanks/Thank you*
Salamat sa iyo	*Thank you* (used with friends, informal, and family members)
Salamat sa inyo	*Thank you* (formal)
Salamat sa inyong lahat	*Thank you all* (informal)
Salamat po sa inyo	*Thank you* (very formal)
Maraming salamat po sa inyo	*Thank you very much* (very formal)
Maraming salamat	*Thank you very much*
Maraming salamat sa iyo	*Thank you very much* (informal)
Maraming-maraming-salamat	*Thank you so very much*
Maraming-maraming salamat sa iyo	*Thank you so very much* (informal)
Maraming-maraming salamat sa inyo	*Thank you so very much* (very formal)
Naku, nag-abala ka pa, salamat	*Oh, you should not have bothered! Thank you*
Naku. Nag-abala pa kayo, salamat	*Oh, you should not have bothered! Thank you* (very formal)
Salamat na lang	*I can only say thank you*

☑ Exercise 6

Which of the forms of 'thank you' would you use with the following people? Can you see more than one answer for some of them?

a. Guest to waiter   _____
b. Waiter to guest   _____
c. Guest to guest (of same age)   _____
d. Young guest to an older guest   _____
e. Older guest to a young guest   _____

When someone says 'thank you' to you in any of these ways, a simple and polite response is **walang anuman**. Cover up the list of common expressions. How many different ways of saying 'thank you' can you remember? Try to recall five of them and use them on your Filipino friends. They will be impressed not only by your knowledge of Tagalog, but also by your good manners!

Language skills

3 Hindi *No/not*

Hindi is the most common and versatile way of saying *no* in Tagalog. **Hindi** transforms a positive statement into a negative statement. The word **hindi** comes before the comment (what is said about the subject) and the subject. For example, hindi masarap ang pagkain = the food is not tasty; **hindi** mainit ang kape = the coffee is not hot; **hindi** malayo ang palengke = the market is not far.

	Tagalog	Literal translation	English
Hindi + noun	Hindi doktor si Fred.	Not doctor Fred	*Fred is not a doctor.*
Hindi + adjective	Hindi malinis ang kotse.	Not clean the car	*The car is not clean.*
Hindi + ba	Hindi ba nars si Letty?	Not nurse Letty?	*Isn't Letty a nurse?*
Hindi + pa	Hindi pa hinog ang mangga.	Not yet ripe the mango	*The mango is not ripe.*
Hindi + verb	Hindi umiinom ang bisita.	Not drink(ing) the visitor	*The visitor isn't drinking.*
Hindi + personal pronoun	Hindi siya Pranses.	Not he/she French	*He/she is not French.*
Hindi + pronoun	Hindi ito sariwa.	Not this fresh	*This is not fresh.*

✅ Exercise 7

Look at the pictures. Each picture is followed by a statement. Using the word **hindi**, turn each of these sentences into a negative statement.

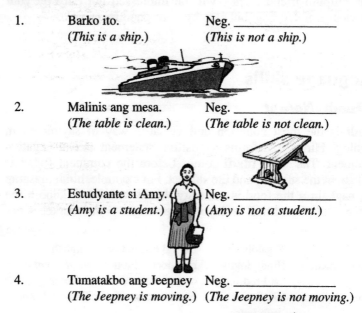

1.   Barko ito.   Neg. _____
            (*This is a ship.*)   (*This is not a ship.*)

2.   Malinis ang mesa.   Neg. _____
            (*The table is clean.*)   (*The table is not clean.*)

3.   Estudyante si Amy.   Neg. _____
            (*Amy is a student.*)   (*Amy is not a student.*)

4.   Tumatakbo ang Jeepney   Neg. _____
            (*The Jeepney is moving.*)   (*The Jeepney is not moving.*)

4. Wala *None*

The word **wala** expresses absence of something. **Wala** is a reply to a **may** or **mayroon** question. Unlike **hindi**, **wala** is followed by a ligatured pronoun. Example: Wala akong lapis, *I don't have a pencil*. Wala kaming guro, *We don't have a teacher*. Wala itong takip, *This has no cover*. However, when followed by a noun, **wala** takes a ligature. Example: Walang kotse si Shirley, *Shirley doesn't have a car*. Walang pera si Maria, *Maria doesn't have money*. Walang panahon si Julie, *Julie doesn't have time*. Look at the sample sentences:

Question	Reply:
May pera ba si Ginoong Cruz?	Wala. Walang pera si Ginoong Cruz.
Has Mr Cruz got money?	*No. Mr Cruz hasn't got money.*
May asawa ba kayo? (formal)	Wala. Wala akong asawa.
Do you have a husband/wife?	*No. I don't have a husband/wife.*
May problema ka ba? (informal)	Wala. Wala akong problema.
Do you have a problem?	*No. I don't have a problem.*
May bus na ba?	Wala. Wala pa.
Is there a bus now?	*No. There's no (bus) yet.*
May pagkain ba dito?	Wala. Walang pagkain dito.
Is there food here?	*No. There's no food here.*
May Coke o Pepsi ba kayo?	Wala. 7-Up lang.
Do you have Coke or Pepsi?	*No. Just 7-Up.*

Exercise 8

Using the formula already given in the sample sentences, give the reply to the following questions:

1. May sasakyan ba sa bus stop?   Neg._____
   Is there a vehicle at the bus stop? *No. There is no vehicle at the bus stop.*

2. May yelo ba kayo?   Neg._____
   Do you have any ice? *No. We have no ice.*

3. May katulong ba si
   Ginoong Reyes?   Neg._____
   Has Mr Reyes got a helper? *No. Mr Reyes has no helper.*

More on Hindi? *No/not?* Wala? *No/none?*

It is common for English speakers to experience some confusion between the use of **hindi** and **wala**. When we use the word 'none' in English, the Tagalog translation of this is '**wala**'. The problem arises when we realise that in English, the word 'no' can also be used to mean 'none'. For example, the response to the question, 'do you have a ticket?' can be 'no'. In this situation, the word 'no' expresses an absense of something. That's why non-Tagalog speakers sometimes make the mistake of saying **hindi** instead of **wala** when they mean 'none'; for **hindi** also means 'no'! Confused? Don't panic! Study the sample sentences:

Sentence	Negative	Question	Reply
Amerikano si Jim.	Hindi British si Jim.	British ba si Jim?	Hindi.
Jim is American.	*Jim is not British.*	*Is Jim British?*	*No. Jim is American.*
Tagalog si Elvie.	Hindi Bisaya si Elvie.	Bisaya ba si Elvie?	Hindi.
Elvie is Tagalog.	*Elvie is not Visayan.*	*Is Elvie Visayan?*	*No. Elvie is Tagalog.*
Malaki ang Australia.	Hindi maliit ang Australia?	Maliit ba ang Australia?	Hindi.
Australia is big.	*Australia is not small.*	*Is Australia small?*	*No. It is big.*

Remember: If you want to express the absence of something or someone, then the correct word to use is **wala**.

One-minute phrases

Walang wala (*wah-lang-wah-lah*) Literally, *no nothing*. This commonly used Tagalog phrase means: *I have no money* or *I'm broke*.

May sama ng loob (*my-sa-mah-nang-law-awb*) Literally, *having a bad feeling inside*. If Filipinos feel hurt or offended, they will typically not express their feelings in a direct manner. This phrase suggests a common Filipino way of expressing feelings in more general terms. 'May sama ako ng loob sa kaniya.' *I have a bad feeling towards her/him.*

Magmahabang dulang (*mag-ma-hah-bang-doo-lang*) Literally, *a long dining table*. This expression indicates a forthcoming marriage. 'Magmamahabang dulang ang anak ni Ginoong Cruz.' *The son of Mr Cruz is getting married.* The long dining table is typical of buffet-style meals used during Filipino festivals.

May sinasabi (*my-see-nah-sa-bee*) Literally, *to have something to say*. This Tagalog expression denotes wealth. 'May sinasabi ang pamilya Santos.' *The Santos family are well-heeled/wealthy.*

Maraming kuskos-balungos (*mah-rah-ming-kus-kus-bah-loo-ngoos*) Literally, *a lot of scrubbing and fussing*. This expression is used in connection with a person who has difficulty in making his or her point. 'Maraming kuskos-balungos si Pedro.' *Pedro beats around the bush a lot.*

Cultural Tip

You may have noticed some Filipinos kissing the hand of a senior member of the family or people of social standing. This custom, known as **mano**, is seen as a mark of respect. Do not be surprised if Filipino children do this to you! It is also a way of showing respect to the visitor.

4 | NASAAN ANG POST OFFICE?
Where's the post office?

In this unit you will learn how to

■ ask 'where?'
■ buy stamps and send a parcel
■ use adjectives

💬 Asking 'where?'

📼 Dialogue 1

Louise Cook wants to go to the post office. Let's join her as she asks the hotel receptionist how to get there. Listen carefully to the sound of the words. You will notice that when a question is asked, the tone of the final word goes up. All question words in Tagalog have this feature.

Louise	**Na**saan ang pinakama**la**pit na post office **di**to?
Receptionist	**Na**sa Kalye Maningning po.
Louise	**Puwe**de bang la**ka**rin?
Receptionist	Aba, **o**po.
Louise	Maaari bang big**yan** mo a**ko** ng direksi**yon**?
Receptionist	Ganito *po*. Pagla**bas** ni**nyo** sa hotel, tuma**wid** ka**yo** at ku**ma**nan. Dumi**ret**so ka**yo**. Pagka**ta**pos kuma**li**wa ka**yo** sa Kalye Rondolo. Ikali**mang** gu**sa**li **bu**hat sa **kan**to ang post office.
Louise	Ma**ra**ming sa**la**mat.
Receptionist	*Wala* pong anuman.

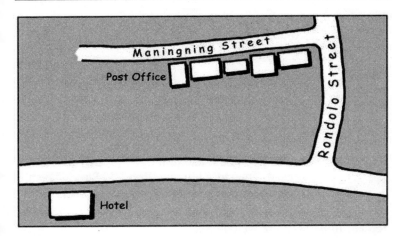

Talasalitaan	*Vocabulary*
nasaan	*where*
pinakamalapit	*nearest*
nasa	*at/on/in/at the/on the/ in the*
puwede bang	*is it possible*
lakarin	*to walk (it)*
aba	*of course/hey/my*
opo	*yes* (formal)
maaari bang	*is it possible* (see also puwede bang)
bigyan mo ako	*give me*
direksiyon	*direction*
ganito po	*like this*
paglabas ninyo	*once you've come out*
tumawid kayo	*you cross (the street)*
dumiretso kayo	*walk straight ahead*
kumanan	*turn right*
pagkatapos	*then*
kumaliwa	*turn left*
ikalimang gusali	*fifth building*
kanto	*corner*
wala pong anuman	*you're welcome* (formal)

Translation

Louise	Where's the nearest post office here?
Receptionist	It's located at Maningning Street ma'am.
Louise	Can I walk it?
Receptionist	Yes, ma'am.
Louise	Could you give me directions? [Could you tell me where it is?]
Receptionist	It's like this ma'am. When you leave the hotel, cross [the street] and turn right. [You] Walk straight ahead. Then turn left onto Rondolo Street. The post office is the fifth building from the corner.
Louise	Thank you very much.
Receptionist	You're welcome.

 Exercise 1

Listen carefully to the 'direction' words on your tape. The pictures should help you.

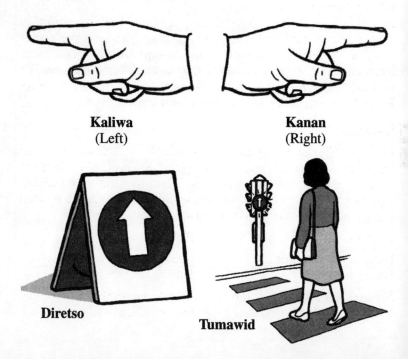

Kaliwa
(Left)

Kanan
(Right)

Diretso

Tumawid

Match the Tagalog with the correct English:

English	Tagalog
1. Turn left	kumanan
2. Turn right	diretso
3. Straight ahead	tumawid kayo
4. Right	kaliwa
5. Cross (the street)	kumaliwa
6. Left	kanan

Language skills

1 Nasaan? *Where?* (location)

In Dialogue 1, Louise Cook introduced you to a new question word: '**nasaan**' or 'where'? She asked: 'Nasaan ang Post Office?' (*Where is the post office?*). **Nasaan** is a commonly used question word which asks where a thing or a place is located. e.g. **nasaan** ang aklat ko? (where is my book?), **nasaan** ang immigration office? (where is the immigration office?). Notice that the hotel receptionist began her reply with **nasa**. This has nothing to do with American astronauts but is the way to answer a **nasaan** question in Tagalog. The reply to **nasaan** should always begin with the word **nasa** followed by the location of the subject of the sentence. For example, '**nasaan** ang bahay mo?' (*where is your house?*), '**nasa** Kalye Cruz ang bahay ko (*my house is in Cruz Street*).

Exercise 2

Listen to the following **nasaan** questions and answers on your tape. Repeat what you hear until you feel confident. Why not try to make up a few **nasaan** questions for yourself? Ask your Filipino friends to help you. First try asking the **nasaan** question, then change places and try giving the **nasa** answers.

Question	Reply:
Nasaan ang Maynila? *Where is Manila?*	**Nasa Pilipinas** ang Maynila. *Manila is in the Philippines.*
Nasaan ang Mayon Volcano? *Where is the Mayon Volcano?*	**Nasa Albay** ang Mayon Volcano. *Mayon Volcano is in Albay.*

Nasaan ang barko?	**Nasa dagat** ang barko.
Where is the ship?	*The ship is on the ocean.*
Nasaan ang mga bata?	**Nasa bahay** ang mga bata.
Where are the children?	*The children are at home.*
Nasaan ang sombrero?	**Nasa silya** ang sombrero.
Where is the hat?	*The hat is on the chair.*

Note: In English, two vowels may occur commonly together (a, e, i, o, u) and be pronounced as one sound. For example, hoop, keep, people, tea, beach. These double vowel sounds are known as diphthongs. In Tagalog, each vowel is pronounced separately and so there are no diphthongs. For example, the word **nasaan** is not pronounced *nasan* but rather *nah-sah-an*. Both a's are pronounced separately. **Remember:** This applies to all Tagalog words where two vowels occur together.

 Exercise 3

Look at the pictures. Roy Cook is confused and doesn't know where each of these places are. He needs to ask a passer-by for help. What question would Roy ask and what reply would the passer-by give? For example: 'Nasaan ang Robinson's Shopping Mall?' 'Nasa Edsa ang Robinson's Shopping Mall.' Use the clue words accompanying each picture to help you formulate your answers.

1.

Clues:
Simbahan
Sto.
Domingo

2.

Clues:
Jeepney stop
Guzman
Street

3.

Clues:
Palengke
Cubao

4.

Clues:
Bangko
Makati

Read out your answers and practise them with your Filipino friends. You will be surprised how quickly you can ask where something or somewhere is!

Buying stamps and sending a parcel

Dialogue 2

Louise Cook has arrived at the post office and is talking to a clerk.

Louise Gusto kong bumili ng selyo para sa mga postcards ko.

Clerk Saan *po* ang punta ng mga postcards?

Louise Sa Inglatera at sa Amerika.

Clerk 3.80 *po* ang isang selyo. Ilang selyo *po* ang kailangan ninyo?

Louise Labinlima. May pakete rin ako papunta sa Inglaterra, airmail.

Clerk 57.00 pesos *po* ang selyo. Pakilagay *po* sa timbangan ang pakete. Ano *po* ang laman ng pakete?

Louise Isang aklat. Magkano naman ito?

Clerk 240.00 pesos ang pakete. Paki-abot *po* sa akin ang pakete.

Louise Salamat. Eto ang bayad ko.

Clerk *Wala* pong anuman.

Talasalitaan	*Vocabulary*
gusto ko	*I like/ I want*
bumili ng selyo	*buy some stamps*
para sa mga	*for* (plural)
saan	*where* (direction)
ang punta	*the destination / going to*
isang selyo	*one stamp*
ng mga	*of the* (plural)
ilang selyo	*how many stamps*
ang kailangan ninyo	*what you need*
labinlima	*fifteen*
papunta sa	*going to*
pakilagay	*please put/place*
sa timbangan	*on the scales*

ang pakete	*the parcel*
ang laman	*the contents*
isang aklat	*one book/ a book*
paki-abot sa akin	*please pass to me/ hand to me*
magkano naman	*how much is it?*
eto	*here is*
bayad ko	*my payment*

Translation

Louise   I want to buy some stamps for my postcards.

Clerk   Where are they going to?

Louise   To England and to America.

Clerk   One stamp costs 3.80. How many stamps do you want?

Louise   Fifteen (stamps). I also have a parcel going to England by airmail.

Clerk   The stamps cost 57 pesos. Please put the parcel on the weighing machine. What is the content of the parcel?

Louise   A book. How much is it?

Clerk   The parcel will be 240 pesos. Could you please hand me the parcel?

Louise   Thank you. Here's my payment (money).

Clerk   You're most welcome.

Exercise 4

Read through Dialogue 2 again. Imagine that you too are making a trip to the post office. Using the dialogue and the vocabulary box provided to help you, how would you say the following in Tagalog?

1. I want to buy stamps for my parcel.
2. I want to buy stamps for a letter to America.
3. How much are the air letters each?
4. Where are the scales?
5. Kindly weigh the parcel for me.

 Listen to the tape. The clerk at the post office asks you: 'Ano pong maipaglilingkod ko sa inyo?' or 'How may I help you?' You may respond by using the answers you have already provided in this exercise.

Talasalitaan	*Vocabulary*
papunta sa	*going to*
sulat	*letter*
magkakano	*how much (each)*
para sa akin	*for me*

 Exercise 5

Listen to the following words on the tape and then try repeating them. Cover the list up and try to see how many you can recall without looking at the book. Why not ask your Filipino friends to help you?

Listen and repeat

stamp	selyo
envelope	sobre
parcel	pakete
scales	timbangan
to post	ihulog
letter	sulat
pen	bolpen
string	tali
box	kahon
wrapping paper	pambalot

Exercise 6

Look at the drawings. Listen to the list of items read out on the tape and tick or circle the ones you can see:

Language skills

2 Adjectives, words that 'describe'

Pretty, tall, good, large, far, terrific, amusing, runny, fat, tired etc. All of these words are describing words. They create a picture of a person or a thing. These words are known in English as adjectives; words that describe a noun (the name of person or thing). Remember pronouns we first met in Unit 1 (page 8)? Adjectives also describe pronouns. For example, he is tall, they are old, we are wealthy. Sometimes we use both adjectives and nouns together. When we do this, then the adjective always comes before the noun it describes. Confused? Don't panic! Look at these examples: clean (adjective) table (noun) = clean table. Good (adjective) news (noun = good news. Short (adjective) story (noun) = short story. The good news is that this is written the same way in Tagalog (adjective followed by noun). In Tagalog, there is only one simple addition to remember: if the adjective ends with a vowel (a, e, i, o, u), then 'ng' is added to the end of the adjective. If the adjective ends with a consonant (any letter other than a vowel), then 'na' comes in between the adjective and the noun. Let's take a look at some examples.

Adjective + **ng**	+ noun	= phrase
maganda + ng	bahay	= magandang bahay (*beautiful house*)
mahaba + ng	pila	= mahabang pila (*long queue*)
mabuti + ng	guro	= mabuting guro (*good teacher*)
maligaya + ng	Pasko	= maligayang pasko (*happy Christmas*)
matalino + ng	estudyante	= matalinong estudyante (*intelligent student*)
Adjective + **na**	+ noun	= *phrase*
masarap + na	pagkain	= masarap na pagkain (d*elicious food*)
maliit + na	kotse	= maliit na kotse (*small car*)
mahirap + na	buhay	= mahirap na buhay (*hard life*)
madilim + na	kuwarto	= madilim na kuwarto (*dark room*)
pagod + na	kabayo	= pagod na kabayo (*tired horse*)

Exercise 7

Look at the four cartoon drawings. Each one is numbered. Now listen carefully to a description of three of the women. Can you identify which ones are being described? Use the examples and vocabulary just given to help you. Can you write down a description of the woman who is not mentioned on the tape?

Exercise 8

Look carefully at the following pictures. Using the vocabulary box below, describe what you see in as many different ways as possible, using as many adjectives as you can. For example, 'Magandang, maliit na bahay' (*beautiful, small house*)

1.

2.

3.

4.

Well done! Whether you are in the house, taking a break at the office or sitting outside, look around you for a moment. Try to describe some of the things you see using the vocabulary you have learned so far in this book. Why not try it out with your Filipino friends, too?

Talasalitaan	*Vocabulary*
mabango	*fragrant*
maganda	*beautiful/pretty*
malaki	*big*
masaya	*happy*
mabilis	*fast*
makulay	*colourful*
mabaho	*bad smelling*
mabait	*kind*
mahaba	*long*
siksikan	*crowded*
mabagal	*slow*
maikli	*short*

malinis	clean
marumi	dirty
kaakit-akit	attractive

One-minute phrases

Balat-sibuyas (*bah-laht see-boo-yahs*) Literally, 'onion-skinned' or 'thin-skinned'. This phrase is used when referring to a *very sensitive person.*

Pabigla-bigla (*pah-beeg-lah beeg-lah*) – lacking in self-control, hasty, abrupt, impulsive. For example **Kung magsalita siya'y pabigla-bigla**. *He/she has an abrupt way of speaking.*

Suwerte sa buhay (*soo-wer-teh sah boo-high*) Literally, *lucky in life.* A common Tagalog phrase meaning someone has been bringing *good luck* to the family. The opposite is:

Malas sa buhay (*mah-lahs sah boo-high*) Literally, *bad luck in life.* A common Tagalog phrase meaning someone has been bringing *bad luck to the family.*

Malinis sa katawan (*mah-le-nees sah kah-tah-wahn*) Literally, *clean in the body* This expressions refers to a person who likes being physically clean and tidy.

(i) Cultural tip

Filipinos will rarely use their hands or fingers to point when giving directions. Instead, they may purse their lips or even nod their heads to indicate the general direction you need to go in. This is normal, so don't be surprised if it happens.

5 | PERA
Money

In this unit you will learn how to

- ask the price of goods and haggle
- ask 'how much?' and 'how much each?'
- change currency/travellers' cheques at the bank
- tell the time

Asking the price of goods

Dialogue 1

All over the Philippines you will find small stores selling basic items such as food and school supplies. These small businesses sell various and 'assorted' items. The Tagalog word for assorted is **sarisari**. These small shops are known in the Philippines as 'sarisari stores'. In this dialogue, we join Bill Cook at a local sarisari store.

Bill	Tao po!
Owner	Maganda**ng ha**pon *po*.
Bill	Maganda**ng ha**pon *po* nam**an**. May s**o**bre ba kay**o**?
Owner	Mayroon *po*, mali**it** *po* ba o mala**ki**?
Bill	Iy**o**ng mali**it** lang. Magka**no** nam**an**?
Owner	Lim**ang pi**so *po* is**ang** dosena.
Bill	O s**ige**, is**ang** dosena *nga*. At ang **bol**pen?
Owner	Tig-tat**long pi**so *po*. A**nong** kulay *po*?
Bill	It**im**. Big**yan** mo *nga* ak**o** ng is**a**.
Owner	**He**to *po*. Disi-**ot**so pesos po la**hat**-la**hat**. A**no** pa *po* sir?
Bill	Iy**an** lang. **He**to ang bayad ko.
Owner	Sal**a**mat *po*.

Talasalitaan	*Vocabulary*
may	*has/ have*
mayroon	*has/ have* (used in replies)
bigyan	*give*
itim	*black*
limang piso	*five pesos*
isang dosena	*one dozen*
sige	*all right/ okay*
nga	*please/indeed/really*
iyan lang	*that's all (just those)*
tig-tatlong piso	*three pesos each*
anong kulay	*what colour*
tao po?	*anyone at home?*
naman	*to you too/on the other hand*
heto	*here you are*
disi-otso pesos	*eighteen pesos*
lahat-lahat	*all in all/altogether*
ano pa?	*anything else/what else?*
bayad ko	*my payment*

Translation:

Bill   Anyone at home?

Owner   Good afternoon.

Bill   Good afternoon to you, too... do you have any envelopes?

Owner   Yes we have sir, small or large (ones)?

Bill   Just the small ones. And how much are they?

Owner   Five pesos a dozen sir.

Bill   All right, a dozen please. And the ballpens?

Owner   Three pesos each sir. What colour?

Bill   Black. I would like to buy one.

Owner   Here you are sir. Eighteen pesos altogether. Do you want anything else?

Bill   That's all. Here you are. (*lit., here's my payment*)

Owner   Thank you sir.

Language skills:

1 Isa, dalawa, tatlo, etc. *One, two, three, etc.*

Filipinos tend to use both Tagalog, Spanish *and* English when counting. This is hardly surprising when we look at the history of the country. The Philippines was under Spanish rule for over 300 years and American rule for 50 years. Both countries have left their mark on the Philippines in both its culture and language. Note, however, that the Spanish spelling and pronunciation used in the Philippines is not the same as the standard Spanish spelling and pronunciation. Look at this table:

Listen to the correct pronunciation on your tape and repeat the words.

English	Tagalog	Filipino Spanish spelling
one	isa	uno
two	dalawa	dos
three	tatlo	tres
four	apat	kuwatro
five	lima	singko
six	anim	sais
seven	pito	siyete
eight	walo	otso
nine	siyam	nuwebe
ten	sampu	diyes

Memorising tip

Cover up both the Tagalog and Filipino Spanish columns. Try repeating first the Spanish numbers, then the Tagalog numbers. How many can you remember? Do not move on to the next set of numbers until you feel confident with numbers one–ten. If you want to memorise the numbers effectively, then try not to swallow too much at once. You will be surprised to see how much more quickly and effectively you are learning! Follow this pattern for all subsequent groups of numbers.

 Listen to the correct pronunciation on your tape and repeat the words

English	Tagalog	Filipino Spanish spelling
eleven	labing-isa	onse
twelve	labindalawa	dose
thirteen	labintatlo	trese
fourteen	labing-apat	katorse
fifteen	labinlima	kinse
sixteen	labing-anim	disisais
seventeen	labimpito	disisiyete
eighteen	labingwalo	disiotso
nineteen	labinsiyam	disinuwebe

Follow the memorising tip!

 Listen to the correct pronunciation on your tape and repeat the words

English	Tagalog	Filipino Spanish spelling
twenty	dalawampu	beinte
twenty one	dalawampu't isa	beinte uno
twenty two	dalawampu't dalawa	beinte dos
twenty three	dalawampu't tatlo	beinte tres
twenty four	dalawampu't apat	beinte kuwatro
twenty five	dalawampu't lima	beinte singko
twenty six	dalawampu't anim	beinte sais
twenty seven	dalawampu't pito	beinte siyete
twenty eight	dalawampu't walo	beinte otso
twenty nine	dalawampu't siyam	beinte nuwebe

Follow the memorising tip!

For the following numbers, repeat the process as in 21–29 in both Tagalog and Spanish.

English	Tagalog	Filipino Spanish spelling
thirty	tatlumpu	treinta
forty	apatnapu	kuwarenta
fifty	limampu	singkwenta
sixty	animnapu	sisenta
seventy	pitumpu	sitenta
eighty	walumpu	otsenta
ninety	siyamnapu	nubenta

Listen to the correct pronunciation on your tape and repeat the word.

English	Tagalog	Filipino Spanish spelling
one hundred	isandaan	siyento
two hundred	dalawandaan	dos siyentos
three hundred	tatlongdaan	tres siyentos
four hundred	apatnaraan	kuwatro siyentos
five hundred	limandaan	singko siyentos
six hundred	animnaraan	sais siyentos
seven hundred	pitongdaan	siyete siyentos
eight hundred	walongdaan	otso siyentos
nine hundred	siyamnaraan	nuwebe siyentos
one thousand	isanlibo	mil

Exercise 1

Why not try out your new knowledge of Spanish and Tagalog numbers?

1. What is the Spanish number for **19**?
2. What is the Tagalog number for **64**?
3. What is the Spanish number for **99**?
4. What is the Tagalog number for **27**?
5. What is the Spanish number for **115**?
6. What is the Tagalog number for **480**?

Exercise 2

Louise Cook was delighted to discover that there is also a weekly lottery draw in the Philippines. She chose the numbers 4, 11, 16, 34, 39 and 45. Can you help Louise to check her lottery ticket? Listen to this week's numbers as they are broadcast on the radio.

2 Counting money

The Philippine peso comes in the following denominations:

Tagalog	Spanish	English
piso	peso	*one peso*
dalawang piso	dos pesos	*two pesos*
tatlong piso	tres pesos	*three pesos*
apat na piso	kuwatro pesos	*four pesos*
limang piso	singko pesos	*five pesos*
anim na piso	sais pesos	*six pesos*
pitong piso	siyete pesos	*seven pesos*
walong piso	otso pesos	*eight pesos*
siyam na piso	nuwebe pesos	*nine pesos*
sampung piso	diyes pesos	*ten pesos*

Exercise 3

Louise Cook found some peso notes in her purse. Using what you have learned so far in this unit, can you help her count the money? Put the subtotal in the column on the right. How much money does she have in her purse altogether?

Sub-total:

1. Limang piso + sampung piso =
2. Limang piso + limang piso =
3. Dalawampung piso + limampung piso =
4. Limampung piso + limampung piso =
5. Limandaang piso + limandaang piso =

_____

Total

Now try repeating this exercise, this time using Spanish numbers.

3 Anong oras na? *Telling the time*

Now that you feel confident with numbers, you will be pleased to hear that telling the time in the Philippines is done almost exclusively in Filipino Spanish. The hours in Filipino Spanish are as follows:

Filipino Spanish	English
Ala-una	One o'clock
Alas dos	Two o'clock
Alas tres	Three o'clock
Alas kuwatro	Four o'clock
Alas singko	Five o'clock
Alas sais	Six o'clock
Alas siyete	Seven o'clock
Alas-otso	Eight o'clock
Alas nuwebe	Nine o'clock
Alas diyes	Ten o'clock
Alas-onse	Eleven o'clock
Alas dose	Twelve o'clock

To say **'half past'** the hour, simply mention the hour followed by **'y medya'** (pronounced: *'eeh mehd-yah'*). For example, 3.30 would be **'alas tres y medya'**.

To say XX minutes <u>**past**</u> the hour, simply mention the hour followed by the minutes in Filipino Spanish (see table). For example, twenty five minutes past six would be *'alas sais beinte singko'*. Quarter past ten would be: **'Alas diyes kinse'**.

To say XX minutes <u>**before**</u> the hour, simply say: 'menos XX _____ [*number of minutes*] **para alas** _____ [*the hour*]'.

For example, twenty minutes to three: **'menos beinte para alas tres'**. Ten minutes to eleven would read: **'menos diyes para alas onse'**, and so on.

To ask the time, simply say: **'Anong oras na?'**

☑ Exercise 4

'Anong oras na?' Can you tell the time?

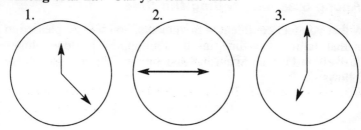

1.　　　　　2.　　　　　3.

4.   5.   6.

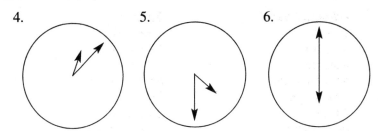

2 Magkano, magkakano *How much, how much each?*

In Dialogue 1 of this unit, Bill Cook purchased some envelopes from the local sarisari store. The question word he used was **magkano** (how much). He said: 'Magkano naman?' (How much is it?). **Magkano** simply means how much. For example: 'Magkano ang Tee-shirt?' *How much is the tee-shirt?* Magkano may also refer to the total sum of your purchase/s. Be careful, however, not to confuse **magkano** (how much) and **magkakano** which means how much each. For example, if there are many mangoes in a basket, unless you want to buy the whole basket of mangoes, you need to ask: 'magkakano ang mangga? How much are the mangoes each?

Responding to 'magkano' and 'magkakano'

Now that you are confident in asking 'how much' or 'how much each', how do you respond to these questions? There are two basic ways of responding: 1) Replace **magkano** or **magkakano** with the price of the item and then repeat the whole sentence; 2) simply give the price.

Question	Reply	Quick reply
1. **Magkano** ang isang yarda ng lace?	₱35.00 ang isang yarda ng lace.	₱35.00.
How much is a yard of lace?	*A yard of lace costs ₱35.00.*	*₱35.00.*
2. **Magkano** ang sombrero?	₱95.00 **po** ang sombrero	₱95.00 **po.**
How much is the hat?	*The hat costs ₱95.00* (formal)	*₱95.00 sir/madam.* (formal)

3. **Magkakano** ang   ₱15.00 ang isa.   ₱15.00.
   kandila?
   How much each are   *The candles are*   ₱ 15.00.
   the candles?   *₱ 15.00 each*

💿 Haggling

📻 Dialogue 2

While sightseeing Louise Cook finds herself at an open market. She begins speaking with a woman standing behind one of the market stalls.

Tindera	Bili na, bili na. **Mu**rang-**mu**ra.
Louise	Magkakano ang sombrero?
Tindera	Ma'am **mu**ra lang *po*. Tig-siy**en**to sing**kwen**ta **pe**sos *po*.
Louise	**Mu**ra? Kay m**a**hal *nga* eh!
Tindera	Aba, magan**da** *po* iyan. Bunt**al** *po*, **ting**nan nin**yo** – isukat *po* nin**yo**.
Louise	(Isinukat) **Med**yo mali**it**. *Wala* bang **ta**wad?
Tindera	**Mu**ra na *po*. Mag**kan**o ba ang **gus**to nin**yo**?
Louise	Sit**en**ta y **sing**ko **pe**sos.
Tindera	Kay**o** naman! *Hindi po*. Malul**u**gi *po* ako. **Si**ge, siy**en**to **bein**te **pe**sos *po*.
Louise	Eto lang ang **pe**ra ko, ots**en**ta **pe**sos.
Tindera	Isand**aan** *po*, **mu**ra na *po* iy**an**.
Louise	Ots**en**ta lang tal**a**ga.
Tindera	Nob**en**ta *po*, may**a**man nam**an** kay**o**.
Louise	O, **si**ge, ots**en**ta y **sing**ko, kung *hindi, hindi* na **ba**le.
Tindera	**Si**ge na *po*, ots**en**ta y **sing**ko.
Louise	Salamat, **e**to ang **ba**yad ko.

Talasalitaan	*Vocabulary*
tindera	*vendor*
bili na	*come and buy*
murang-mura	*very cheap*
tig-siyento singkuwenta pesos	*₱150.00 each*

kay mahal nga	*in fact it's expensive*
buntal	*a kind of Philippine fibre*
tignan ninyo	*you have a look*
isukat ninyo	*you try*
medyo maliit	*slightly small*
wala bang tawad?	*any chance of a discount?*
gusto ninyo	*you like*
kayo naman	*Oh, you*
malulugi	*I'll lose*
eto lang	*just this*
talaga	*really*
mayaman naman kayo	*anyway you are rich*
o, sige	*all right/ okay*
kung hindi	*if not*
hindi na bale	*never mind*

Translation

Vendor Come and buy, come and buy. Very cheap.

Louise How much each are the hats?

Vendor Ma'am so cheap. (They're) ₱150.00 each.

Louise Cheap? Actually they're expensive!

Vendor They're pretty. Made of buntal. Just look at them – why don't you try one?

Louise (*Trying one on*) A little bit small. No discount?

Vendor That's ever so cheap. How much do you want to pay (for it)?

Louise ₱75.00.

Vendor Please! I can't. I'll lose out. (It won't even pay for my overheads!).Okay, ₱120.00 ma'am.

Louise This is all the money I've got, ₱80.00.

Vendor One hundred pesos ma'am, that's ever so cheap.

Louise I can only really pay ₱80.00.

Vendor ₱90.00 ma'am, anyway you are rich.

Louise Okay, ₱85.00, if not, never mind (I won't buy it).

Vendor Okay ma'am, ₱85.00.

Louise Thank you, here you are. *(lit, here's my payment)*

Exercise 5

Imagine you are at a local market in the Philippines. Try asking how much different items are, using both **magkano** and **magkakano.** Use the vocabulary box to help you. Why not ask your Filipino friends to help you, too!

Talasalitaan	Vocabulary
mangga	*mango*
guyabano	*soursop*
dalandan	*oranges*
papaya	*papaya*
pinya	*pineapple*
saging	*banana*
lanzones	*lanzones* (tropical fruit, similar to lychee)
bayabas	*guava*
talong	*eggplant* (aubergine)
ampalaya	*bitter melon*
kalabasa	*squash*
sili	*hot pepper*
kamatis	*tomatoes*
pechay	*pakchoi* (Chinese cabbage)
repolyo	*cabbage*

 # Changing currency and travellers' cheques at the bank

Dialogue 3

Bill and Louise Cook want to change some money at the bank. Bill strikes up a conversation with one of the bank tellers.

Teller   Maga**ndang** um**a**ga *po*. Ano *po* ang maipag**lili**ng**kod** ko sa in**yo**?

Bill   Maga**ndang** um**a**ga nam**an. Gus**to kong **mag**papa**lit** ng sterling pounds.

Teller   Ma**gka**no *po*?

Bill   Lim**an**daang sterling pounds. Ma**gka**no ba ang pal**it**?

Teller   Sis**en**ta y **ot**so **pe**sos po sa is**ang** sterling pound.

Bill   O s**i**ge. **He**to. (Iniab**ot**)

Teller (Bumilang). O, **he**to *po* ang **pe**ra at re**cí**bo nin**yo**.
Bill Nag**pa**palit din ba ka**yo** ng travellers cheques?
Teller Opo. Pero si**sen**ta **pe**sos *po* ang pa**lit**. Kai**la**ngan *po* **na**min
ang pasa**por**te nin**yo**.
Bill **He**to ang travellers cheques at ang pasaporte ko.
Teller **Sige** *po*, pirmahan lang *po* nin**yo** ang mga **tse**ke.
Bill Sa**la**mat.

Talasalitaan	*Vocabulary*
ano po ang maipaglilingkod ko	*what (service) can I do?*
gusto kong magpapalit ng	*I want to change some*
ang palit	*the exchange rate*
sa isang	*to one/ against one*
iniabot	*handed over*
bumilang	*counted*
pera at recibo ninyo	*your money and receipt*
nagpapalit din ba kayo	*do you also change?*
kailangan po namin	*we need*
pasaporte ninyo	*your passport*
pirmahan lang	*(just) please sign*
ang mga tseke	*the cheques*

Translation

Teller Good morning sir. What can I do for you?
Bill Good morning to you too. I'd like to change some sterling pounds.
Teller How much sir?
Bill £500.00 What (*how much*) is the exchange rate?
Teller (It's) 68 pesos to a sterling pound.
Bill Okay. Here you are. (*Handing him the money*)
Teller (*Counting*). Here's your money and receipt sir.
Bill Do you also change travellers' cheques?
Teller Yes sir. But the exchange rate is 60 pesos to a sterling pound. We'll need your passport.
Bill Here are my travellers' cheques and my passport.
Teller Kindly (*please*) sign the cheques, sir.
Bill Thank you.

Exercise 6

How much of the conversation at the bank can you remember? Listen to the tape again and follow Dialogue 3 (page 72). The following statements or questions appeared in the dialogue.

True or false?:

1. Ano po ang maipaglilingkod ko sa inyo?   True / False
2. Magkano ba ang palit?   True / False
3. Sisenta pesos po ang palit.   True / False
4. Nagpapapalit din ba kayo ng sterling pounds? True / False
5. Pirmahan lang po ninyo ang mga tseke.   True / False

 Exercise 7

How do you ask the following in Tagalog?

1. I'd like to change some dollars.
2. What is the exchange rate?
3. The exchange rate is 40 pesos.
4. Do you also exchange Australian dollars?

Use the dialogue and the vocabulary box provided to help you.

Exercise 8

Listening and understanding

A common form of recreation for Filipino men is cockfighting. Many men rear and train fighting cocks in the hope of winning prestige and of course, making money. Let us now join a group of men at a 'sabungan' (cockfighting pit).

1. How much money are they betting on the red fighting cock? ('sa pula')?

2. How much are they betting on the white fighting cock ('sa puti')?

One-minute phrases

Atik (*ah-teek*) Street word for **pera**, *money*. Someone who has a lot of money is **maatik**.

Perahin na lang (*peh-rah-heen nah lahng*) Literally, *just to make into money*, meaning *just give cash/money instead of goods etc.*

Nakatuntong sa numero (*nah-kah-toon-tawng sah noo-meh-raw*) Literally, *stepping on numbers*. This Tagalog expression is used to refer to someone who is constantly subject to scrutiny, *making him/her feel uneasy*. A person who has to constantly *watch his/her ps and qs*.

Isang katutak (*ee-sahng kah-too-tahk*) Literally, *One/a load of/more than plenty*. This phrase is used in connection with surplus or abundance. For example: **Isang katutak ang pagkain sa pinggan ko!** *I've got plenty of food on my plate!*

Nagmimiron (*nahg-mee-mee-rawn*) Derived from the verb **nagmamayroon** meaning *pretending to possess something*. This phrase is often used in connection with a person who is seen to be 'showing off' or 'bragging', or for someone who is ogling.

Cultural tip

As in so many countries around the world, prices often increase when the shopkeeper, vendor or salesperson sees that the customer is a foreigner. Be patient with this. Don't be afraid to try out your Tagalog, even if they speak back to you in broken English. You will find that with a smile and even a little Tagalog, the price will go down. Don't be afraid to haggle in the markets and in small stores. Don't try to haggle in big stores as prices there are fixed.

6 | SAAN KA NAKATIRA?
Where do you live?

In this unit you will learn how to
- use the question word **saan**
- follow directions

👄 Using the question word *saan*

📼 Dialogue 1

Roy Cook is waiting at a bus stop. He's off to Makati, the heart of the business and commercial district of Manila. While waiting, Roy notices his old friend Manny and strikes up a conversation with him.

Roy   O, ano Manny, ku**mus**ta ka?
Manny Roy, ik**aw** ba tala**ga**? Bakas**yon** ka **ba**?
Roy   Ako *nga*. Oo kasama ko ang mga ma**gu**lang ko.
Manny S**aan** ang **pun**ta mo?

Roy	Sa Makati Mega Mall lang kasi masyadong mainit ngayon.
Manny	Doon din ang punta ko. Sabay na tayo.
Roy	Mabuti. Saan kayo nakatira ngayon?
Manny	Sa Sikatuna Village, malapit sa Diliman.
Roy	Saan sa Sikatuna Village? May kilala ako doon.
Manny	Sa may simbahang Katoliko, numero uno, tres, otso. Pumunta ka sa bahay ha? Heto ang mapa.
Roy	Salamat. O, Makati na pala ito!!!

Talasalitaan	*Vocabulary*
ikaw ba talaga	*is it really you?*
sa	*in /on/ at/ in the/ on the/ at the*
bakasyon ka ba	*are you on vacation?*
nga	*indeed/ it's true*
kasama ko	*I'm with*
mga magulang ko	*my parents*
saan	*where* (direction)
ang punta mo	*your destination*
masyadong mainit	*too/very/quite hot*
ngayon	*now/today*
doon	*there*
din	*also/ too/ as well*
sabay na	*do it together/ at the same time*
nakatira	*living / residence*
may kilala ako	*I know someone*
sa may	*near*
simbahan	*church*
numero	*number*
uno, tres, otso	*one, three, eight*
pumunta ka	*you go / you visit / stop by*
sa bahay	*at my place*
ang mapa	*the map*
Makati na pala ito	*ah, we've arrived in Makati already*
	(literally; so this is Makati already)

Translation

Roy	Hey, Manny, how are you?
Manny	Roy, is it really you? Are you on vacation?
Roy	I am indeed. I'm with my parents.
Manny	Where are you going?
Roy	To Makati Mega Mall because it's so hot today.
Manny	I'm also going there. Let's go together.
Roy	Good. Where are you living now?
Manny	At Sikatuna Village, near to Diliman.
Roy	Where in Sikatuna Village? I know someone there.
Manny	Near the Catholic Church, number one, three, eight (Why not) Stop by the house? Here's the map.
Roy	Thanks. Ah, we've arrived in Makati already!

Language skills

1 Saan? *Where?*

In Dialogue 1, Roy Cook introduces us to a new question word: **saan** or 'where'. He asks Manny: '**Saan** ang punta mo? (*Where are you going?*). 'Saan kayo nakatira? (Where do you live?) Be careful not to confuse **saan** with the question word **nasaan** we first met in Unit 4. Although both **saan** and **nasaan** can be translated into English as 'where', both question words perform different functions in Tagalog and so need to be addressed separately.

Saan has two major uses: 1) it represents the place where the action expressed in a sentence occurs. For example: Saan ka bumili ng selyo? (*Where did you buy stamps?*); 2) it represents a continuing condition. Example: **Saan** ka nakaupo? (*Where are you seated?*) When using saan as a question word, the reply should begin with '**sa**' followed by the place where the action occurred in the sentence.

In summary, the difference between **nasaan** and **saan** is quite simple: whereas both questions may refer to location ('where?'), only **saan** questions refer to either the *place of action*, or to *a continuing condition*. For example: **Nasaan** si Richard? Where [location] is Richard? **Saan** matutulog si Richard? Where will

Richard sleep [action]? Don't worry if this sounds a bit heavy going. It will soon become clear to you. Study the following examples and then re-read the explanation.

Examples:

1. Tagalog: **Saan** tayo kakain?
   Literal: Where we will eat?
   English: Where are we going to eat?
   Reply: **Sa** Dad's (At Dad's)

2. Tagalog: **Saan** ka nagpagupit?
   Literal: Where you have a haircut?
   English: Where did you have a haircut?
   Reply: **Sa** Rudy's Barber Shop (At Rudy's Barber Shop)

3. Tagalog: **Saan** sila matutulog?
   Literal: Where they will sleep?
   English: Where will they sleep?
   Reply: **Sa** bahay ko (At my house)

4. Tagalog: **Saan** mag-aaral si Tessie?
   Literal: Where will study Tessie?
   English: Where will Tessie study?
   Reply: **Sa** St Paul's (At St Paul's)

5. Tagalog: **Saan** nakahiga ang bata?
   Literal: Where lying down the child?
   English: Where is the child lying down?
   Reply: **Sa** kama (On the bed)

6. Tagalog: **Saan** sila nakatayo?
   Literal: Where they standing?
   English: Where are they standing?
   Reply: **Sa** harapan (At the front)

7. Tagalog: **Saan** naupo ang babae?
   Literal: Where sat the woman?
   English: Where did the woman sit?
   Reply: **Sa** bagong silya (On the new chair)

8. Tagalog: **Saan** bumili ng sorbetes ang mga bata?
   Literal: Where bought ice cream the children?
   English: Where did the children buy ice cream?
   Reply: **Sa** Ben & Jerry's (At Ben & Jerry's)

Talasalitaan	*Vocabulary*
kakain	will eat
nagpagupit	had a haircut
matutulog	will sleep
mag-aaral	will study
nakahiga	lying down
nakatayo	standing
naupo	sat
bumili	bought
sorbetes	ice cream

 ## Exercise 1

Listen to Dialogue 1 again and follow the conversation on page 76. You will notice that the dialogue has been repeated for a second time on the tape, but this time, Manny's voice has been omitted. Using the text provided, why not try out the role of Manny.

Exercise 2

 Here are some sentences with the word jumbled up. Can you put the words back into the correct order to make a good **saan** sentence? Use the explanation and examples to guide you.

1. nakatira / sila / saan.
   Answer: _____
   Translation: Where do they live?

2. kayo / matutulog / saan.
   Answer: _____
   Translation: Where will you sleep?

3. Nag-aaral / saan / sina Lucy.
   Answer: _____
   Translation: Where do Lucy and her friends study?

4. bumibili / saan / po kayo/ ng sorbetes.
   Answer: _____
   Translation: Where do you buy ice cream? (formal)

5. Si Adam / kakain / saan / ng almusal.
   Answer: _____
   Translation: Where will Adam eat breakfast?

Talasalitaan	*Vocabulary*
nag-aaral	*studying/study*
bumibili	*buying/buy*

Finding an address on a map
Dialogue 2

Roy decided to call Manny on the telephone. Manny is giving Roy instructions on how to get to his house.

Roy   Hello Manny, si Roy ito.

Manny Kumusta Roy, **pu**punta ka ba **ri**to?

Roy   Oo, **pe**ro paki**u**lit mo nga ang tirahan mo. *Hindi* ba masyadong malayo iyan?

Manny Okey lang. Masyadong ma**la**pit nga eh! Ting**nan** mo ang **ma**pa. Nakiki**ta** mo ba ang sim**ba**hang Katoliko?

Roy   Oo. **Na**sa Kalye Vito ito.

Manny Una, *bumaba* ka sa McDonald's. **Iyan** ay **Ka**lye Sanchez. Dumi**ret**so ka **bu**hat sa McDonald's. Nakiki**ta** mo ba ang **Ka**lye Roxas?

Roy   Oo.

Manny Tuma**wid** ka do**on** – **iyan** ang **kal**ye **na**min, **Kal**ye Simeon. **Kami** ay **nu**mero **uno**, tres, **o**tso. May ka**sa**ma ka ba?

Roy   *Wala*. Nag-**ii**sa a**ko**. Hinta**yin** mo a**ko**.

Talasalitaan	*Vocabulary*
pupunta ka ba	*are you going to*
pakiulit mo nga	*please repeat*
tirahan	*residence/ address*
nakikita mo	*you see/ you are seeing*
Katoliko	*Catholic*
una	*first*
bumaba ka	*you alight/ get off*
iyan	*that*
kalye namin	*our street*
kami ay	*we are*
kasama	*companion*
nag-iisa	*alone*
hintayin mo ako	*wait for me*

Translation

Roy   Hello Manny, this is Roy.

Manny How are you Roy, are you coming over?

Roy   Yes, but can you repeat your address for me? Isn't it very far?

Manny It's ok. In fact it's quite near. Look at the map. Can you see a Catholic church?

Roy   Yes, it is along Vito Street.

Manny First, get off at McDonald's. That is Sanchez Street. From McDonald's walk straight ahead. Can you see Roxas Street?

Roy   Yes.

Manny Cross there. That's our street, Simeon Street
We are (Our house is) number one three eight. Do you have somebody with you? (Literally, do you have a companion?)

Roy   No, I'm alone. Wait for me.

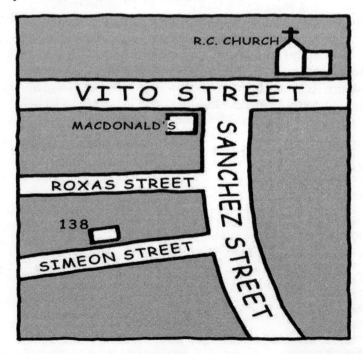

More useful words

Talasalitaan	*Vocabulary*
plaza	*town square*
ospital	*hospital*
munisipyo	*municipal offices*
kapitolyong panglalawigan	*provincial capital*
korte	*court*
istasyon ng pulis	*police station*
sementeryo	*cemetery*
Bulwagang Pambarangay	*Barangay Hall*
palengke	*market*
LRT	*light rail transit*

Exercise 3

Fill in the right word using a word from the box.

> bahay   kasama   ka   mapa   nakikita

1. Pupunta _____ ba sa hotel?
2. Sa Kalye Simeon ang _____ namin.
3. Saan sa _____ ang simbahang Katoliko?
4. _____ mo ba ang McDonald's?
5. Sino ang _____ mo?

Exercise 4

Match up the question with the correct answer:

Question	Answer
1. Masyadong malayo ba ang tirahan ni Manny?	a. Walang kasama si Roy
2. Saan nakatira si Manny?	b. Nasa Kalye Vito ito.
3. Saan dapat tumawid si Manny?	c. Sa Sikatuna Village.
4. May kasama ba si Roy?	d. Hindi. Masyadong malapit ito.
5. Nasaan ang simbahang Katoliko?	e. Sa Kalye Roxas.

▣ Language skills

2 **Masyado** *So, very, quite, too, etc.*

Remember the adjectives (describing words) you met on page 55? Well, the good news is that there are some interesting ways of 'spicing up' your adjectives with small words such as *too, quite, very, so*, etc. These small words are known as 'adverbs'. You can spot them easily because in addition to being small, they always go in front of the adjective. For example, quite (adverb) + handsome (adjective) = quite handsome; so (adverb) + hot (adjective) = so hot, etc. Adverbs give additional information about adjectives. This means that if you want to give extra impact to your adjectives, you need to use an adverb or adverbs. In Tagalog, adverbs such as *so, very, quite, too* are represented by a single word: **'masyado'**. Adverbs work in Tagalog in just about the same way as they do in English. As with English adverbs (e.g. 'quite'), **masyado** can appear on its own. However, when **masyado** is used in connection with an adjective, it is placed before the adjective. In order to help the sentence flow better, **'ng'** is attached to the end of the word **'masyado'**. For example: masyado + ng (very) + marumi (dirty) = masyadong marumi (very dirty); masyadong mataas (too high), masyadong mahaba (very long) and so on. Of course, there are other kinds of adverbs but we will deal with those as they come along.

Here are some examples of adverb + adjective combinations:

Masyado + ng + adjective =			**Combination**	**English**
Masyadong	+	malaki	=	masyadong malaki	*very big*
Masyadong	+	malamig	=	masyadong malamig	*too cold*
Masyadong	+	mabilis	=	masyadong mabilis	*so fast*
Masyadong	+	mainit	=	masyadong mainit	*very hot*
Masyadong	+	madaldal	=	masyadong madaldal	*very talkative*
Masyadong	+	mataas	=	masyadong mataas	*quite high*
Masyadong	+	madilim	=	masyadong madilim	*very dark*
Masyadong	+	malakas	=	masyadong malakas	*quite loud, very strong*
Masyadong	+	mahina	=	masyadong mahina	*too soft (volume), very weak*

Masyadong	+	mabagal	=	masyadong mabagal	*too slow*
Masyadong	+	mahaba	=	masyadong mahaba	*quite long*

Exercise 5 Sentence building

Can you fill in the spaces with the right word combination words that you can find in the box?

Magbabakasyon si Philip at si Tina sa Pilipinas!
Phil and Tina will go on Holiday to the Philippines

Nasa eroplano si Phil at si Tina. _____ sila sa
Pilipinas. _____ _____ (40 c) sa Pilipinas
pero doon sila magbabakasyon. _____
_____ daw ang Pilipinas (17,000 milya _____ ___
Heathrow). Ang eroplano ay _____
_____ na. Sabi ng _____ _____
_____ alas 9:30 daw nang umaga _____
_____ ng eroplano sa paliparan.

Talasalitaan	Vocabulary
masyadong mainit	*very hot*
masyadong mataas	*quite high*
kapitan ng eroplano	*captain of the airplane*
magbabakasyon	*will go on vacation*
ang dating	*time of arrival*
masyadong malayo	*quite far*
buhat sa	*from*

Finding the right Jeepney/bus

Dialogue 3

Roy has decided to take a Jeepney to Manny's place. There are many Jeepneys in Manila so Roy wants to make sure that he gets on the right one.

Roy   Papunta ba ito sa Sikatuna Village?
Drayber Opo. Saan *po* ba doon?
Roy   Sa McDonald's sa Kalye Sanchez.

Drayber   OK *po*, **h**ihinto **it**o sa McDonald's.
Roy   Ma**gk**ano ang pama**sa**he hang**gan**g sa Sikatuna?
Drayber   Dos sing**kw**ent**a** lang *po*.
Roy   **He**to ang **ba**yad. Paki**pa**ra mo sa **Ka**lye Sanchez ha?
Drayber   **O**po.

Talasalitaan	*Vocabulary*
papunta ba ito sa	*is this going to*
saan po ba	*where sir?*
hihinto ito	*this will stop*
ang pamasahe	*the fare*
hanggang sa	*until*
dos singkewenta	*2.50 pesos*
heto ang bayad ko	*here's my fare*
pakipara mo	*please stop at*

Translation

Roy	Is this going to Sikatuna Village?
Driver	Yes sir, where (in Sikatuna Village)?
Roy	McDonald's on Sanchez Street.
Driver	OK sir, we will be stopping there. (literally, this will stop)
Roy	How much is the fare to Sikatuna Village?
Driver	It's 2.50 pesos sir.
Roy	Here's my fare. Please stop at Sanchez Street, OK?
Driver	Yes sir.

Exercise 6

Imagine that you are going to visit a friend in the Diliman area of Metro Manila. Use Dialogue 3 and the vocabulary box to help you form your own dialogue. Use your tape to make the exercise more realistic and more fun:

Ikaw   _____

Drayber   Opo. Saan po ba doon?

Ikaw   _____

Drayber   Okay po, hihinto ito sa _____

Ikaw _____hanggang sa_____
Drayber Tres singkwenta lang po.
Ikaw _____
Drayber Opo.

One-minute phrases

Kilala ko siya (*kee-lah-lah kaw see-yah*) Literally, *I know him/her*. This expression is used to mean that a person knows 'of' someone (has heard of them/shook hands with them or they have been introduced to each other). The expression does not necessarily mean that they know the person as a friend or acquaintance. For example: **Kilala niya ang asawa ng gobernador**. *He/she knows the governor's wife/husband.*

Do not mistake the above with
Kakilala ko siya (*kah-kee-lah-lah kaw-see-yah*) Literally *He/she is an acquaintance*. For example: **Kakilala ko si Bobbie Rodero**. *Bobbie Rodero is my acquaintance.*

Matalik na kaibigan (*mah-tah-leek nah kah-ee-bee gahn*) Meaning *best friend*. For example: **Matalik na kaibigan ko si Jun Terra**. *Jun Terra is my best friend.*

Mabilis magpatakbo (*mah-bee-lees mahg-pah-tahk-boo*) Literally, *fast to run a vehicle*. Meaning: *a fast driver*. For example: **Mabilis magpatakbo ang aming drayber kaya maaga kaming nakarating sa paliparan**. *Ours was a fast driver so we arrived at the airport early.*

Huling biyahe (*hoo-leeng bee-yah-heeh*) Meaning: *last trip*. For example: **Anong oras ang huling biyahe ninyo papunta sa Calapan?** *What time is your last trip to Calapan?*

(i) Cultural tip

The Jeepney is a mode of transport unique to the Philippines. Originally modelled on the US army Jeep, it has since been transformed into the most common form of public transport on Philippine roads. Jeepneys are easily identifiable by their typically colourful and lavish decoration. They are probably the cheapest means of transport available, although not always the most comfortable! If you wish to ride on a jeepney, don't forget that there are few official 'stopping' places and so you will have to inform the driver when and where you want to get off.

Destinations and routes are usually written on both the front and the side of the Jeepney. You can hail Jeepneys in most places except on main roads where stricter traffic regulations apply. If in doubt, ask a local!

7 ANG PAMILYA KO
My family

In this unit you will learn how to

■ introduce the members of your family
■ use **ay** in a sentence
■ use possessive pronouns

Introducing the members of your family

Dialogue 1

At the Abiva house, Tita Abiva is showing her family album to Bill and Louise Cook.

Tita	Ito ay larawan ng pamilya ko. Sa liku**ran**, **bu**hat sa *kaliwa* ay si **Ta**tay, si **a**te Azon at si Jake ang a**sa**wa ni**ya**, si Edith ang a**sa**wa ni Jose, si Louie ang a**sa**wa ni Citta, at ito ay si **Na**nay.
Bill	Ang mga **na**sa harapan?
Tita	Ang mga **na**sa harap**an**, **bu**hat sa *kaliwa* ay si Ely wa**lang** a**sa**wa, si Dino na katabi ko ay bi**na**ta at *pinakabunso* sa pa**mil**ya namin, at ito si Toto ang a**sa**wa ko.
Bill	Malaki-la**ki** ang pamilya nin**yo**.
Tita	Oo, **pe**ro ang mala**king** pamilya ay masa**yang** pamilya.

Talasalitaan	*Vocabulary*
pinakabunso	*youngest*
larawan	*photograph/picture*
ng pamilya ko	*of my family*
sa likuran	*behind/at the back*
ang pamilya ninyo	*your family*
tatay	*father*
asawa	*spouse*
pero	*but*
ang asawa niya	*her/his partner*
binata	*bachelor*
na katabi ko	*(who's) next to me*
katabi ni	*next to*
nasa likuran	*at the back*
ng pamilya namin	*of our family*
ang asawa ko	*my partner*
malaki-laki	*quite big*
ate	*elder sister*
harapan	*front*
malaking pamilya	*big family*
kapag	*if/when*
masayang pamilya	*happy family*
nasa harapan	*in front*

Translation

Tita This is a photograph of my family. At the back, from the left that is (my) father, (my) older sister Azon and her husband Jake, Edith the wife of Jose, Louie, the husband of Citta and this is (my) mother.

Bill [and] Those in the front?

Tita The ones in front, from the left are Ely who is unmarried, Dino (who is) seated next to me, (he) is a bachelor and the youngest in our family, and this is Toto my husband.

Bill Your family is quite big.

Tita Yes, but a big family is a happy family.

Exercise 1

Look at the picture of the Abiva family on page 89. Imagine that Tita Abiva has asked **you** to explain to the Cooks 'who is who' in the picture. Remember, your answer should begin with '**nasa**' as you will need to show the *location* of the person. In your answers, use the words from the box. The dialogue and vocabulary box may also be of help to you.

---

nasa likuran   kaliwa   katabi ni   nasa harapan   kanan

Example: Tatay.   Answer: Nasa likuran, sa kaliwa.

1. Si Ate Azon at si Jake.   Answer:
2. Si Ely.   Answer:
3. Si Tita.   Answer:
4. Si Citta.   Answer:
5. Si Toto.   Answer:
6. Si Dino.   Answer:

The Filipino family tree

Tagalog	Pronunciation	English
nanay/inay	*nah-nigh/ee-nigh*	*mother*
tatay/itay	*tah-tigh/ee-tigh*	*father*
ate	*ah-te*	*older sister*
kuya	*koo-yah*	*older brother*
kapatid	*kah-pah-teed*	*sibling*
kapatid na lalaki	*kah-pah teed nah lah-lah-kee*	*brother*
kapatad na babae	*kah-pah teed nah bah-bah-ee*	*sister*
tiyo	*tee-yaw*	*uncle*
tiya	*tee-yah*	*aunt*
lolo	*law-law*	*grandfather*
lola	*law-lah*	*grandmother*
apo	*ah-paw*	*grandcild*
bayaw	*bah-yao*	*brother-in-law*
hipag	*hee-pahg*	*sister-in-law*
pamangkin	*pah-mahng-keen*	*nephew/niece*
asawa	*ah-sah-wah*	*husband/wife*

⚙ Language skills

1 Ko, mo, niya, namin, natin, ninyo, nila
Possessive pronouns

If you look closely at Dialogue 1, you will notice that the words **ko** (*my*), **niya** (*his her*) and **namin** (*our*) have one thing in common: they express *ownership* or *possession*. These words are known as **possessive pronouns**. Possessive pronouns are used in two basic ways: 1) they tell us about *ownership*, i.e. 'ang pasaporte **ko**' (*my* passport), 'ang guro **namin**' (*our* teacher), 2) they show *relationship* with a person, i.e., 'ang nanay **ko**' (*my* mother), 'ang tatay **namin**' (*our* father). You will notice that in English the possessive pronoun goes in front of the thing (*noun*) it possesses. For example: **your** name, **his** house, **my** father, **our** country and so on. In Tagalog, the order is reversed with the possessive pronoun being placed *after* the word it possesses. For example: pangalan **mo** (*your* name), bahay **niya** (*his* house), tatay **ko** (*my* father), bansa **natin** (*our* country) and so on. One small but important difference to watch out for is the first person plural. In English, we simply say '*our* house', '*our* street', '*our* village'. Tagalog has two possibilities: one which *includes* the listener (**natin**), and another which *excludes* the listener (**namin**). For example, if I were to speak to you about 'tatay **natin**' or '*our* father', then the use of the inclusive form (**natin**) makes it clear that he is also *your* father. If however I talk about 'tatay **namin**', then the use of the exclusive form (**namin**) indicates that he is '*our*' father (me, my brothers and sisters) while not implying that he is also your father. Look at the following table:

Personal possessive pronouns:

Number	English	Tagalog
1st person (singular)	*my*	**ko**
(plural)	*our*	**namin** (exclusive of listener/s)
	our	**natin** (inclusive of listener/s)
2nd person (singular)	*your*	**mo**
(plural)	*your*	**ninyo**
3rd person (singular)	*his/her*	**niya**
(plural)	*their*	**nila**

Here are some example sentences:

English	**Tagalog**

1. He/she is **my friend.**   *Kaibigan ko siya*
2. Is he **your driver?**   *Drayber mo ba siya?*
3. We are **their guest**.   *Bisita nila kami*
4. Cora is **our teacher**.   *Guro namin si Cora*
5. Are you **his friend**?   *Kaibigan ka ba niya?*

Exercise 2

Translate the following sentences, using the vocabulary box to help you:

1. Margaret is my friend.
2. John is his brother.
3. Ann is their visitor.
4. They are my classmates.

Exercise 3 Listening

Talasalitaan	*Vocabulary*
bisita	*guest*
mga kaklase	*classmates*
guro	*teacher*

 Listen carefully to the accompanying exercise, then look at the pictures. Can you tell who is related to whom?

1.

2.

3.    4.

🖸 Language skills

2 Ng Of/of the
Ni/nina + Name of person/s

Another new word used in Dialogue was '**ng**' (pronounced *nang*). **Ng** is also used to show **possession**. For example: 'ang laruan **ng** bata' (literally, *the toy **of** the child = the child's toy*), 'baso **ng** tubig' (a glass **of** water), 'ang pintuan **ng** bahay' (*the doorway **of** the house*). These examples show that **ng** can be translated into English as '**of**' or '**of the**'. Try to remember, however, that in English, the word **of** often disappears completely and is replaced by an **apostrophe** + '**s** For example, 'the mother **of** the bride' becomes 'the bride's mother', 'the book **of** the student' becomes 'the student's book'. When using a person's name, however, we use the word **ni** instead of **ng,** indicating that the person concerned is the <u>possessor</u>. For example, 'Ito ang bahay **ni** Mary' *(this is Mary's house).* If more than one person is involved, then **nina** is used (the plural of **ni**). For example: 'Ka-opisina siya **nina** Tony'. *He is an officemate of Tony and his friend/s.*

Look at the following examples:

Tagalog	**English**
ni Jose	**of** Jose/ Jose's
nina Jose	**of** Jose and his friend/s'
ni Mary	**of** Mary/ Mary's
nina Mary	**of** Mary and her friend/s'
ng bata	**of the** child / the child's
ng mga babae	**of the** women/ the women's
ng Presidente	**of the** President/ the President's
ni Queen Elizabeth	**of** Queen Elizabeth/ Queen Elizabeth's

Here are some full sentences to show this expression in use.

1. Anak **ni** Queen Elizabeth si Prince Charles.
   *Prince Charles is the son **of** Queen Elizabeth.*

2. Kotse **ng** Presidente ito.
   *This is the car **of the** President.*

3. Doktor **ni** Bennie si Doktor Cruz.
   Doctor Cruz is Bennie's doctor.

4. Maleta **ng** mga babae iyan.
   That is the women's suitcase.

Exercise 4

Fill in the blank with the correct word. Refer to the Language skills on pages 94–5.

1. Kailangan mo ba _____ (ng/ni) tulong ko?
2. Hindi _____ (namin/nina) alam ang tirahan ni Phil.
3. Anak _____ (ni/ng) ginoong Abiva si Jobert.
4. Sino ang kapatid _____ (ng/ng mga) guro?
5. Gusto _____ (ko/nina) ang bagong kotse mo.
6. Nasa mesa ang pagkain _____ (ng/ni) mga bisita.
7. Bukas, narito ang guro _____ (niya/nina).

Exercise 5

Look at the pictures and write a sentence about each using either *ng*, *ni* or *nina*.

Using '*ay*' in a sentence

Dialogue 2

At the Abiva house, Bill, Louise and Tita continue their conversation.

Louise	Ilan ang anak ninyo?
Tita	Lima. Isa lang ang walang asawa. Heto ang larawan ng mga anak at mga apo ko.
Louise	Sila ay magaganda.
Tita	Kayo, ilan ang anak ninyo?
Louise	Dalawa lang. Si John at si Roy.

Tita	May anak ba si John?
Bill	Oo. Dalawa. Si Adam at si Lucy.
Tita	Maliit ang pamilya ninyo!
Louise	Oo *nga.*
Katulong	Eto *po* ang **pam**palamig.
Tita	Salamat. Tayo ay magpalamig muna.

Talasalitaan	*Vocabulary*
ilan	*how many*
ang anak ninyo	*your child*
lima sila	*there are five*
isa lang	*only one*
walang asawa	*not married*
ng mga anak	*of the children*
pampalamig	*refreshment*
mga apo ko	*my grandchildren*
dalawa lang	*only two*
anak ninyo	*your children*
pamilya ninyo	*your family*
oo nga	*I agree*
eto po	*here you are*
magpalamig muna	*have some refreshments first*

Translation

Louise	How many children do you have?
Tita	Five. Only one is not (yet) married. Here is a photo of my children and my grandchildren.
Louise	They are beautiful.
Tita	How many children do you have? (*literally, and you, how many children do you have?*)
Louise	Just two. John and Roy.
Tita	Does John have children?
Bill	Yes. Two. Adam and Lucy.
Tita	Your family is small!
Louise	I agree.
Maid	Here is your refreshment ma'am!
Tita	Thank you. Let's have something to drink first (literally, *refreshments*).

✔ Exercise 6

Read the following story. You will notice that several words are
missing from the Tagalog dialogue. Using the vocabulary box
provided, fill in the missing words. Use the English translation to
help you.

Donna visits Chit's family in Batangas

Donna	Magandang araw po. Kumusta po kayo? Si Donna po ako. _____ ako ni Chit.
Host	Ikaw ba si Donna? Pasok ka. _____ ka pala. Ilan kayong _____?
Donna	Tatlo po. Ako, ang _____ , si Eloisa ang pangalawa, at si Mila, ang _____. Lahat po kami walang asawa.
Host	Ganoon ba? Kumusta ang mga magulang mo?
Donna	Mabuti po naman sila. Kayo po, ilan po ang _____ _____?
Host	Apat ang _____ _____.
Donna	_____ ang may asawa?
Host	Isa lang _____ _____. Si Zeny at dalawa na _____ _____ _____. Magpalamig ka muna.
Donna	Maraming salamat po. Ang sarap nito! Kung gayon may _____ na pala kayo.
Host	Oo at maligaya naman ako!
Donna	Mabuti naman at nakilala ko kayo sa wakas.
Host	Ako rin!

Translation

Donna	Good morning (*polite*). How are you? I am Donna – Chit's friend.
Host	Are you Donna? Ah, please come in! You are indeed tall! How many brothers and sisters do you have?
Donna	Three ma'am. I'm the eldest, Eloisa the second and Mila is the youngest. We are all still single.
Host	I see. And how are your parents?
Donna	They are fine ma'am. And how about you ma'am, how many children do you have?

Host	I have four children.
Donna	Are any of them married yet?
Host	Only one so far. Zeny. She has two children. Please have some refreshment.
Donna	Thank you. This is delicious! So, you now have grandchildren!
Host	Yes, and I am very happy about that!
Donna	It is so nice to meet you at last.
Host	You too!

Talasalitaan	Vocabulary
pinakabunso	youngest
matangkad	tall
magkakapatid	siblings
apo	grandchild
pinakamatanda	eldest
ang anak niya	her children
ang may-asawa	(the) married (one)
anak ko	my children
ilan	how many

Exercise 7

Which question matches which answer?

1. Anak mo ba siya?

2. Nasa silangan ng Pilipinas ang Davao.

3. Ano ang tawag sa matandang kapatid na lalaki?

4. Asawa kaya ni Azon si Jake?

5. Sa ospital tayo bumibili ng selyo.

A. Oo. Asawa yata ni Azon si Jake.

B. Kuya.

C. Hindi. Sa tindahan tayo bumibili ng selyo.

D. Hindi. Hindi ko siya anak.

E. Wala. Nasa Timog ito.

☑ Exercise 8 Speaking and listening activity

Listen to the dialogue on the tape. How many of the words or phrases from the conversation between Pepot and Donna can you remember ? Listen to the tape again. Here are some snatches from the dialogue. Fill in the missing parts. When you have completed the task, why not ask one of your Filipino friends to help you act out the dialogue?

Donna O, tuloy ba _____ _____ _____ kina Peps? *(our picnic)*

Pepot Sino ba ang _____ _____ ___ _____? *(older of the two?)*

Donna _____ _____ ang tanda ni Romy kay Peps. *(three years)*

Pepot _____ _____ si Peps. *(younger)*

Donna _____ _____ng anak ni Romy. *(what is the name)*

Pepot _____ ____ _____ _____. *(Don't you know?)*

Donna Oo. _____ _____ ____ ____ ____. *(she is my mother's sister).*

Pepot Bibili ako _____ _____ ____ _____ . *(some cold drinks)*

Donna Sa palagay ko, magiging masaya _____ _____ ____ ___ *(this picnic).*

⚙ Language skills

3 Ay

Life and language would seem rather boring if we had only one set way of communicating correctly with one another. Fortunately, we can vary sentences in order to add spice, variety and colour to our language. For example, *'Hello Bob, how are you this morning?'* becomes *'Morning Bob, how are you?'* or perhaps *'How are you this morning, Bob?'*. All of these simple sentences communicate the same message, but all are slightly different. Tagalog does much the same thing with the simple word **ay** (pronounced *eye*). This little word has no direct English translation but is a veritable gold nugget when it comes to adding variety to our spoken Tagalog. The good news for English speakers is that the word **ay** follows the normal English language sentence structure. It *inverts* the usual sequence of Tagalog words making it resemble its English equivalent. For example, *he is good* (**mabuti siya**) becomes *siya ay mabuti*. You may be forgiven for thinking that **ay** means 'is' or that **ay** is the equivalent of the English verb 'to be', but this is not so. A sentence involving the use of **ay** does not differ in meaning from the sentence without **ay**. It simply offers variety and assists the flow of the sentence. **Ay** can also be used as a more formal style and as such is commonly found in writing, lectures, sermons and so on, although this is only used after vowels. You will no doubt have noticed the use of **ay** in Dialogue 1, together with the shortened form of **'y**. Both forms are correct. You will notice that the shortened **'y** form is most commonly used when following words which end with a vowel. This is not always the case however. For example: **Ito'y maganda**, *This is pretty.* **Ikaw'y guro**, *You are a teacher.*

Here are some more examples.

English	Tagalog	Inverted (ay sentence)
They are Americans	Amerikano sila	Sila *ay* Amerikano
The queue is long	Mahaba ang pila	Ang pila *ay* mahaba
Is the chair clean?	*Malinis ba ang silya?*	*Ang silya ba ay malinis?*
Ann is industrious	Masipag si Ann.	Si Ann *ay* masipag
They are nurses	Mga narses sila.	Sila'*y* mga narses
The vegetable is fresh	Sariwa ang gulay	Ang gulay *ay* sariwa.
The mango is sour	Maasim ang mangga	Ang mangga'*y* maasim
The car is at the garage	Nasa garahe ang kotse	Ang kotse'*y* nasa garahe
He is a doctor here	Doktor siya dito	Siya *ay* doktor dito

Exercise 9

Convert the following standard Tagalog sentences into their equivalent **ay** form sentences:

1. Anak mo siya.
2. May tiket ako.
3. Malamig ang tubig.
4. Mainit ngayon.
5. Masarap ang handa mo.

Talasalitaan	*Vocabulary*
tiket	*ticket*
malamig	*cold*
tubig	*water*
masarap	*delicious*
handa	*food preparation*

One-minute phrases

Maghabol sa tambol mayor (*mahg-hah-bawl sah tahm-bawl mah-yor*) Literally, *to chase the principal drum (of a marching band)*. This expression is applied to somebody who has been cheated (i.e. in money, relationships, financial deals etc.). The expression implies that the victim has no chance of finding justice. Marching bands are a common sight in the Philippines, especially during fiestas, funerals and weddings. *To chase the principal drum*, as the saying goes, takes some doing, as it is a heavy instrument to run away with! The phrase is similar in meaning to the English expressions, *caught napping* or *caught with his pants down!*

Mukhang Biyernes Santo (*mook-hahng beeyer-ness sahn-taw*) Literally, *a face like Good Friday!* This expression is applied to a person who looks gloomy. As a Christian country, the Philippines traditionally observes the celebration of Holy Week. Part of Holy Week is the observance of Good Friday, the solemn remembrance of the day Jesus died. Filipinos tend to disapprove of festivities on Good Friday as a sign of respect for the **Santo Intiero** or *Dead Christ*. Anyone who wears a solemn expression on their face at other times may find themselves on the receiving end of the comment, **Mukhang Biyernes Santo ka!** *You've got a face like Good Friday!*

Parang pinagbiyak na bunga (*pah-rahng pee-nahg-bee-yahk nah boo-ngah*) Literally, *Looks like a fruit chopped in two*. When a piece of fruit is chopped into two halves, the two halves are generally identical. This expression is commonly used therefore to refer to twins.

Kaibigang matalik/matalik na kaibigan (*kah-ee-bee-gahng mah-tah-leek/mah-tah-leek na kah-ee-bee-gahn*) a term which means *best friend.*

Kasa-kasama (*kah-sah-kah-sah-mah*) This expression is used to identify a person commonly seen with another person. For example: **Laging kasa-kasama ni Jun si Bobbie.** *Bobbie is always seen in Jun's company.*

Cultural tip

When meeting the family of a Filipino friend for the first time do not be surprised if they appear to be more 'formal' than relaxed with you. This is normal. Many Filipinos often feel initimidated by foreigners, but as they gradually get to know you, they will begin to feel more relaxed. Don't be afraid to try out your Tagalog, even if you make mistakes. They will appreciate your efforts and will warm to you more quickly.

8 SA RESTAWRAN
At the restaurant

In this unit you will learn how to

■ order your drinks
■ choose some typical Filipino food
■ ask for your bill
■ make words plural using '**mga**'

Ordering your drinks

Dialogue 1

Bill, Louise and Roy have decided to eat dinner at the local *Kamayan* restaurant.

Waiter Magan**dang** ga**bi** *po*. Mali**gay**ang pagda**ting** sa 'Ka**may**an'.
Bill May **me**sa ba ka**yo** pa**ra** sa tat**lo**?
Waiter May**roon** *po*. **He**to *po* ang **me**sa ni**nyo**.
Bill Salamat. (*Naupo* ang mag-**a**nak)
Waiter Sir, **he**to *po* ang menu **na**min. **A**no *po* ang **gu**sto ninyong inu**min**?
Bill Sanda**li** lang. Louise?
Louise Malam**ig** na **tu**big lang **mu**na. May mineral water ba ka**yo**?
Waiter May**roon** *po*. Ka**yo** *po* sir?
Bill San Miguel beer.
Waiter (kay Roy) Sa in**yo** *po*, sir?
Roy White wine ang sa **a**kin.
Waiter Okey *po*. Pu**lu**tan sir, **I**big *po* ba ni**nyo**.
Bill Oo. **A**no ang pulu**tan** nin**yo**?
Waiter **Ta**pa at lit**son** *po*. I**sang** pla**to** o i**sang** pla**ti**to *po*?

Bill   Parang masarap. O sige. Isang plato. Salamat.
Waiter   Wala pong anuman.

Talasalitaan	*Vocabulary*
maligayang pagdating	*welcome*
may mesa ba kayo	*do you have a table*
para sa tatlo	*for three*
malamig na tubig	*cold water*
ang mesa ninyo	*your table*
ang menu namin	*our menu*
ang gusto ninyo	*what you like*
platito	*saucer*
muna	*first/for the time being*
parang	*seems/like*
kay	*to* (+ *name*)
ang sa akin	*mine*
pulutan	*finger food to go with drinks*
tapa	*sliced fried beef*
litson	*suckling pig*
plato	*plate*

Translation

Waiter Good evening sir. Welcome to *Kamayan*.
Bill   Do you have a table for three?
Waiter Yes sir. Here is your table, sir.
Bill   Thank you. (The family sits down)
Waiter Sir, here's our menu. What would you like to drink?
Bill   Just one moment. (You) Louise?
Louise I'll have cold water (for the time being). Do you have any mineral water?
Waiter Yes, we have ma'am. And you sir?
Bill   San Miguel beer.
Waiter (to Roy) And you, sir?
Roy   I'll have a white wine.
Waiter OK sir. Finger foods (to go with the drinks) sir, would you like some?
Bill   Yes. What are your pulutan?
Waiter Sliced fried beef and suckling pig sir. One plate sir, or one saucer?

Bill   Seems delicious. OK, one plate (of finger foods). Thank
              you.
Waiter   You're welcome sir.

🐦 Exercise 1

Can you say the following?

1. There are four of us. (We are four)
2. Do you have a table for four persons?
3. I want (a glass of) cold water.
4. I would like (a bottle of) San Miguel beer.
5. Do you have a big table?

🐦 Exercise 2

Look at Dialogue 1 again. Based on this dialogue, can you tell
which of the following sentences are true and which are false?

1. Para sa dalawa ang mesa.
2. Ang mesa ay para sa tatlo.
3. Mabuti para kay Louise ang malamig na tubig.
4. Gusto ni Louise ng malamig na beer.
5. Hindi gusto ni Bill ang inumin.
6. San Miguel Beer yata ang gusto ni Bill.

📽 Language skills

1 Mga *Making words plural*

Dialogue 1 introduced us to the word 'mga' (pronounced *mah-
ngah*). In jargon, this word is known as a pluraliser. A pluraliser is
a word which lets us know that more than one person, place or
thing is being referred to. In English, there are three basic ways of
indicating the plural: 1) by adding the letter 's' to the end of the
pluralised word. Hence, suitcase becomes 'suitcases'; 2) by
changing a single letter in the pluralised word. Here, woman
becomes women; 3) by adding 'es' to the pluralised word. Here,
mango becomes mangoes . Tagalog has a far less complex way of
making words plural. Simply add the word mga before the noun
you wish to pluralise. For example: **tiket** (*ticket*) becomes **mga
tiket** (*tickets*); **babae** (*woman*) becomes **mga babae** (*women*);

Pilipino (*Filipino*) becomes **mga Pilipino** (*Filipinos*). What could be easier?!

Exercise 3

Find the correct Tagalog words for the following and then pluralise them.

Did you know...?

Sometimes Tagalog will pluralise adjectives, too. For example **mabuti** (*good*) can become **mabubuti**, **malaki** (*big*) can become **malalaki**. Here the **mga** pluraliser is dropped in favour of repeating the second syllable of the word. In this type of sentence the plural adjective must always precede a plural noun or pronoun. For example: **maliit siya – maliliit sila**. Don't worry if this seems to complicated for you at this time – you can come back to it later when you feel more confident. Just stick to the **mga** form for the moment.

Exercise 4

Using the vocabulary box provided arrange the following muddled up words into correct Tagalog sentences.

1. bisita/ sa bahay/ na/ mga/ may.
2. kayo/ mga/ ba/ estudyante?
3. pilipino/ sila/ mga/ hindi.
4. kailangan/ ang/ ko/ at mesa /mga silya.
5. sariwa/ mga prutas/ na ito/ ang.

Talasalitaan	Vocabulary
na	*already*
estudyante	*student*
hindi	*no*
kailangan	*need*
silya	*chair*
sariwa	*fresh*
prutas	*fruit*

Choosing some typical Filipino food

Dialogue 2

The Cook family are ready to order. The waiter approaches them.

Waiter Ibig n'yo na *po* bang um**or**der?
Bill O**o**. A**ko**, **gus**to ko ng a**do**bong pus**it**, me**cha**do at gini**sang gu**lay. Ik**aw**, Louise? **Ano** ang order mo?
Louise A**ko**, **gus**to ko ng apri**ta**da, sini**gang** na ba**ngus** at **ka**nin. May na**pi**li ka na ba, Roy?
Roy O**po**. Muk**hang** masa**rap** ang a**do**bong ma**nok**. **Gus**to ko rin ng pan**sit** at pini**ri**tong **lum**piya.
Waiter Ano *po* ang starter nin**yo**? **May**roon pong **so**pas ma**nok** o kaya'y sa**ri**wang **lum**pia.
Bill Sari**wang lum**pia!
Waiter Sari**wang lum**pia, sir. Masa**rap** *po* ang **sar**sa.
Bill Sala**mat**.
Waiter *Wala* pong anu**man**.

Talasalitaan	*Vocabulary*
ibig n'yo na	*would you like now*
umorder	*to make your order*
sopas manok	*chicken soup*
adobong pusit	*squid adobo*
mechado	*mechado*
ginisang gulay	*sauteed vegetables*
ano	*what*
apritada	*apritada*
sinigang na bangus	*fish*
kanin	*boiled rice*
may napili	*has selected/chosen*
mukhang masarap	*seems tasty*
abobong manok	*chicken adobo*
starter ninyo	*your starter*
o kaya'y	*or*
sariwa(ng) lumpia	*fresh spring rolls*
rekomendado	*recommended*
sarsa	*sauce/dressing*
gusto ko rin	*I also like*

Translation

Waiter Would you like to order now?

Bill I would like adobong pusit, michado and sauteed vegetables. (And) You Louise? What would you like to order?

Louise I would like apritada, sinigang na bangus [fish] and rice. Have you chosen, Roy?

Roy Yes, mum. The chicken adobo looks tasty. I would also like noodles and fried lumpia.

Waiter Sir, what would you like for your starter? There is chicken soup or fresh lumpia.

Bill Fresh lumpia!

Waiter Fresh lumpia sir. The salad dressing is delicious!

Bill Thank you.

Waiter You're welcome.

Mang Simeon's Kamayan Restaurant
Roxas Boulevard, Manila

Starter:

Tapang baka	₱175.00
Sopas Manok	₱100.00
Lumpiang ubod	₱125.00
Sariwang lumpia	₱125.00
Ensaladang seafood	₱200.00
Pansit luglog	₱125.00

Ulam:

Adobong manok sa gata	₱250.00
Adobong baboy at baka sa toyo	₱300.00
Pansit bihon	₱280.00
Pansit miki	₱280.00
Pansit miki at bihon	₱280.00
Kaldereta	₱300.00
Sinigang na bangus	₱280.00
Pritong tilapia	₱280.00
Ginisang pusit	₱300.00
Menudo	₱200.00
Sinigang na bakang may saging	₱250.00
Kanin	₱100.00
Chinese fried rice	₱120.00

Gulay:

Ginisang munggo	₱65.00
Chop suey	₱150.00
Inihaw na talong	₱60.00

Pamutat:

Leche Flan	₱100.00
Halo-halo	₱150.00
Sorbetes	₱150.00
Minatamisang saging na may yelo	₱150.00

Inumin:

San Miguel beer	₱35.00
Soft Drinks	₱25.00
Fruit Shake	₱40.00
Kape	₱25.00

Service charge not included

Exercise 5

Choose from the list of condiments in the box and tell the waiter what you want. Use the dialogue to help you.

Waiter   Para sa inihaw na bangus po ba?
You   (Clue: ask for some vinegar for your bangus.)
Waiter   Bakit, matabang po ba?
You   (Clue: ask for some salt.)
Waiter   Ito po ay para sa ensalada
You   (Clue: ask for some sauce/ salad dressing.)
Waiter   Ibig po ba ninyo ito para sa pansit?
You   (Clue: ask for some soy sauce.)

Talasalitaan	*Vocabulary*
toyo	*soy sauce*
paminta	*pepper*
suka	*vinegar*
sarsa	*sauce/salad dressing*
asin	*salt*
ibig po ba ninyo	*would you want*
gusto ko ng	*I would like/I want*

Cultural tip

Whether at corner stores or in small (**turo-turo**) restaurants along the highway, some delicacies are always on the menu and are sure to tickle Filipino taste buds. Here are a few of the most popular dishes:

Leche flan – A sweet dish consisting of evaporated milk, condensed milk, egg yolks, sugar, lemon peel and vanilla essence. Similar in appearance and taste to *crème caramel*. It is always the main attraction on the buffet table at fiestas and celebrations.

Bilobilo – this popular snack is prepared by mixing water and sticky rice flour. The mixture is then shaped into small balls which in turn are dropped into a pan quarter filled with boiling coconut milk where sugar, shredded jack fruit, pineapple and vanilla have already been added.

Bibingka – Cooked in smouldering coconut husks, **bibingka** has its own unique taste. It is prepared from rice flour, sugar and the flesh of a young (i.e. unripe) coconut. **Bibingka** is placed under a smouldering coconut husk until it turns a slightly brownish colour. Sometimes the top of the **bibingka** is decorated with chopped cheese. Nice to eat when warm, but tends to harden when cold.

Adobong manok – Made by marinating pieces of chicken in vinegar, pepper, garlic, then cooked in coconut milk until tender and aromatic. Seasoned with soy sauce. Served hot as a side dish. **Masarap!**

🗣 Language skills

2 Other uses of Mga

Mga is also used in Tagalog to express approximation. When used in connection with numbers, it can be understood to mean 'approximately', 'about' or 'around'.

Examples:

Tagalog: **Mga** apat na kilo ang kailangan ko.
English: *I need about 4 kilos.*

Tagalog: **Mga** pito siguro ang darating.
English: *Perhaps around seven* (people) *will be arriving.*

Tagalog: Mga isang yarda ang bilhin mo.
English: *You* [need to] *buy around one yard.*

Mga can also be used when approximating time.

Examples:

Tagalog: Mga alas dos nang hapon ako babalik.
English: *I'll be back by around 2.00 p.m.*

Tagalog: **Mga** alas onse sila natulog kagabi.
English: *They slept at about 11.00 last night.*

Tagalog: **Mga** alas sais nang umaga ang simula ng misa.
English: *The mass starts at around 6.00 a.m.*

Exercise 6

Complete the following sentences:

1. Gusto ko ng (around 2 kilos) dalanghita.
2. Kailangan namin ng (approximately 3 yards).
3. (Around 2 o'clock) ba ang alis ng bus?
4. (Approximately nine) ang mga bisita nila.
5. Siguro (about eight people) are in the Jeepney.

Talasalitaan	Vocabulary
gusto ko	I like/want
dalanghita	oranges
kailangan	need
alis	departure
siguro	perhaps

Dialogue 3

The Cook family are enjoying their meal, but they would like to order some more food.

Bill   Um**o**rder pa **ta**yo ng pansit. U**bos** na.

Louise   U**bos** na rin ang **gu**lay at **hi**pon.

Roy   At *saka* a**do**bong ma**nok**. **Tu**big rin.

Bill   (to waiter) **Gu**sto pa **na**min ng: isang **pla**tong pans**it**, isang **pla**tong **gu**lay, i**sang pla**tong **hi**pon at a**do**bong ma**nok**.

Waiter   **Ka**nin rin *po* sir?

Bill   Oo. At *saka* mala**mig** na **tub**ig.

Waiter   **O**po sir. Sal**am**at *po*.

Bill   Wa**lang** anu**man**.

Talasalitaan	*Vocabulary*
umorder pa tayo	*let's order some more*
ng pansit	*some noodles*
ubos na	*ran out/consumed*
tubig rin	*water too*
gulay at hipon	*vegetables and prawns*
at saka	*and also*
gusto pa namin ng	*we want some more*
isang plato(ng)	*a plate of*
gulay	*vegetables*

Translation

Bill   Let's order some more noodles. (There's) Nothing left!
Louise   No more vegetables and prawns either.
Roy   And chicken adobo too! Water also.
Bill   (to waiter) We would like another plate of noodles, some more vegetables, also prawns and chicken adobo.
Waiter   Rice as well sir?
Bill   Yes, and some cold water too.
Waiter   Yes sir. Thank you.
Bill   You're welcome.

✔ Exercise 7

On the tape you can hear people ordering different dishes at a Manila Kamayan restaurant. Did you notice what each person ordered? Look at the waiter's ordering slip. Write down what each person has ordered.

Mang Simeon's Kamayan Restaurant
Roxas Boulevard, Manila

Customer 1: *Miss Buyco* _____

_____

Customer 2: *Mrs Vito* _____

_____

Customer 3: *Miss Guanzon* _____

_____

Table *14*   Waiter *Domingo*

Asking for the bill

Dialogue 4

The Cook family have enjoyed their meal. Bill Cook now wants
to pay.

Bill	Ang chit *nga* **na**min.
Waiter	Aba **o**po. *Sandali* lang *po*. (Waiter returns and hands him the bill)
Bill	(Pointing at something) **A**no ito?
Waiter	Iyan *po* ang starter ni**nyo**.
Bill	Iyan, a**no** iy**an**?
Waiter	Iyan *po* ang **i**numin ni**nyo**.
Bill	Gano**on** ba? Ka**sa**ma ba ang service charge **di**to?
Waiter	*Hindi po*.
Bill	O, a**no** na**man** ang mga i**to**?
Waiter	Ang mga i**yan** *po* ang pul**u**tan ni**nyo**.
Bill	Gano**on** ba? Okey, ma**bu**ti. **He**to ang **ba**yad ko.
Waiter	Sa**la**mat *po* sir.
Bill	Wa**lang** anu**man**.

Talasalitaan	*Vocabulary*
ang chit nga namin	*our bill please*
aba opo	*sure, sir*
medyo nagulat	*somewhat surprised*
ano ito	*what is this?*
ang mga ito	*these*
ang mga iyan	*those*
magkano	*how much*
pangalawang order	*second order*
kasama ba	*is it included*
heto ang bayad	*here's the payment*

Translation

Bill	(May we have) Our bill please.
Waiter	Of course sir. One moment please.
Bill	(Checking bill) What is this?

Waiter	That's your starter sir.
Bill	And that, what is that?
Waiter	That is (those are) your drinks, sir.
Bill	Is that so? Is the service charge included here?
Waiter	No, sir.
Bill	What are these here?
Waiter	Sir, those are your side dishes that came with the drinks.
Bill	Is that so? Ok, that's fine. Here's the payment.
Waiter	Thank you sir.
Bill	You're welcome.

Ito

Iyan

Iyon

📻 Language skills

3 Ito, iyan, iyon *This, that, that (over there)*

Ito (pronounced *ee-taw*) '*This*' refers to something close to the speaker, approximately within arm's reach. For example: **Relos ko ito**. *This is my watch.*

Iyan (pronounced *ee-yahn*) '*That*' is used to refer to anything close to the person/s addressed (approximately within arm's reach) but not too close to the speaker. For example: **Sariwa ba iyan?** *Is that fresh?*

Iyon (pronounced *ee-yawn*) '*that*' is used to refer to things at a distance from both the speaker and the person/s addressed. For example: **Anong halaman iyon?** *What* [kind of] *plant is that* [over there]?

Practise reading the following sentences:

Tagalog	Literal	English
Pasaporte ko ito	Passport my this	*This is my passport*
Ito ba ang pila?	This ? the queue	*Is this the queue?*
Ilog Pasig iyan	River Pasig that	*That is Pasig River*
Bulkang Mayon iyon	Volcano Mayon that	*That (over there) is Mayon volcano*
Masarap ito	Delicious this	*This is delicious*
Bolpen ko rin iyan	Pen my also that	*That is also my pen*
Hindi ba barko iyon?	Not ? ship that	*Isn't that a ship (over there)?*

4 Mga + ito, iyan, iyon

Remember **mga** from page 106? By adding the pluraliser **mga** to **ito**, **iyan**, and **iyon**, we get **mga ito**, **mga iyan**, **mga iyon**. Strictly speaking, as **ito**, **iyan** and **iyon** are pronouns, it is theoretically correct just to add **mga**. In practice however, this does not happen. The problem is solved by simply annexing **ang** before **mga**, thus **mga ito** becomes **ang mga ito**, **mga iyan** becomes **ang mga iyan** and **mga iyon** becomes **ang mga iyon**. Look at the explanation:

	Process	Meaning
ang **mga** ito	the /pluraliser /this	= *these*
ang **mga** iyan	the/ pluraliser /that	= *those*
ang **mga** iyon	the/ pluraliser /that	= *those* (over there)

Here are some further examples:

Singular	Plural

1. Tagalog: Maleta ko ito.

   Maleta ko ang mga ito or
   Mga maleta ko ang mga ito.

   English: *This is my suitcase.*   *These are my suitcases.*

2. Tagalog: Malinis ba iyan?   Malilinis ba ang mga iyan?
   English: *Is that clean?*   *Are those clean?*

3. Tagalog: Bahay iyon.   Mga bahay ba ang mga iyon?
                                    Bahay ba ang mga iyon?

   English: *Is that a house*   *Are those houses*
            (over there)?   (over there)?

One-minute phrases:

Dala-dala (*dah-lah dah-lah*) Literally, *load-load*. Meaning *a load carried around*. For example: **Laging maraming dala-dala si Bing**. *Bing has always a lot to carry around*.

May padala (*meh pah-dah-lah*) Literally, *has something* (an item) *to be delivered*. Meaning *a delivery*. Something sent either through the post or delivered in person. **May padala(ng) Barong Tagalog si Ate Ely sa akin**. *Ate Ely sent me a Barong Tagalog*.

Mabuting makisama (*mah-boo-teeng mah-kee-sah-mah*) Literally, *nice to conform with others*. Meaning *a person who gets along well with everybody*. For example: **Mabuting makisama si Doktor Rivera**. *Doctor Rivera gets along well with everybody*.

Tirhan mo ako (*teer-hahn maw ah-kaw*) Meaning *leave some* (food) *for me*. **Tirhan** is derived from the verb **tira** meaning *to portion out*. For example: **Tirhan mo ako ng leche flan**. *Leave some leche flan for me*.

Sabi-sabi (*sah-bee sah-bee*) Literally, *say-say/talk-talk*. This phrase is used to refer to *idle gossip*. A common and very popular Tagalog saying is as follows: **Ang maniwala sa sabi-sabi walang bait sa sarili**. *You are not kind to yourself if you believe in gossip*.

(i) **Cultural tip**

In rural Philippines, it is still very common for people to eat with their hands. This was the way Filipinos ate for hundreds of years before the arrival of the Spanish. *Kamayan* restaurants (**kamayan** comes from the Tagalog word **kamay** which means *hand*) offer people the opportunity to sample local delicacies in this traditional way. Why not try it out for yourself? If you show a willingness to enter into Filipino traditions, it can only serve to strengthen the ties with your Filipino friends.

9 SA BOTIKA
At the pharmacy

In this unit you will learn how to

■ ask for medication
■ consult a doctor
■ name the parts of the body

Asking for medication

Dialogue 1

Louise Cook is at the pharmacy. She wants to buy some medicine for Roy who has been experiencing stomach trouble.

Louise	May ga**mot** ba kayo para sa **pag**tatae?
Pharmacist	**Me**ron *po*. **Par**a sa in**yo** *po* ba?
Louise	*Hindi*. **Pa**ra sa a**nak** ko.
Pharmacist	**A**nong e**dad** po ang a**nak** nin**yo**?
Louise	Dalawam**pung** ta**on** siya.
Pharmacist	**He**to *po* ang ga**mot** sa **pag**tatae. Masa**kit** din *po* ba ang **u**lo ni**ya**?
Louise	*Hindi* na**man**. Kai**lan**gan ba ni**ya** ng re**se**ta ng dok**tor**?
Pharmacist	*Hindi* na *po*. **I**inumin *po* ni**ya** i**to** tat**long be**ses i**sang ar**aw. **I**wa**san** lang *po* ni**yang** umi**nom** ng **tu**big na may **ye**lo.
Louise	Ma**ra**ming sa**la**mat. **He**to ang **bay**ad.
Pharmacist	*Wala* pong anu**man**.

Talasalitaan	*Vocabulary*
may gamot	*has/have medicine*
(para) sa pagtatae	*for diarrhoea*
anong edad	*how old*
anak ninyo	*your child*
dalawampung anyos	*20 years old*
ang gamot	*the medicine*
masakit	*hurting/painful*
ang ulo niya	*his/her head*
hindi naman	*not quite*
reseta ng doktor	*doctor's prescription*
hindi na po	*not anymore*
iinumin	*will swallow*
tatlong beses isang araw	*three times a day*
iwasan lang	*please avoid*
uminom	*to drink*
tubig na may yelo	*water with ice*

Translation

Louise	Do you have anything for diarrhoea ?
Pharmacist	Yes ma'am. Is it for you?
Louise	No. It's for my son.
Pharmacist	How old is your son?
Louise	Twenty years old.
Pharmacist	Here's the medicine for diarrhoea. Does he have a headache too?
Louise	No. Does he need a doctor's prescription?
Pharmacist	No. He must take this three times a day. He needs to avoid drinking water with ice.
Louise	Thank you very much. Here's the payment.
Pharmacist	Don't mention it.

☑ Exercise 1

How much do you remember from the dialogue between Louise Cook and the pharmacist? Can you match column A and column B?

A	B
1. gamot	a. para sa anak ko
2. reseta	b. tubig
3. edad	c. ulo
4. para sa inyo po ba?	d. doktor
5. masakit	e. dalawampung anyos
6. uminom	f. sa pagtatae

Other items commonly found at the pharmacy can be found in the vocabulary box.

Talasalitaan	*Vocabulary*
termometro	*thermometer*
'band aid'	*sticking plaster*
antiseptik krema	*antiseptic cream*
gamot sa pagtatae	*medicine for diarrhoea*
gamot sa sakit ng ulo	*headache tablet*
gamot sa sipon	*medicine for colds*
bulak	*cotton wool*
gamot sa nagsusuka	*medicine for vomiting*
'bandage' or pantapal	*bandage*
tintura de yudo	*iodine*
gamot sa ubo	*cough medicine*

Language skills

1 Para sa *For*

When Louise Cook asked the pharmacist for some medicine for her son, she said: 'May gamot ba kayo **para sa pagtatae**? Do you have (any) medication for diarrhoea? The Tagalog words '**Para sa**' used in this example are translated into English as 'for'. **Para sa** can be used in three different ways:-

1. To indicate where or who something is for: for example, '**Para sa guro ang bolpen**', *The ballpen is for the teacher*. '**Para sa kusina ang mga silya**', *The chairs are for the kitchen*. Sometimes Tagalog drops the word '**para**' and so the sentence becomes simply '**sa guro ang bolpen**' or 'sa kusina ang mga silya'. When **para** is deleted, however, the resultant sentence is often ambiguous, since the **sa** phrase may be interpreted as a

possessive **sa** phrase '**sa guro ang bol pen**' may also mean *the pen belongs to the teacher*. **Para**, therefore, cannot be dropped. When the name of an individual is involved, then **para sa** becomes **para kay,** for example, '**Para kay Amy ang silid na ito**' or simply '**kay Amy ang silid na ito**', *This room is for Amy.*

2. To indicate favour or support for an individual or group: for example, '**Para sa Partido Mabuhay si Ignacio**', *Ignacio is for the Mabuhay Party*', '**Para sa Newcastle United F.C. si John**', *John is for Newcastle United F.C.* Once again, sometimes the word '**para**' is dropped and the sentences become 'sa **Partido Mabuhay si Ignacio**' and 'sa **Newcastle United F.C. si John**'.

3. To indicate the purpose of or for something: for example, '**Para sa paglalaba ang sabon**', *The soap is for washing clothes*; **Para sa pagtulog ang kulambo**', *The mosquito net is for sleeping*; '**Para sa pagsulat ang lapis**', *The pencil is for writing*. Notice that in this type of sentence, the word **para** cannot be dropped.

2 Para kanino *For whom*
Para saan *For what*

The related Tagalog question words are '**para kanino**' (for whom?) and '**para saan**' (for what?). Both question words look for an answer in the '**para sa**' form. For example: '**Para kanino ang pasalubong?**' (*for whom is the gift?*), '**para kay Alice ang pasalubong**' (*the gift is for Alice*). **Para saan ang gatas?** (*what is the milk for?*), **para sa kape ang gatas** (*the milk is for the coffee*). Use the following table to guide you through the different variations of the **para sa** form:

	Tagalog	English	Question word
1st person	para sa akin	*for me*	Para kanino
	para sa amin	*for us* (exclusive)	Para kanino
	para sa atin	*for us* (inclusive)	Para kanino
2nd person			
	para sa iyo	*for you*	Para kanino
	para sa inyo	*for you* (plural and singular formal)	Para kanino

3rd person	para kay	*for* + person's name =	para kanino
	para kina	*for* + person's and friend/s' names =	para kanino
	para sa kaniya	*for him/her*	para kanino
	para sa kanila	*for them*	para kanino
	para sa tao	*for a person* (personal noun)	para kanino
	para sa paa	*for the foot* (thing)	para saan
	para sa bintana	*for the window* (place)	para saan

Take a look at the following examples:

Tagalog:	Para sa bata ang gatas
English:	*The milk is for the child*

Tagalog:	Para sa lola ang pamaypay
English:	*The fan is for grandmother*

Tagalog:	Para kay Patricia ang mga bulaklak
English:	*The flowers are for Patricia*

Tagalog:	Para sa akin ba ang mga ito?
English:	*Are these for me?*

Tagalog:	Hindi para sa kanila ang pagkain
English:	*The food is not for them*

Tagalog:	Para sa bagong meyor ako
English:	*I am for the new mayor*

Tagalog:	Para sa mga bata ang mga laruan
English:	*The toys are for the children*

Tagalog:	Para sa organisasyon ko ba si Liam?
English:	*Is Liam for my organisation?*

Exercise 2

Now try answering the questions by saying what each item is for.
Choose the correct answer from the vocabulary box provided.

Example:
Para saan ang mantikilya?   Para sa tinapay ang mantikilya.

1. Para saan ang gatas?   _____
2. Para saan ang kurtina?   _____
3. Para saan ang selyo?   _____
4. Para saan ang payong?   _____
5. Para saan ang kama?   _____
6. Para saan ang maleta?   _____
7. Para saan ang yelo?   _____

Talasalitaan	*Vocabulary*
ulan	*rain*
mantikilya	*margarine*
gatas	*milk*
silid-tulugan	*bedroom*
kurtina	*curtain*
selyo	*stamp*
tsaa	*tea*
bintana	*window*
biyahe	*travel*
kama	*bed*
maleta	*suitcase*

Consulting a doctor

Dialogue 2

Roy Cook's stomach trouble had still not cleared up by the following day and so he decided to pay a visit to the doctor. We now join him at the surgery.

Doktor   **Anong** masa**kit** sa i**yo**?
Roy   Masa**kit** *po* ang ti**yan** ko at nag**ta**tae a**ko**. May bini**li** a**kong** gam**ot** sa botika **para** sa **pag**tatae.
Doktor   Ma**bu**ti. **Ano** ba ang ki**na**in mo?
Roy   Pansit, lits**on** at San Miguel beer.
Doktor   **Ting**nan ko nga ang ma**ta** mo.
Roy   (Ibinu**ka** ang ma**ta**)

Doktor **Ting**nan ko na**man** ang bi**big** mo at i**la**bas mo ang **di**la mo.

Roy (Ibinu**ka** ang bi**big** at inila**ba**s ang **di**la).

Doktor **I**lang **be**ses kang nag**ta**tae sa i**sang a**raw?

Roy Mga li**mang be**ses *po*.

Doktor **So**bra si**gu**ro ang na**ka**in mo. **Bi**bigyan ki**ta** ng dalaw**ang** re**se**ta. **I**sa **pa**ra sa sa**kit** ng ti**yan**.

Roy **Pa**ra sa**an** *po* i**tong i**sa?

Doktor **Pa**ra sa **pa**gtatae. Toasted bread lang **mu**na ang ka**i**nin mo.

Roy Salamat *po*.

Doktor Wa**lang** anu**man**.

Talasalitaan	*Vocabulary*
ang tiyan ko	*my stomach*
nagtatae ako	*I'm having diarrhoea*
may binili ako(ng)	*I bought*
ang kinain mo	*what you ate*
tingnan ko nga	*let me see/examine*
ang mata mo	*your eyes*
ibinuka	*opened*
ang bibig mo	*your mouth*
ilabas	*show*
ang dila mo	*your tongue*
ilang beses	*how many times*
sa isang araw	*in one day*
mga lima	*about five*
sobra siguro	*perhaps too much*
ang nakain mo	*what you have eaten*
bibigyan kita	*I'll give you*
dalawang reseta	*two prescriptions*
para sa sakit ng tiyan	*for stomach ache*
para sa pagtatae	*for diarrhoea*
lang muna	*first*
ang kainin mo	*what you have to eat*

Translation

Doctor	Where are you feeling the pain?
Roy	I have a stomach ache and I've got diarrhoea. I bought some medication for diarrhoea from the pharmacy.
Doctor	Good. What have you eaten?
Roy	Noodles, suckling pig and San Miguel beer.
Doctor	Let me examine your eyes.
Roy	(Opening his eyes)
Doctor	Now let me look in your mouth. Show me your tongue.
Roy	(Opening his mouth and showing his tongue).
Doctor	How many times a day are you going to the toilet?
Roy	About five times sir.
Doctor	Perhaps you've over eaten. I will give you two prescriptions. One for your stomach ache.
Roy	What is the other one for?
Doctor	For your diarrhoea. Just eat toast for the meantime.
Roy	Thank you.
Doctor	Don't mention it.

▣ Naming the parts of the body

Mga bahagi ng katawan *Parts of the body*

Listen to the tape for the correct pronunciation of each word. Use the pronunciation guide to help you remember the words.

English	Tagalog	Pronounced
1. *ankle*	bukongbukong	*boo-kawng-boo-kawng*
2. *arm*	bisig	*bee-seeg*
3. *back*	likod	*lee-kawd*
4. *backside*	puwit	*poo-weet*
5. *breast*	dibdib	*deeb-deeb*
6. *cheek*	pisngi	*pees-ngee*
7. *chin*	baba	*bah-bah*
8. *ears*	tainga/tenga	*teh-ngah*
9. *elbow*	siko	*see-kaw*
10. *eye(s)*	mata	*mah-tah*
11. *eyebrow*	kilay	*kee-ligh*
12. *eyelashes*	pilikmata	*pee-leet-mah-tah*

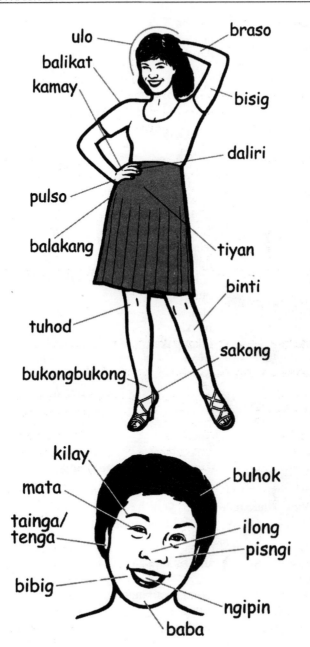

13. *face*	mukha	*mook-hah*
14. *foot*	paa	*pah-ah*
15. *fingers/toes*	daliri	*dah-lee-ree*
16. *hand*	kamay	*kah-migh*
17. *hair*	buhok	*boo-hawk*
18. *head*	ulo	*oo-law*
19. *heel*	sakong	*sah-kawng*
20. *hips*	balakang	*bah-lah-kahng*
21. *jaw*	panga	*pah-ngah*
22. *knee*	tuhod	*too-hawd*
23. *leg*	binti	*been-tee*
24. *lower arm*	braso	*brah-saw*
25. *mouth*	bibig	*bee-beeg*
26. *nape*	batok	*bah-tawk*
27. *neck*	leeg	*leh-ehg*
28. *nose*	ilong	*ee-lawng*
29. *palm*	palad	*pah-lahd*
30. *penis*	buto	*boo-taw*
31. *scalp*	anit	*ah-neet*
32. *shoulder*	balikat	*bah-lee-kaht*
33. *sole*	talampakan	*tah-lahm-pah-kahn*
34. *stomach*	tiyan	*tee-yahn*
35. *teeth*	ngipin	*ngee-peen*
36. *tongue*	dila	*dee-lah*
37. *vagina*	puki	*poo-kee*
38. *waist*	baywang/bewang	*beh-wahng*
39. *wrist*	pulso	*pool-saw*

☑ Exercise 3 Understanding and speaking

Imagine that you are at the pharmacy. Complete your part of the following dialogue. Once you have completed the dialogue, why not ask one of your Filipino friends to act out the dialogue with you:

Parmasyotika Magandang umaga po, sir.
Ikaw _____ _____. (Say good morning)
Parmasyotika Ano po ang kailangan nila, sir?
Ikaw Masakit ang _____ _____. (Say: I have a toothache) May _____ (medicine) ba kayo para dito?

Parmasyotika	Opo. Mayroon po.
Ikaw	___ ___. _____ __ (Say all right. Thank you (formal).)
Parmasyotika	Gusto po ba ninyo ay yung iinumin?
Ikaw	(Say Yes, that's fine)
Parmasyotika	O sige po. heto po ang tabletas. Iinumin ninyo ito tatlong beses isang araw.
Ikaw	_____ _____? (Ask how much it is)
Parmasyotika	Treynta pesos po.
Ikaw	Heto _____ _____. (Say Here's the payment)
Parmasyotika	Maraming salamat po.
Ikaw	_____ _____. (Say don't mention it)

Exercise 4

Can you place the following list of body parts in their correct order? For the correct order, begin with the top of the body and work down to the feet.

1. ulo
2. paa
3. mata
4. daliri
5. binti
6. kamay
7. buhok
8. panga
9. talampakan
10. tiyan

Exercise 5

Say whether the following statements are **tama** (true) or **mali** (false). Use the vocabulary box to help you. **Remember**: a **mali** answer should follow this format: Nasa _____ ang _____.

Example: Nasa kamay ang mata.   Answer: Mali. Nasa mukha
ang mata.

1. Nasa gitna ng binti ang tuhod.   Answer:
2. Nasa likuran ang dibdib.   Answer:
3. Nasa kamay ang mga daliri.   Answer:
4. Nasa bisig ang talampakan.   Answer:
5. Nasa tenga ang labi.   Answer:
6. Nasa bisig ang kamay.   Answer:

Talasalitaan	*Vocabulary*
nasa harapan	*at the front*
nasa tabi ng	*beside/next to the*
nasa gitna ng	*in the middle of*
nasa pagitan ng	*between the*
nasa ilallim ng	*at the bottom of*
nasa ibaba ng	*below the*
nasa itaas ng	*above the*
nasa likuran	*at the back/behind*

☑ Exercise 6 Listening and understanding

Look at the pictures. On the tape you will hear a number of people complaining about their ailments. Can you match up the picture with the ailment?

One-minute phrases

Parang kabute pronounced (*pah-rahng kah-boo-teh*) Literally, *'like mushroom'*. This term is applied to a person who seems to have the ability to *appear and disappear*. In Filipino tradition, mushrooms are said to appear almost overnight. An example of this is the child who regularly plays truant from school, attending class only occasionally.

Ang sakit ng kalingkingan ay damdam ng buong katawan (*ang-sah-keet nahng kah-leeng-kee-ngahn igh dahm-dahm nahng booawng kah-tah-wahn*) This is a popular Filipino saying which can be translated as *the pain of the little finger is felt by the whole body*. For example, in a situation where a worker makes a mistake, the consequences of that mistake may be experienced by all or many of his / her co-workers.

Ganito 'yon (*gah-nee-taw 'yawn*) Literally, *it's like this...* A phrase roughly equivalent to the English expression, 'beating around the bush'. The expression is often used when someone wants to give a long (boring ?) explanation. Example: **Saan ka galing? Ganito 'yon...** . *Where have you been? Well, it's like this... .*

Nakapamburol (*nah-kah-pahm-boo-rawl*) Literally, *dressed in funeral attire*. This is a very common Tagalog expression applied to a person dressed in his/ her Sunday best (best clothing). Similar in meaning to the English expressions, *dressed to the nines* or *dressed to kill*. Example: **Nakapamburol si Mario kasi abay siya sa kasal**. *Mario is dressed to kill because he will be a sponsor at the wedding.*

Dedbol na ako (*ded-bol-nah-ahkaw*) Literally, *I'm like a dead bull*. Similar in meaning to the English expressions *I'm exhausted, I'm shattered.*

Cultural tip

Filipino people are generally very modest about their bodies, particularly the women. Revealing swimming costumes and other garments are not commonly worn, especially in rural areas. In Filipino culture, modesty and respectability go hand in hand. Respecting local culture in this regard will ensure a healthy respect for the visitor too! Tourist beaches and resorts do, however, offer a more relaxed environment for the sun worshipper. Don't forget the after-sun lotion!

10 | TULONG?
(Need) Help?

In this unit you will learn how to
- ask for help
- use the **sa** possessives and **kanino** (*whose*)
- shop for a gift
- use **sa** as a preposition

Asking for help

Dialogue 1

Bill Cook needs some assistance. He bought a tee-shirt but it doesn't fit him. He's gone back to the department store.

Tindera	Magan**dang ha**pon *po*. **Ano** pong maipaglilingkod ko sa in**yo**?
Bill	Magan**dang ha**pon naman. **Itong** T-shirt na binili ko dito, mali**it** sa **akin**. Size L lang ito.
Tindera	Gano**on** *po* ba? Sa in**yo** *po* ba? Ano pong size nin**yo**?
Bill	Size XXL ako. Oo sa **akin**. May XXL ba ka**yo**?
Tindera	Sa palagay ko *po*. Sumun**od** *po* kayo sa **akin** sa T-shirt department. **Di**to *po* ba ninyo ki**nu**ha iyan?
Bill	Oo. **Di**to sa lu**gar** na i**to**.
Tindera	Pumili *po* kayo ng size nin**yo** at **pa**palitan **na**min i**yan**.
Bill	Mara**ming** salamat.
Tindera	*Wala* pong anu**man**.

Talasalitaan	*Vocabulary*
tindera	*assistant* (female)
itong T-shirt	*this tee-shirt*
na binili ko dito	*that I bought here*
maliit sa akin	*small for me*
lang ito	*this is only*
ganoon po ba	*is that so*
sa palagay ko	*in my opinion*
sumunod po kayo sa akin	*please follow me*
ninyo kinuha iyan	*you got that*
sa lugar na ito	*here in this place*
pumili po kayo	*please choose*
ng size ninyo	*your size*
papalitan namin iyan	*we will replace that*

Translation

Tindera	Good afternoon sir. What can I do for you?
Bill	Good afternoon to you, too. The tee-shirt I bought here, it's small for me. (It's) Only size L.
Tindera	Is that so sir? Is it yours sir? What size do you take?
Bill	I take XXL. Yes it's mine. Do you have size XXL?
Tindera	I think so sir. Please follow me to the tee-shirt department. Did you get that from this department?
Bill	Yes. Here in this area.
Tindera	Please choose your size and we'll exchange it.
Bill	Thank you.
Tindera	You're welcome sir.

Exercise 1

Can you supply the correct question to Bill's answer?

1. Bill: 'Itong T-shirt na binili ko dito, maliit sa akin.'

   Did the tindera ask:

   a. Gusto po ba ninyo ng T-shirt?
   b. Ano pong maipaglilingkod ko sa inyo?
   c. Magandang hapon po.

2. Bill: 'Size L lang ito.'

   Was he asked:

      a. Sa inyo po ba?
      b. Anong size po?
      c. Ganoon po ba?

3. Bill: 'Size XXL ako.'

   Did the tindera ask:

      a. Ganoon po ba?
      b. Size L po ba?
      c. Ano pong size ninyo?

4. Bill: 'Oo. Dito sa lugar na ito.'

   The tindera asked:

      a. Saan po ninyo kinuha iyan?
      b. Dito ba ninyo kinuha iyan?
      c. Dito mo ba kinuha iyan?

Language skills

1 Sa akin, sa iyo, sa kaniya *Mine, yours, his/hers*

The words mine, yours, his/hers, ours, yours, and theirs all tell us about who owns or possesses something. In English these words are known as possessives (see also Unit 7). There are two main ways in which the possessive is expressed in Tagalog: 1) by the use and of **may** or **mayroon** (see Unit 2), 2) by the use of the possessive **sa** form. In the possessive **sa** form (**sa akin, sa iyo, sa kaniya, sa amin, sa atin, sa inyo, sa kanila** and **sa** + personal / common noun) **sa** is used together with the possessor in order to express possession of the subject. For example: **Sa akin ang aklat.** *The book is mine.* **Sa inyo ba ang maletang ito?** *Is this suitcase yours?* **Sa babae ang payong.** *The umbrella belongs to the woman.* **Remember**: the **sa** form changes depending on who or what is the possessor. For example, **sa** becomes **kay** or **kina** when used with a person or people's names. Try not to worry about this. You will pick up more as you go along. Just look at the following examples:

1. **Sa bata** ang bisikleta — *The bicycle belongs to the child*
2. **Kay Joe** ang malamig na inumin — *The cold drink is Joe's*
3. **Kina Ely** ang regalo — *The gift belongs to Ely and her friends*
4. **Sa atin** ba iyan? — *Is that ours?*
5. **Sa Amerikano** daw ang lapis — *Apparently the pencil belongs to the American*

Sa possession table

	Tagalog	English
1st person	sa akin	mine
	sa amin	ours (exclusive)
	sa atin	ours (inclusive)
2nd person		
	sa iyo	yours
	sa inyo	yours (plural and singular polite)
3rd person		
	kay Sally	Sally's
	kina Gary	Gary's and his friend/s'
	sa kaniya	his/hers
	sa kanila	theirs
	sa + personal noun	belong/s to
	sa + common noun	belong/s to

Exercise 2

Using what you have learned so far in this chapter, re-arrange the following jumbled up sentences into their correct form. The literal English translation should give you a clue.

1. Tagalog: maletang / ito / ang / sa akin
   Correct order: _____
   Literal: Mine the suitcase this.

2. Tagalog: Sa bata / bisikleta / ang / ba?
   Correct order: _____
   Literal: Belonging to the child the bicycle?

3. Tagalog: ang / Jeepney / bagong / sa kanila .
   Correct order: _____
   Literal: Belongs to them the new Jeepney.

4. Tagalog: sa /iyan / hindi / iyo.
   Correct order: _____
   Literal: Not yours that.

5. Tagalog: tsinelas / Beth / ang / kay.
   Correct order: _____
   Literal: Beth's the slippers.

6. Tagalog: ito / kina / ba / Philip?
   Correct order: _____
   Literal: Belong to Philip and his friend/s does this?

2 Mga kulay *Colours*

We have already met some of the Tagalog words for colours. Here
is a fuller list:

Tagalog	Pronunciation	English
berde	behr-deh	*green*
azul	ah-sool	*blue*
pula	poo-lah	*red*
puti	poo-tee	*white*
dilaw	dee-lao	*yellow*
itim	ee-teem	*black*
rosas	raw-sahs	*pink*
kayumanggi	ka-you-mang-gee	*brown*
kulay dalandan	koo-lie da-lan-dan	*orange*
kulay-abo	koo-lie-ah-bo	*grey*
biyoleta/murado	bee-yaw-let-ah	*purple*
kulay-pilak	koo-lie-pee-lak	*silver*
kulay-ginto	koo-lie-gin-taw	*gold*

✔ Exercise 3

Read through the list of Tagalog colour words again. Now cover
the list up and line up the English words with their correct Tagalog
equivalents:

1.	yellow	berde	_____
2.	white	kulay-pilak	_____
3.	red	itim	_____
4.	blue	puti	_____
5.	silver	biyoleta	_____
6.	purple	kulay ginto	_____
7.	black	dilaw	_____
8.	green	pula	_____
9.	gold	azul	_____

Exercise 4 Reading and listening

Listen to the tape. Margaret, Bob and family are on a visit to Mines View Park in Baguio. They are trying to decide who will carry each of the bags. Follow the text then try to answer the questions that follow.

Sa Mines View Park sa Baguio

Nasa Mines View Park sa Baguio si Margaret at ang asawa niyang si Bob. Marami silang bag dahil kasama nila si Stephen, Amy, Lucy at Paul. Pakinggan natin sila:

Margaret Kanino itong pulang bag?
Amy Sa akin po.
Bob Kanino naman ang itim na tote bag?
Stephen Hindi sa akin. Kay Paul iyan.
Margaret Kanino ang dilaw na plastic bag?
Paul Kay Lucy yata.
Bob Itong itim na duffel bag, sa iyo ba ito, Stephen?
Stephen Opo. Salamat po.
Margaret Sa iyo ba ang denim na tote bag, Paul?
Paul Hindi po. Kay tatay iyan.

Talasalitaan	*Vocabulary*
nasa parke	*at the park*
ang asawa niyang	*her husband*
marami	*many/plenty*
dahil sa	*because*
kasama nila	*accompanied by*
kanino	*whose*
pulang handbag	*red handbag*
itim	*black*
hindi sa akin	*not mine*
dilaw	*yellow*
yata	*I think*
itong itim	*this black (one)*

Translation

Margaret   Whose red bag is this?
Amy   (It's) mine mum.
Bob: (And) who does this black tote bag belong to?
Stephen   Not mine. That is Paul's.
Margaret   Whose is the yellow plastic bag?
Paul   I think that's Lucy's.
Bob   This black duffel bag, is this yours, Stephen?
Stephen   Yes sir. Thank you.
Margaret   Is the denim tote bag yours, Paul?
Paul   No ma'am. That belongs to Dad.

Answer in complete sentences.

1. Kay Paul ba ang itim na tote bag?
2. Kay Stephen ba ang pulang plastic bag?
3. Kay Paul ba ang duffel bag?
4. Kanino ang denim na tote bag?
5. Kay Lucy ba ang dilaw na plastic bag?

Shopping for a gift

Dialogue 2

The Cook family are at a handicraft shop shopping for **pasalubong**.

Louise	Magaganda ang mga panyolito, pamaypay at burdadong napkins **dito**. Bibili ako ng isang dosenang panyolito.
Bill	Tama. Para kanino ang mga panyolito?
Louise	Para sa mga ka-opisina ko.
Bill	Kanino ang mga pamaypay?
Louise	Sa akin. Bibili ako ng tatlo.
Bill	Bibili naman ako ng laruang Jeepney.
Louise	Kanino ang laruang Jeepney?
Bill	Kanino pa? 'di sa akin at kay Roy.
Louise	Kanino naman ang burdadong napkins?
Bill	Sa kapitbahay natin. Pasalubong!
Louise	Tama.

Talasalitaan	*Vocabulary*
magaganda	*beautiful* (plural)
ang mga panyolito	*the handkerchiefs*
mga pamaypay	*fans*
burdado(ng)	*embroidered*
sa kapitbahay natin	*for our neighbours*
bibili ako ng	*I'll buy/I'm going to buy*
isang dosenang	*one dozen*
tama	*that's right*
para kanino	*for whom*
para sa	*for*
mga ka-opisina ko	*my officemates*
laruan(g)	*toy*
kanino pa	*whose else*
'di sa akin	*of course it's mine*
pasalubong	*gift*

Translation

Louise	The handkerchiefs, fans and embroidered napkins here are gorgeous. I'm going to buy a dozen handkerchiefs.
Bill	All right. For whom are the handkerchiefs?
Louise	For my officemates.
Bill	Whose are the fans?
Louise	Mine. I'm going to buy three.
Bill	I'm going to buy a toy Jeepney.
Louise	Whose is the toy Jeepney?
Bill	Who else's? Of course, it's for Roy and me.
Louise	And whose are the embroidered napkins?
Bill	They are for our neighbours. Homecoming gifts!
Louise	Exactly!

Language skills

3 Kanino *Whose*

Whenever we use a **sa** form sentence to express possession by a person or persons, then the accompanying question word is always **kanino** (*whose*). For example, '**Kanino ang payong?**', *Whose is the umbrella? / To whom does the umbrella belong?* or *Who does the umbrella belong to?* You will notice that there are three variations given in English. The Tagalog form is much simpler using only **kanino**. To form a **kanino** question, simply use **kanino** in place of the **sa** possessor. Note that Tagalog sometimes uses **kanino** in connection with **ng** as a linker, thereby becoming **kanino + ng = kaninong**. The main difference is that **kanino** is used on its own to represent the question word '*whose*', whereas **kaninong** may only be used when followed by the noun it describes or modifies. It can never stand alone. Here are some examples of this form:

1. **Kaninong** sombrero (noun) iyan? *Whose hat is that?* **Kaninong** kotse (noun) ang nasa garahe? *Whose car is in the garage?* **Kaninong** anak (noun) si Sophie? *Whose child is Sophie?*

2. **Kanino** ang lapis? *Whose is the pencil?* **Kanino** ang kotseng itim? *Whose is the black car?*

Look at the following examples:

Question: **Kanino** ang mga maleta?
Reply: **Sa amin** ang mga maleta.

Question: **Kanino** ang bansang Pilipinas?
Reply: **Sa mga Pilipino** ang bansang Pilipinas.

Question: **Kaninong anak** si Prince Charles?
Reply: **Kay Queen Elizabeth na anak** si Prince Charles *or* **Kay Queen Elizabeth**.

Question: **Kaninong pamasahe** ito?
Reply: **Sa aking pamasahe** ito.

Question: **Kaninong pasaporte** ang nasa mesa?
Reply: **Kay Corang pasaporte** ang nasa mesa.

Question: **Kanino** ang computer dito?
Reply: **Sa mga estudyante** ang computer dito.

Exercise 5

Why don't you translate the following sentences into Tagalog? Use **kanino** or **kaninong** + noun.

Example: Whose is this?   **Kanino** ito?
Whose child is Beth?   **Kaninong anak** si Beth?

1. Whose are those?
2. Whose house is this ?
3. Whose teacher is Cora?
4. Whose is that?
5. Whose are these vegetables?
6. Whose are the green mangoes?
7. Whose is this suitcase?
8. Whose child is Joanna?
9. Whose is this suitcase?
10. Whose camera is that?

Exercise 6 Listening and speaking

Listen to the tape. You will hear items mentioned that belong to one of the groups of people in the cartoons. Can you identify which item belongs to which group? You will be asked: **Kanino ang [+ item]?** Your reply should be:

1. **sa mga tao sa beach**,   2. **sa mga turista**   or   3. **sa mga bata.**

Use the vocabulary box provided to help you.

Talasalitaan	*Vocabulary*
beach ball	*beach ball*
pala	*spade*
balde	*bucket*
tuwalya	*towel*
pasaporte	*passport*
tiket	*ticket*
lapis	*pencil*
notbuk	*notebook*
pisara	*blackboard*
kamera/Kodak	*camera*
sunglasses	*sunglasses*
radyo	*radio*
alimango	*crab*
desk	*desk*

Language skills

4 Sa *To/to the, in/in the, on/on the, at/at the*

We have already met 'sa' and looked at its uses in connection with other words. A further use of 'sa' is that it represents the place where the action expressed in a sentence occurs. For example: **Bumili si Roy ng posporo sa tindahan.** *Roy bought some matches from the store.* By far the most common usage of sa is when it represents the English words *in/in the, on/on the, at/at the.* English refers to these words as prepositions. Prepositions tend to be used in two main ways: 1) to represent a place, 2) to represent time. We can try to make this a little clearer by looking at a few examples of each: **Lumalangoy si Louie sa dagat,** *Louie is swimming in the sea.* **May kumakain ba sa kusina?,** *Is someone eating in the kitchen?* **May pagkain na sa mesa,** *There is food on the table now.* **Umiyak siya sa simula ng tula,** *He/she cried at the beginning of the poem.* All of these are prepositions of place. Prepositions can also be used to express the time in which an action occurred. For example: **Matutulog ako sa hapon,** *I will sleep in the afternoon.* **Mananahi ako sa Sabado,** *I will do some sewing on Saturday.* **Nagtatrabaho si Greg sa gabi,** *Greg works at night.*

Study these further examples:

Tagalog: Bibisita ka ba **sa kamakalawa**?
English: *Will you be visiting in a fortnight?*

Tagalog: Wala kami **sa bahay** kahapon.
English: *We weren't at home yesterday.*

Tagalog: Pupunta ka ba **sa kaarawan ko**?
English: *Are you coming to my party?*

Tagalog: Kayo ba ang manedyer **sa tindahang ito**?
English: *Are you the manager in this store?*

The vocabulary box contains some useful time words and phrases.

Talasalitaan	*Vocabulary*
ngayon	*today*
kahapon	*yesterday*
bukas	*tomorrow*
sa isang araw	*the day before yesterday*
sa isang araw	*the day after tomorrow*
ngayong linggo	*this week*
noong isang linggo	*last week*
sa isang linggo	*next week*
ngayong umaga	*this morning*
ngayong hapon	*this afternoon*
mamayang gabi	*tonight*
kahapon nang hapon	*yesterday afternoon*
kagabi	*last night*
bukas nang umaga	*tomorrow morning*
bukas nang gabi	*tomorrow night*
bukas nang hapon	*tomorrow afternoon*
bukas nang tanghali	*tomorrow midday*
mamaya	*later*
linggo-linggo	*every week*
tuwing Linggo	*every Sunday*

Exercise 7

Fill in the space with the correct **sa** (preposition of place) reply. Use the vocabulary box to help you.

Talasalitaan	*Vocabulary*
dagat	*sea*
tindahan	*store*
palengke	*market*
palaruan	*playground*
kalye	*street/road*
tindahan ng laruan	*toy store*
paliparan	*airport*

1. Bibili (buy) si Boy ng sorbetes _____.
2. Maraming eroplano (aeroplanes) _____.
3. Maliligo (bathe) ka ba _____.
4. Magaganda ang mga laruan (toys) _____.
5. Sariwa (fresh) ang mga gulay (vegetables) _____.
6. Naglalaro (play) sina Eileen _____.
7. Tumatakbo (run) ang mga sasakyan (transportation)

   _____.

Exercise 8

This time, provide a **sa** (preposition of time) reply. Use the vocabulary from the box to help you.

Talasalitaan	*Vocabulary*
tanghali	*midday*
gabi	*at night*
hapon	*afternoon*
umaga	*morning*
Sabado	*Saturday*
Linggo	*Sunday*
hatinggabi	*midnight*

Example: Aalis daw siya **sa umaga**.
                Appparently he/she is leaving in the morning.

1. Narito ang mga magulang (parents) ni Elizabeth
   _____. (afternoon)
2. _____ kami sisimba. (will go to church)
3. Maraming bituin (stars) _____ .
4. Mainit (hot) ang araw _____. (midday)
5. Lumulubog (sets) ang araw _____.
6. Sumisikat (shine) ang araw _____.
7. Pupunta (will go) si Jayne at si John dito _____.

One-minute phrases

Sigurado ka ba? (*see-goo-rah-daw kah bah*) Literally, *sure you are?* This phrase is commonly used to express doubt about information. For example: **Sigurado ka bang darating ang bisita mo mamaya?** *Are you sure your visitor will be arriving later?*

Palabiro (*pah-lah-bee-raw*) Literally, *fond of joking.* A person with a good sense of humour! For example: **Palabiro si Juanito kaya laging masaya ang barkada niya.** *Juanito is fond of cracking jokes that's why his friends are always in a happy mood.*

Tayo-tayo (*tah-yaw tah-yaw*) Literally, *we-we* or *us-us.* First person plural. This phrase seems grammatically unusual. Anybody who uses the expression 'tayo-tayo' automatically excludes other people from their group. For example: **Sinu-sino ang iimbitahin mo sa party mo?** *Who are you going to invite to your party?* Reply: **Wala. Tayo-tayo lang.** *No-one. Just ourselves.*

Sila-sila (*see-lah-see-lah*) Literally, *they-they*, exactly the same connotation as 'tayo-tayo' except that this time, it is in the third person plural. For example: **Sila-sila lang ang nag-uusap.** *They themselves are just talking to one another.*

Maasim ang mukha (*mah-ah-seem ahng mook-hah*) Literally, *the face is sour.* This applies to someone whose facial expressions indicate disapproval. For example: **Parang galit si Mister Cruz, maasim ang mukha eh.** *I think Mr Cruz is angry, his face looks sour.*

) **Cultural tip**

For the visiting westerner, clothing in the Philippines can seem very good value for money. Be careful, however, as things may not always be as they seem! Always check a garment carefully. As regulations tend to be more relaxed, there are plenty of 'fake' goods on the market. Check the size carefully, too. Filipinos tend to be smaller in physical stature than their western cousins. A good rule of thumb would be to always try the next size up. For example, if you normally buy XL tee-shirts at home, look for a Filipino size XXL.

11 GUSTO KONG MAGPAGUPIT
I want a haircut

In this unit you will learn how to

■ make an appointment
■ describe what you want done
■ use pseudo-verbs

Making an appointment

Dialogue 1

Bill Cook wants to have his hair cut. He telephones a nearby barber shop.

Bill	Magand**ang** um**a**ga. **Gu**sto kong **mag**pagu**pit**.
Barbero	Magand**ang** um**a**ga *po* na**man**. A**no**ng **o**ras *po* ang **i**big nin**yo**?
Bill	Kail**an**gan kong **mag**pagupit ngay**ong** al**as** dos. **Puwe**de ba?
Barbero	**Ti**tingnan ko *po*. A**ba**, may ba**kant**e *po* ka**mi**. **Puwe**de *po*. Kung **gust**o *po* nin**yo**, mas ma**a**ga.
Bill	**A**yaw ko nang mas ma**a**ga. Al**as** dos na lang.
Barbero	**O**po. Mar**a**ming sal**a**mat *po*.
Bill	Wal**ang** anu**man**.

Talasalitaan	Vocabulary
gusto ko(ng)	*I like/want*
magpagupit	*have a haircut*
ang ibig ninyo?	*what you want?*
ngayon(g) alas dos	*today at two o'clock*
puwede ba	*is it possible*
titingnan ko	*let me see*
aba	*oh!/say!*
may bakante	*has/have a vacancy*
ayaw ko	*I don't like*
mas maaga	*earlier*

Translation

Bill	Good morning. I want to have a haircut.
Barber	Good morning to you, too. What time do you have in mind?
Bill	I need to have a haircut today at 2.00 p.m. Is this possible?
Barber	Let me see. Yes, we have a vacancy. It's possible sir. If you like, we have an earlier time.
Bill	I don't want an earlier time. 2.00 p.m. would be all right.
Barber	Yes sir. Thank you very much.
Bill	Don't mention it.

Inday & Nenet Styling Salon
Del Pilar Street
Iloilo City 5000
Telephone: 56534

Price List

Gupit (lalaki)	₱50.00
Kulot (perm)	₱200.00
Manicure	₱60.00
Pedicure	₱60.00
Masahe	₱75.00
Hair Colour & Wash	₱300.00
Wax	₱400.00
Cut & Wash	₱150.00

Tumatanggap kami ng Home Bookings

Exercise 1

Listen once again to Dialogue 1 on the tape. Try playing the part of the barber, then reverse roles and play the part of Bill Cook.

🔊 Language skills

1 Pseudo-verbs

kailangan	need(s) (to), ought to, must, should
dapat	ought to, must, should
maaari	can, may, could, might
puwede	can, may, could, might
gusto	like(s) (to), would like (to) want(s) (to)
ibig	like(s) (to), would like (to), want(s) (to)
nais	like(s) (to), would like (to), want(s) (to)
ayaw	do(es)n't like (to), wouldn't like (to)

Just one look at this lengthy list is probably enough to send a chill down the spine of the most hardened language learner... – but fear not! Although the list looks complicated, it is in fact quite straightforward. All of the words in the list appear at first glance to be ordinary verbs (doing words). However, although they do have verb-like meanings, they do not change in the same way that genuine verbs do and are therefore called pseudo-verbs. As the translations show, some of the pseudo-verbs are similar to one another in meaning: **kailangan** and **dapat**; **maaari** and **puwede**; **gusto**, **ibig** and **nais**. There are however certain subtle differences.

For example, in sentences where **kailangan** or **dapat** occur, **kailangan** suggests internal necessity or need, whereas **dapat** suggests external necessity or appropriateness. Look at the following sample sentences: a. **Kailangan** matalino ang estudyante b. **Dapat** (na) matalino ang estudyante, may be translated as *The student must be intelligent*. Sentence (a) suggests that the student feels the need to be intelligent, whereas sentence (b) requires that the student be intelligent.

In sentences where **maaari** or **puwede** occur, both denote ability, permission or possibility. **Maaari** is common in both formal and informal contexts; **puwede** is common only in informal contexts.

Gusto, **ibig** and **nais** all denote preference or desire. The three differ from one another in level of usage and in some cases, in connotation as well. **Gusto** is the most common. **Ibig** is more formal than **gusto**, and occurs more frequently in writing than in speech. **Nais** is the most formal and is rare in ordinary conversation.

Ayaw is the contrary of **gusto**, **ibig** and **nais** in that it expresses dislike.

These pseudo-verbs are commonly used in conjunction with **ng** which we first met in Unit 7 (more on this later in this unit). The usage table will help you to decide which is the most appropriate pseudo verb to use:

Usage table

Pseudo-verb	English	Use
gusto	*like(s) (to), would like (to), want (s)*	most common; mild inclination to a stronger desire
ibig	*like(s) (to), would like (to), want (s)*	more formal than **gusto** and occurs more frequently in writing than in speech; a fairly strong desire
nais	*like(s), (to) would like (to), want (s)*	specify stronger preferences than **gusto**; a strong desire
ayaw	*do(es)n't like (to), wouldn't like (to)*	contrary of **gusto**, **ibig**, **nais** (similar in meaning to **hindi**)
dapat	*ought to, must, should*	connotes external necessity or appropriateness
kailangan	*need(s) (to), ought to, must, should*	connotes internal necessity or need
maaari	*can, may, could, might*	denotes ability, permission, or possibility; common in both informal and formal contexts
Puwede	*can, may, could, might*	denotes ability, permission, or possibility; common only in informal contexts

Examples:

Tagalog: **Kailangan** mo ba ito?
English: *Do you need this?*

Tagalog: Hindi ko **gusto** ang pagkain kagabi.
English: *I didn't like the food last night.*

Tagalog: **Puwede** tayong matulog doon.
English: *We can sleep (over) there.*

Tagalog: Ito ba ang **nais** mo?
English: *Is this what you want?*

Tagalog: Iyan ang **ibig** ko sa kaniya.
English: *That's what I like about him.*

Tagalog: **Ayaw** ko ng kapeng walang gatas.
English: *I don't like coffee without milk.*

Tagalog: **Dapat** na narito sila bukas.
English: *They should be here tomorrow.*

Tagalog: **Maaari** bang dito muna tayo?
English: *Might we stop here first?*

☑ Exercise 2

Complete the following sentences with an appropriate pseudo-verb.

1. Ano ang (gusto, kailangan, ibig, nais) [like] mo?
2. (Kailangan, nais, ibig) [need] namin ng malamig na tubig.
3. Bakit (ayaw, ibig, gusto) [doesn't like] niya ng halo-halo?
4. (Dapat, nais, ayaw) [should] nasa bahay na ang mga bata.
5. Ano ang (ibig, puwede, dapat) [want] kainin ng bisita?

🔊 Describing what you want done

▣ Dialogue 2

Bill Cook is at the barber's. He is describing to the barber the haircut he wants.

Barber   Sir, ano **pong** gu**pit** ang **gus**to nin**yo**?
Bill   **Gus**to ko *hindi* mas**ya**dong ma**ha**ba.
Barber   Ibig *po* ba nin**yo** hang**gang** ita**as** ng **ba**tok?
Bill   **Puwe**de na, **pe**ro *hindi* ko **gus**to ang crew cut.
Barber   **Nai**s *po* ba nin**yo** *maikli* sa ta**bi**?
Bill   Oo. **Pe**ro kai**lang**an **med**yo maka**pal** sa tuk**tok**.
Barber   Okay lang *po*. **Hu**hugasan ko lang *po* ang inyong bu**hok**.
Bill   O **si**ge, **gus**to ko rin ng **kon**ting masahe.

Barber Opo sir.
Bill Salamat.
Barber *Wala* pong anu**man**.

Talasalitaan	*Vocabulary*
ano pong gupit	*what (kind of) haircut*
sa tabi	*at the sides*
hindi masyado(ng)	*not very*
mahaba	*long*
ibig po ba ninyo	*do you want*
hanggang itaas	*reaching the top*
batok	*nape*
puwede na	*will suffice*
gusto ko rin	*I'd also want*
hindi ko gusto	*I don't like*
nais po ba ninyo	*do you want*
medyo	*slightly*
maikli	*short*
makapal	*thick*
sa tuktok	*at the top*
huhugasan ko lang	*I'll just wash*
ang inyong buhok	*your hair*
konting masahe	*a little massage*

Translation

Barber Sir, what kind of haircut would you like?
Bill I like it not too long.
Barber Would you like it just above the nape of the neck?
Bill That would do, but I don't want a crew cut.
Barber Would you like it to be short at the sides?
Bill Yes. But it needs to be thick on top.
Barber That's OK sir. I just have to wash your hair.
Bill OK, I'd also want a massage.
Barber Yes sir.
Bill Thank you.
Barber You're welcome sir.

Exercise 3 Writing and speaking

Sagutin sa Tagalog (respond in Tagalog):

1. Anong klaseng gupit ang gusto ni Bill?
2. Gusto ba ni Bill ng crew cut?
3. Saan dapat maikli ang gupit?
4. Ano muna ang gagawin ng barbero?
5. Ano pa ang gusto ni Bill na gagawin ng barbero?

Language skills

2 More about pseudo-verbs

Since **kailangan**, **gusto**, **ibig**, **nais**, **maaari**, **puwede**, **ayaw** and **dapat** are considered as action words, it is clear that they have to be used in connection with a word which identifies those actually 'doing' the 'action' ('subjects' or, perhaps more appropriately, we can refer to them as 'actors').

In Tagalog, the general rule is as follows: pseudo-verbs take only **ng** form 'actors'. The **ng** form consists of the following: **ni** (of / singular – personal), **nina** (of / plural – personal), **ko** (my), **mo** (your), **niya** (his / her), **namin** (our / exclusive), **natin** (our / inclusive), **ninyo** (your / plural), **nila** (their), **nito** (of this), **niyan** (of that), **noon** (of that over there) and **ng** (of). These pseudo-verbs may also need an object or objects.

Remember the difference between a definite and an indefinite object? A definite object is always preceded by the word 'the', whereas an indefinite object is always preceded by the word 'a'. The connecting word used with an indefinite object is **ng** whereas **ang** is used for definite objects. Although this may sound horribly complicated, try not to feel intimidated by the jargon. Look carefully at the table below and then study the examples:

Pseudo-verb	Actor	Object		
		Definite	**or**	**indefinite**
	A	B		C
kailangan (**ng**)	ni,nina, ko, mo,	(**ang**) si sina, ako,		(**ng**)
gusto	niya, namin, natin	ka, siya, kami		same as A
ibig	ninyo, nila, nito	tayo, kayo,sila		
nais	niyan, noon	ito, iyan, iyon		
puwede	**ng** + noun	**ang** + noun		
ayaw				
dapat				
maaari				
(**Note**: ko + ka = kita)				

To produce a pseudo-verb sentence: 1. Choose a pseudo-verb. 2. Choose an 'actor' from column A. 3. Choose a definite object from column 'B' 'or' 4. Choose an indefinite object from column C.

The basic formula is as follows:

Pseudo-verb +A + B or C = sentence

Look at the following example sentences. Note the differences between a pseudo-verb and actor used in connection with a definite object, then with an indefinite object.

Pseudo-verb	Actor	Indefinite object	Definite object
Ayaw	ni Judy	**ng hilaw na mangga**	
Judy doesn't like unripe mangoes			
Ayaw	ni Judy		**ang hilaw na mangga**
Judy doesn't like the unripe mango			
Gusto	mo [ba]		**ito?**
Do you want/like/Would you want/like this?			
Gusto	mo [ba]	**nito?**	
Do yu want/like Would you want/like some of this?			
Kailangan	ko	**ng bagong sapatos**	
I need a new (pair of) shoes			
Kailangan ko			**ang bagong sapatos**
I need the new (pair of) shoes			

Did you notice...?

The first example could be literally translated as 'doesn't like of Judy unripe mangoes'. However, as explained earlier, all pseudo-verbs require **ng** form actors. Although these **ng** form actors are required in Tagalog, we do not need to translate them into English. The correct translation of the sentence thus reads, *Judy doesn't like unripe mangoes.*

Exercise 4

Match up columns A (pseudo-verb with **ng** actor) and B (definite / indefinite object) correctly. When you have done this, use a preposition of time or space from the box to expand the sentence further.

Example:

A	B	Place
Gusto namin	ng malamig na Pepsi	sa bahay

A (pseudo-verb with 'actor')	B (definite or indefinite object)
Gusto ni Tessie	magpagupit
Kailangan nila	ng malamig na kape
Nais po ba ninyo	ang bagong kotse
Hindi ko gusto (ng)	ng katulong
Ayaw ng mga bisita	ng aking tulong

Exercise 5

Fill in the space with a pseudo-verb and then translate your sentence into English.

1. _____ mo ba ng lapis (pencil)?
   Translation:

2. _____ bumili ni Baby ng saging (banana) sa palengke.
   Translation:

3. Bakit mo _____ ng malaking pisara (blackboard)?
   Translation:

4. Sino ang _____ mong isama (go with you) sa sine?
   Translation:

5. _____ mo ba ng malamig (cold) na Pepsi?
   Translation:

Dialogue 3

Louise Cook is at the hairdresser's. She is discussing hairstyles with the hairdresser (HD).

HD	Maganda *po* ang bu**h**ok ni**n**yo ma'am, **Ano** *po* ang **gus**to ni**nyo**ng ga**win** ko?
Louise	Puwede bang cut, and blow dry?
HD	Maaari *po*. **Gus**to *po* ba ni**n**yo ng *mai**kli***?
Louise	**Ba**gay ba sa **a**kin ang maik**l**ing gu**pit**?
HD	**O**po. Ba**ba**gay *po* sa in**yo**. Magan**da** *po* sa in**yo** ang maik**l**ing bu**hok**.
Louise	Mas **ba**gay **ya**ta sa **a**kin ang ma**h**a**b**a.
HD	**Ba**gay *po* sa in**yo** ang ma**h**aba at mai**kli**.
Louise	O **si**ge, mai**kli**.
HD	Okay *po*. Huhu**ga**san ko **mu**na ang bu**h**ok ni**n**yo.
Louise	Sa**la**mat.
HD	*Wala* pong anu**man**.

Talasalitaan	*Vocabulary*
maikling buhok	*short hair*
ang buhok ninyo	*your hair*
ang mahaba	*a longer one*
gawin ko	*I'd do*
puwede ba(ng)?	*is it possible?*
maaari po	*it's possible* (formal)
bagay ba sa akin	*does it suit me*
ang maikling gupit	*short cut*
babagay po sa inyo	*it will suit you*
mas bagay	*suits better*
huhugasan ko muna	*I will wash first*
maganda sa inyo	*beautiful/nice on you*

Translation

HD	You're hair is pretty madam. What would you like me to do?
Louise	Can I have a 'cut and blow dry'?
HD	It's possible ma'am, would you like a short cut?
Louise	Does a short cut suit me?
HD	Yes ma'am, it would suit you. A short cut would be nice on you.
Louise	I think a longer (one) is prettier.
HD	Long hair and short hair both suit you.
Louise	OK, a short one.
HD	OK ma'am. I'll have to wash your hair first.
Louise	Thank you.
HD	Don't mention it.

Exercise 6

Try playing the part of the hairdresser. Based on the dialogue, tell Mrs Cook the following:

1. Her hair is very long.
2. That long hair suits her too.
3. You'll have to wash her hair.

More words used at the barber shop / hairdresser can be found in the vocabulary box.

Talasalitaan	*Vocabulary*
magpakulot	*to have a perm*
magpagupit	*to have a cut*
putulin/gupitin	*to cut* (the hair)
putulan/gupitan	*to give the hair/person a cut*
i-set	*to set the hair*
gunting	*scissors*
tuwalya	*towel*
silya	*chair*
tuwid na buhok	*straight hair*
minamanikyur	*being given a manicure*
pinipedikyur	*being given a pedicure*

Exercise 7

Listen carefully to the tape. You will hear three different people explaining to their hairdresser / barber what they want. Use Dialogue 3 and vocabulary boxes to help you understand. Write down on the task sheet what each customer is asking for:

Toto Mario's Unisex Hair Salon

476 Pereira Street
Quezon City

Phone 01915-5550

Stylist: *Mario*   Date: *March 19, 2000*

Customer 1 _____
Pangalan: _____
Kailangan:_____
_____
_____

Customer 2 _____
Pangalan: _____
Kailangan:_____
_____
_____

Customer 3 _____
Pangalan: _____
Kailangan:_____
_____
_____

Exercise 8 Understanding and speaking

You are off to the stylist to have your own hair cut. Listen to the tape and respond to your stylist's questions:

Stylist Magandang umaga po. Welcome sa Toto Mario's.
Ikaw   (Say good morning)

Stylist	Ano po ang maitutulong ko sa inyo?
Ikaw	(Tell him you want to have your hair cut)
Stylist	Ibig n'yo na po bang magpagupit ngayon o gumawa ng appointment para bukas?
Ikaw	(Tell him you would like it now, if possible)
Stylist	Aba opo. Gusto rin po ba ninyong hugasan ko ito?
Ikaw	(Tell him no thank you. You just want it cut)
Stylist	Ibig po ba ninyo mahabang gupit o maikli?
Ikaw	(Tell him you want it cut short)
Stylist	Ibig rin po ba ninyo ng masahe?
Ikaw	(Tell him politely you just want the haircut)
Stylist	Okay lang po sir.
Ikaw	(Say thank you very much)

Tips

1. Don't forget to tip 10–15%
2. Ask if they have worked with non-Asian hair before (if you are non-Asian)
3. Ask them to repeat what you have requested (to make sure they have understood)
4. Stylists often love to chat. Don't lose the opportunity to practice your Tagalog!

☝ Language skills!

3 More on the sa preposition

During the conversation between Louise Cook and the hairdresser, the hairdresser said: **Babagay po sa inyo. Maganda po sa inyo and maikling buhok**. It will suit you ma'am. A short cut would be nice on you. In this example, the word 'sa' was used in yet another way. It wasn't used as a preposition of time or place, but rather with the describing word **maganda**. **Sa** can also be used with adjectives. For example: **Mabait sa akin si Cora**. Cora is nice to me. **Mabuti sa kanila ang mga guro**. The teachers are

good to them. **Mapagmahal si Jonathan sa mga kapatid niya.**
Jonathan is affectionate to his brothers. When **sa** is used as an
ordinary preposition, then it is translated into English as either **to**,
for, **on**, **in**, **into**, **about**, or **at**.

Some further examples:

1. Tagalog: Malaki **sa iyo** ang blusa mo
   English: *Your blouse is big on you*

2. Tagalog: Maliit **sa bata** ang sapatos
   English: *The shoes are small on the child*

3. Tagalog: Maluwang **kay Larry** ang sombrerong ito
   English: *This hat is loose (big) on Larry*

4. Tagalog: Mabuti raw **sa iyo** ang gamot
   English: *Apparently, the medicine is good for you*

Exercise 9

Why don't you see how much you have remembered – choose the
correct answer from the box:

1. Magalang _____ (to the old people) si Rosita.
2. Mabuti _____ (to you) ang magpahinga.
3. Malaki yata _____ (on him) ang tsinelas.
4. Hindi ba maliit _____ (on me) ang pantalong ito?
5. Mabait _____ (to us) ang bisita ni Margaret.
6. Masyadong mahaba _____ (on her) ang damit na ito.

One-minute phrases

> **Matigas ang ulo** (*mah-tee-gahs ahng oolaw*) Literally; *hard the
> head.* Meaning hardheaded/stubborn. For example: **Matigas
> ang ulo ni Boy**. *Boy is stubborn.*
>
> **Hindi yata pupuwede** (*heen-dee yah-tah poo-poo-weh-de*h)
> Literally; *not I think it will do* Meaning *I don't think it's possible./
> I don't think it can.*
>
> **Pagbutihin mo** (*pahg-boo-tee-heen ma*w). Meaning *make it
> good*. This phrase is commonly used when offering
> encouragement. For example: **Pagbutihin mo ang pag-aaral**

para maging doktor ka pagdating ng araw. *Study hard so that you'll become a doctor in the future.*

Lakad-takbo (*lah-kahd tahk-baw*) Literally; *walk-run.* Meaning a brisk walking pace. For example: **Lakad-takbo ang ginawa ko para maabot ko ang huling biyahe ng tren.** *I half walked, half-ran in order to catch the last train.*

Mabilis pa sa alas-singko (*mah-bee-lees pah sah ah-lahs-seeng-kaw*). Literally, *faster than five o'clock.* This phrase goes back to the time in the 1950s and 1960s when Filipino employees in Manila used to listen out for the five o'clock whistle from the port area of the city. The whistle signalled the end of the shift for the dock workers. Anyone finishing their work before the five o'clock whistle was deemed by his or her workmates to be *faster than the five o'clock* [whistle].

(i) **Cultural tip**

Whether you want to make an appointment with a hairdresser or buy something from a department store, you may sometimes find it difficult to attract the attention of a shop assistant. Invariably, they know that you are there but are hesitant to give you eye contact or approach you because of a lack of confidence in their own English. The assumption is always that foreigners do not understand Tagalog. This is just shyness and can easily be overcome with a warm and friendly smile, coupled with a few words of Tagalog. Never be afraid to try out your Tagalog. Even a few words will go a long way towards giving you a positive and memorable experience of the Philippines.

12 BAGAY BA SA AKIN?
Does this suit me?

In this unit you will learn how to

■ try something on in a store
■ use the passive
■ describe the weather

Trying something on in a store

Dialogue 1

Louise Cook is trying something on in the changing room of a departmental store.

Store assistant	**Gus**to *po* ba nin**yo** i**yan**? Mag**su**kat pa *po* ka**yo** ng i**ba**. **Pal**da at **blu**sa po kung **a**yaw nin**yo** ng di**ret**so. May i**bang ku**lay rin po. Mag**su**kat *po* ka**yo** ng **pal**da at **blu**sa.
Louise	**Si**ge. (Isi**nu**kat) **Med**yo masi**kip ya**ta ang **blu**sa **pe**ro malu**wang na**man ang **pal**da. **Gus**to kong pu**mi**li pa.
Store assistant	**Si**ge *po*. Pu**mi**li pa *po* ka**yo**. I**to** pong may bulak**lak**? Di**ret**so po i**to**.
Louise	**Na**pakagan**da** ni**yan** at kung **ta**ma ang **su**kat, **bi**bili a**ko** ng dala**wa**. **Gus**to ko ring bu**mi**li ng ban**da**na.
Store assistant	Ma**ra**mi *po* ka**ming** ban**da**na. **Na**sa kabi**lang** departa**men**to *po* ang mga **i**to.
Louise	Ma**ra**ming sa**la**mat.
Store assistant	*Wa**la*** pong anu**man**.

Talasalitaan	*Vocabulary*
gusto po ba ninyo	*do you like/would you like*
magsukat pa	*try some more*
ng iba	*other ones*
may palda at blusa	*we have blouses and skirts*
kung ayaw ninyo	*if you don't like*
diretso	*straight* (dress)
ibang kulay rin	*other colours also*
bibili ako	*I will buy*
isinukat	*tried it on*
medyo masikip	*slightly small*
ng bandana	*a scarf*
pero maluwang	*but loose*
pumili pa	*choose some more*
may bulaklak	*with flowers*
napakaganda	*so pretty*
niyan	*that*
kung tama	*if right*
ang sukat	*the size*
ang kamay	*the arms*
nasa kabila(ng) departamento	*in the department store*

Translation

Store assistant Do you like that ma'am? Why not try a few others. We have skirts and blouses if you don't want a dress. They come in other colours too. Why not try on a skirt and a blouse ma'am.

Louise All right. (*trying*) I think the blouse is a little tight but on the other hand the skirt is loose.

Store assistant Okay ma'am. Please try on some others. How about this flowery dress?

Louise That is so pretty, and if it's my size, I will take two. I would also like to buy a scarf.

Store assistant We have many scarves. They're in the department next door.

Louise Thank you very much.

Store assistant You're welcome.

Exercise 1

Drawing from what you have learned so far, replace the words in italics with a different adjective, verb, noun or pronoun, to form coherent Tagalog sentences.

Example: Gusto po ba ninyo *iyan*?
Answer: Gusto po ba ninyo *ito*?

1. May palda at blusa po kung *ayaw* ninyo ng diretso.
2. Magsukat po kayo ng *palda at blusa*.
3. Medyo *masikip* yata ito.
4. Ito pong may *bulaklak*?
5. Napakaganda niyan at kung *mabuti* ang sukat, bibili ako ng dalawa.
6. Gusto ko ring *bumili* ng bandana.
7. Marami po kaming *bandana*.

Language skills

1 Verbs: Active voice / passive voice Transitive / intransitive

When forming a simple sentence, action words play a key role: they let us know what is being done. These action words are known as verbs. Verbs have two distinct ways of indicating an action, each giving a different flavour or 'voice' to the sentence. We can call these distinct flavours the active voice and the passive voice. The 'voice' of a sentence tells us something about the relationship between: 1) the subject of the verb; 2) the 'doer' of the verbal action; 3) the person or thing that the verbal action is done to.

We use the active voice when the subject of the verb is the 'doer' of the action. The active voice is used in most English speech and writing, because we usually want to inform our listeners or our readers about who or what carried out the action of the verb. For example: Roy read a book yesterday. Jack and Jill carried a pail of water. I bought a pair of slippers.

The passive voice is used when the subject is not the person or thing 'doing' the action of the verb. It is the person or thing that is acted upon by the verb. For example: The ball was thrown by the boy. The ribbon was cut by the mayor. These words were said by him. We also use the passive voice to direct our listener's attention to the most important part of our message. The passive voice can be used when we do not know who carries out the action expressed by the verb. For example: The food has been eaten.

Before moving on to **um** verbs, it is important for us to understand the difference between transitive and intransitive verbs. Very simply, a transitive verb is a verb that has a direct object. For example: **Bumili si Roy ng sombrero** (*bumili* is the verb while **ng sombrero** is the direct object). *Roy bought a hat.* An intransitive verb, by way of contrast, is a verb that has no direct object. For example: **Namili si Mary**. *Mary went shopping.* Some verbs are always transitive (with an object), others are always intransitive (without an object), but just to keep us on our toes, many verbs are used both transitively and intransitively. We will further explore both transitive and intransitive verbs as we go along.

2 The um verb

We now turn to the first active verb type, known as the **um** verb. The **um** verb type forms major transitive and intransitive verbs. There are two major ways of forming **um** verbs: 1) by adding **um** in front of a verb stem or 'root' that begins with a vowel. (A verb root is a verb in its simplest form. For example, the verb **kumain** *to eat*. The root / stem of **kumain**, is **kain** = *eat*); or 2) by inserting **um** inside a verb root that begins with a consonant (non-vowel). Look at some examples.

How to change the tense of an **um** verb stem beginning with a vowel:

Example: Verb stem: **alis** (*leave*)

um + alis	= umalis (to leave)	infinitive
a + alis	= aalis	future
um + a + alis	= umaalis	present
um + alis	= umalis	past

Note: Did you notice that in the **um** verb the infinitive and past tense look the same? They are distinguished only by their use. While the infinitive is only used in commands, suggestions and requests, (For example: **Umalis ka!** '*You go*'), the past tense usually takes a time element in the sentence (for example: Kumain **kami kagabi**, *We ate last night*).

Four major ways of changing verb tenses in Tagalog

1. Infinitive (used in commands, suggestions and requests only)
   For example:
   Command: Huwag kang **tumayo** diyan! *Don't [you] stand there!*
   Suggestion: **Kumain** na tayo. *Let's eat now*
   Request: Puwede bang **kumuha** ka ng plato sa kusina?
   Could you fetch a plate from the kitchen?

2. Future: will/shall + infinitive, the future perfect tense (will have + past participle), be going to + infinitive the future progressive tense (will be + present participle)
   For example: **Uuwi ako.** *I am going home. I will/shall go home*

3. Present: the simple present tense, the present progressive tense
   For example: **Kumakain** ako ng gulay araw-araw. *I eat vegetables every day*

4. Past: the simple past tense, the past progressive tense
   Example: **Bumili** si Ronald ng sorbetes. *Ronald bought some ice-cream*

 Listen to the pronunciation of each of the following verbs, then try to pronounce each word yourself, without the help of the tape.

Verb root	Meaning	Infinitive	Future	Present	Past
akyat	*climb*	umakyat	aakyat	umaakyat	umakyat
asa	*rely upon*	umasa	aasa	umaasa	umasa
inom	*drink*	uminom	iinom	umiinom	uminom
iyak	*cry*	umiyak	iiyak	umiiyak	umiyak
uwi	*go home*	umuwi	uuwi	umuuwi	umuwi
utang	*borrow money*	umutang	uutang	umuutang	umutang

How to change the tense of an **um** verb stem beginning with a consonant:

Example: Verb stem: **basa** (*read*)

b + um + asa	= bumasa (to read)	infinitive
ba + basa	= babasa	future
b + um + abasa	= bumabasa	present
b + um + asa	= bumasa	past

 Listen to the pronunciation of each of the following verbs, then try to pronounce each word yourself, without the help of the tape.

Verb root	Meaning	Infinitive	Future	Present	Past
bili	*buy*	bumili	bibili	bumibili	bumili
kain	*eat*	kumain	kakain	kumakain	kumain
kuha	*get*	kumuha	kukuha	kumukuha	kumuha
gawa	*make*	gumawa	gagawa	gumagawa	gumawa
hiram	*borrow*	humiram	hihiram	humihiram	humiram
lakad	*walk*	lumakad	lalakad	lumalakad	lumakad

More verbs can be found listed at the back of this book.

This is the formula:

Verb	+ actor
Kumain	si Louie
Ate	Louie

Louie ate

Verb	+ actor	+ object
Kumain	si Louie	ng sorbetes
Ate	Louie	ice cream

Louie ate (some) ice cream

Verb	+ actor	+ object	+ place
Kumain	si Louie	ng sorbetes	sa restawran
Ate	Louie	ice cream	at the restaurant

Louie ate (some) ice cream at the restaurant

Verb	+ actor	+ object	+ place	+ time
Kumain	si Louie	ng sorbetes	sa restawran	kahapon
Ate	Louie	ice cream	at the restaurant	yesterday

Louie ate (some) ice cream at the restaurant yesterday

Did you notice how you are able to expand a very simple sentence easily? You can lengthen a sentence by merely adding a preposition of time or place or an adverb etc.

Exercise 2

Using the sentence structure provided (verb + actor + object + place + time), build a Tagalog sentence around each of the following verbs. Use the vocabulary box provided to help you:

1. Bibili
2. Kumakain
3. Gumawa
4. Humihiram
5. Iinom

Talasalitaan	*Vocabulary*
kahapon	*yesterday*
ngayon	*today*
humihiram	*borrowing*
ng kape	*coffee*
kumakain	*eating*
iinom	*will drink*
ng laruan	*toy*
araw-araw	*every day*
gumawa	*to make*
bibili	*will buy*

A note about recent action

There is a minor, yet important, aspect of active Tagalog verbs known as the recent action. The recent action is used to express events in the very recent past. It is formed by prefixing **ka** to the future tense of the verb. For example, the future tense of the **um** verb **alis** is **aalis**. To form the recent action aspect of the verb, we simply add **ka** + **aalis** = **kaaalis**. Remember, however, that the recent action takes the **ng** form as the 'doer' of the action. In order to underline how recent the action is, the word **lang** (*only/just/only just*) is always used with the recent action form. For example, **Kaaalis lang ni Stephen at ni Amy**, *Amy and Stephen have only just left*. **Huwag na tayong magmeryenda, kakakain lang natin ng tanghalian**, *Let's not have a snack as we've only just eaten lunch*. **Kadarating mo lang ba?**, *Have you just arrived?*

Asking about alterations

Dialogue 2

Louise Cook is at the dressmaker's.

Louise   Maganda**ng ha**pon.

Modista Maganda**ng ha**pon *po* na**man**.

Louise   Bumili a**ko** ng **te**lang pambis**tida** sa pal**e**ng**ke, at **gus**to kong *magpatahi* ng bes**tida**.

Modista Aba **o**po. **Na**saan *po* ang **te**la n'yo?

Louise   **He**to. Ay**o**kong mas**ya**dong *maikli* ito.

Modista *Hindi po.* Pu**we**de po bang su**ka**tan ko ka**yo**?

Louise   Aba **oo** na**man**.

Modista Ang **su**kat *po* ng dib**dib** ay tatlum**pu't an**im na pul**ga**da. Ang **bay**wang *po* ay dalawam**pu't** wal**ong** pul**ga**da. Ang hips *po* ay tatlum**pu't** wal**ong** pul**ga**da. Ang mang**gas** *po* ay wal**ong** pul**ga**da. Ang ba**li**kat ay labing-**an**im na pul**ga**da. Ang ha**ba** ng **pal**da ay dalawam**pu't a**pat na pul**ga**da. Iyan lang *po*.

Louise   Kai**lan** ko maa**a**ring ma**ku**ha ang da**mit**?

Modista Sa Biyernes *po*. Mga al**as kwa**tro nang **ha**pon.

Louise   Mar**a**ming sal**a**mat.

Modista *Wala* pong anu**man**.

Talasalitaan	*Vocabulary*
ang sukat ko	*my measurement*
bumili	*bought*
telang pambistida	*dress material*
haba	*length*
sukatan	*to measure*
pulgada	*inches*
paikliin	*be shortened*
nasaan	*where*
heto	*here*
ayoko(ng)	*don't like*
sukat ng dibdib	*bust line*
palengke	*market*
kailan	*when*
magpatahi	*have clothes made*
bukas nang hapon	*tomorrow afternoon*
baywang	*waistline*

hips	*hips*
manggas	*sleeves*
balikat	*shoulders*
palda	*skirt*
makuha	*to collect/get*

Translation

Louise	Good afternoon.
Dressmaker	Good afternoon to you, too.
Louise	I bought some cloth at the market and I would like to have a dress made up.
Dressmaker	Yes ma'am. Where is your cloth?
Louise	Here. I don't want it to be too short.
Dressmaker	No ma'am. Can I take your measurements?
Louise	Of course.
Dressmaker	Your bust line is 36. Your waist line is 28. Your hips are 38. Sleeve length is 8 inches. Armhole is 14 inches. Shoulders are 16. Skirt length is 24 inches. That's all ma'am.
Louise	When will I be able to collect the dress?
Dressmaker	On Friday ma'am, at about 4.00 in the afternoon.
Louise	Thank you very much.
Dressmaker	You're welcome.

Some useful words for a visit to the **sastre** (*tailor*) can be found in the vocabulary box.

Talasalitaan	*Vocabulary*
medida	*tape measure*
sinulid	*thread*
karayom	*needle*
iklian	*to make short*
habaan	*to make long*
lakihan	*to make big*
liitan	*to make small*
palitan	*change*
terno	*go together*
itupi	*to fold*
kalsahan	*to lower the hemline*

Exercise 3

 Listen to the list of items on the tape. The tailor has misplaced his spectacles and can't see where he has left things. Can you help him find them? With a pen or pencil, circle each item mentioned as you hear it.

Exercise 4

How do you say the following in Tagalog?

1. You want a green skirt.
2. You don't want a long skirt.
3. You need it on Monday.
4. Your skirt is at home.

Language skills

3 Verbalisation of adjectives

Louise Cook used the word **umikli** in her conversation with the dressmaker, **ayokong masyadong umikli ito**. **Umikli** is derived from the adjective **maikli** (*short*). In Tagalog, adjectives can also become action words (verbs). When this happens, the resulting meaning of the newly formed action word is 'to become _____'. To do this, simply drop the prefix 'ma' from the adjective, e.g., **maikli** (*short*), add '**um**' = **um** + **ikli** = **umikli** (*to become shorter*). When the adjective root begins with a vowel (e.g. **asim**, '*sourness*'), simply add 'um' before the root word to produce the infinitive (e.g. **um + asim = umasim** *to become sour*). When the adjective root begins with a consonant (e.g. **ganda** *beauty*), then '**um**' is placed after the first letter (e.g. **g + um + anda = gumanda**, t*o become beautiful*). Here are some more examples:

Example: Adjective stem: **sama** (*badness*) source: **masama** (*bad*)

s + um + ama = sumama (to become/ get worse)	infinitive
sa + sama = sasama (will become/ get worse)	future
s + um + asama = sumasama (becoming/ getting worse)	present
s + um + ama = sumama (became/ got worse)	past

Listen to the pronunciation of each of the following verbalised adjectives on the tape. Why not try to repeat them without the help of the tape.

Adjective	Meaning	Infinitive	Future	Present	Past
(ma)laki	*big*	lumaki	lalaki	lumalaki	lumaki
(ma)ganda	*pretty*	gumanda	gaganda	gumaganda	gumanda
(ma)liit	*small*	lumiit	liliit	lumiliit	lumiit
(ma)sarap	*delicious*	sumarap	sasarap	sumasarap	sumarap
(ma)layo	*far*	lumayo	lalayo	lumalayo	lumayo
(ma)buti	*good*	bumuti	bubuti	bumubuti	bumuti
(ma)linis	*clean*	luminis	lilinis	lumilinis	luminis

A further list can be found at the back of this book.

Some example sentences:

Tagalog: **Gumaganda** ang hardin ni Patricia
Literal: becoming more beautiful the garden of Patricia
English: *Patricia's garden is becoming more beautiful*

Tagalog: **Lumilinis** ang kotse mo
Literal: becoming cleaner the car your
English: *Your car is becoming cleaner*

Tagalog: Hindi **bumuti** ang panahon
Literal: (did)not improve the weather
English: *The weather did not improve*

Tagalog: **Bumibilis** yata ang takbo ng relos mo
Literal: becoming fast I think the running of watch your
English: *I think your watch is running fast*

✔ Exercise 5

Provide the correct tense of the following verbalised adjectives. The stem of each adjective is given in the bracket:

1. _____ ang problema ni Jose araw-araw. (laki, present)
2. Ang bahay ni Aling Maria ay _____. (ganda, present)
3. Hindi ba _____ ang kotse ni Les? (linis, past)
4. Kailangang _____ tayo sa gulo. (layo, infinitive)

✔ Exercise 6

See how many verbalised adjectives you can find in the crossword.

		S	A	K	A	L	I	D
	L	U	M	A	L	A	K	I
L	U	M	I	W	A	N	A	G
	M	A		A	H	A	S	H
H	I	R	A	P		P	M	A
I	N	A	K	B	A	Y	A	A
	A	P	A	N	D	A		
A	W		T	A	N	O	T	N

Describing the weather

Dialogue 3

The weather is bad. Bill, Louise and Roy Cook are talking about it in their hotel room.

Bill   Mukhang *sumasama* ang panahon. Babagyo yata!

Louise   Kagabi, umulan nang malakas at humangin din.

Roy   Noong isang linggo, kahit umuulan, sumisikat ang araw.

Louise   Mabuti kung ganooon.

Bill   Mahirap kasi dito sa Pilipinas, kapag umulan, babaha kaagad.

Roy   Dumidilim na naman ang langit.

Louise   Mabuti yata dito muna tayo sa hotel hanggang sa gumanda ang panahon.

Bill   Sang-ayon sa radyo, bubuti raw ang panahon bago gumabi.

Roy   Magbabasa ako ng aklat.

Talasalitaan	*Vocabulary*
umulan	*to rain*
sumasama	*becoming/getting worse*
ang panahon	*the weather*
babagyo	*there will be a typhoon*
na naman	*again*
ang langit	*the sky*
umulan	*rained*
humangin	*was windy*
noong isang linggo	*last week*
kahit	*even though*
umuulan	*raining*
sumisikat	*shining*
ang araw	*the sun*
gumabi	*to become night*
kung ganoon	*if that's the case*
mahirap	*difficult*
kapag	*if/when*
babaha	*will flood*
kaagad	*immediately*
dumidilim	*becoming dark*

dito muna	*here* (for the moment)
hanggang	*until*
gumanda	*to become fine*
sang-ayon sa	*according to*
radyo	*radio*
bubuti	*will become better*
bago	*before*
magbabasa	*will read*

Translation

Bill   The weather seems to be getting worse. I think a typhoon is coming.

Louise   Last night, it rained hard and there was wind too.

Roy   The other week, even though it was raining, the sun was shining.

Louise   It's good (when it's) like that.

Bill   The trouble here in the Philippines is that when it rains there are floods.

Roy   The sky is getting darker again.

Louise   It might be a good idea to stay in the hotel until the weather settles.

Bill   According to the radio, the weather will be fine by tonight.

Roy   I will read a book.

☑ Exercise 7

The following sentences need to be expanded. Can you add an adverb of time (e.g. **bukas**, *tomorrow*) or preposition (e.g. **sa** *in*, *at*) to expand each sentence? Use the vocabulary box provided to help you:

Example: Kumikidlat kanina   add: **pero** hindi yata uulan.

1. Bumubuti ang panahon **kasi**
2. Umuulan nang malakas **lagi**
3. Hindi bumabaha sa Pilipinas **kung**
4. Lumiliwanag ba ang langit **kahit na**
5. Sasama ang panahon bago gumabi **sapagka't**

Talasalitaan	Vocabulary
kasi	*because*
lagi	*always*
kung	*if/when*
kahit na	*even though*
sapagka't	*because*

Language skills

4 Verbalisation of acts of nature

Most Tagalog words describing acts of nature can also be made into verbs. For example, if the sun is shining, Filipinos merely say '**Umaaraw!**' (from **araw** = the sun). If there is a flash of lightning, they exclaim: '**Kumikidlat!**' (from **kidlat** = lightning). **Umulan kasi kaya hindi kami sumimba**, *It rained that's why we didn't go to church*. The following list gives further examples of other verbalised acts of nature. Notice that they also form their tenses in the same manner as the **um** verb.

Examples:

	Infinitive & past tense		Present continuous	Future
baha – *flood*	bumaha	*to flood*	bumabaha	babaha
araw – *sun*	umaraw	*to shine* (sun only)	umaaraw	aaraw
ulan — *rain*	umulan	*to rain*	umuulan	uulan
kidlat – *lightning*	kumidlat	*to flash* (lightning)	kumikidlat	kikidlat
kulog – *thunder*	kumulog	*to thunder*	kumukulog	kukulog
sikat – *shine*	sumikat	*to shine* (sun, moon)	sumisikat	sisikat
lubog – *set*	lumubog	*to set* (sun, moon)	lumulubog	lulubog
bagyo – *typhoon*	bumagyo	*to have a typhoon*	bumabagyo	babagyo
hangin – *wind*	humangin	*to become windy*	humahangin	hahangin
ambon – *drizzle*	umambon	*to drizzle*	umaambon	aambon
lindol – *earthquake*	lumindol	*to have an e'quake*	lumilindol	lilindol

Changing the tenses of the um acts of nature:

	Infinitive	**Future**	**Present**	**Past**
	umulan	uulan	umuulan	umulan
Example:		*It's going to rain*	*It is raining*	*It rained*

Sample sentences:

Tagalog: Sumisikat ang araw sa silangan
Literal: Shine/shining the sun in the east
English: *The sun shines in the east*

Tagalog: Bumabagyo lagi sa may China Sea
Literal: Typhoon always near the China Sea
English: *There's always a typhoon near the China Sea*

Tagalog: Kapag umaambon may bahag-hari daw
Literal: If/when drizzling there is rainbow apparently
English: *Apparently, when it drizzles, a rainbow appears*

✔ Exercise 8

Basing your answers on the verb in italics, supply an appropriate
reply to the following questions:

1. Hindi ba *bumabaha* sa Maynila?
2. *Lumulubog* ba ang araw sa silangan?
3. Mga anong oras *sumisikat* ang araw sa Pilipinas?
4. Wala bang ingay kung *kumukulog at kumikidlat*?
5. *Umaaraw* ba kung *sumisikat* ang buwan?

✔ Exercise 9

Look at the pictures showing some acts of nature. Can you say
them in Tagalog using the tense or form indicated?

Exercise 10

Listen to the radio weather forecast on the tape. In your own words, try to give the following weather forecast. Use the vocabulary box to help you:

> Today's weather: Cloudy, possible rain in northern Luzon.
> Tonight: Warm
> Tomorrow: Plenty of sunshine

Talasalitaan	*Vocabulary*
makulimlim	*cloudy*
maaaring umulan	*it might rain*
hilagang Luzon	*northern Luzon*
mainit	*warm*
mainit ang araw	*plenty of sunshine*
mamayang gabi	*tonight*
sa hapon	*in the afternoon*

One-minute phrases

Ilista sa tubig (*ee-lees-tah sah too-beeg*) Literally, *list in water*. Meaning not to make a note of something, to forget all about it. This phrase is commonly used in connection with a 'conveniently forgotten' debt.

Di-mahulugang karayom (*dee mah-hoo-loo-gang kah-rah-yawm*) literally, *cannot drop a needle* Meaning a crowded area/ a tightly packed space. For example: **Napakaraming tao noong dumalaw ang Papa sa Luneta at ito'y di mahulugang karayom**. *Luneta was so crowded when the Pope visited that it was so difficult to move around* (find a needle).

Sisikat din ang araw (*see-see-kaht deen ahng ah-rao*) Literally, *the sun will also rise*. Similar in meaning to the English proverb:'Every cloud has a silver lining'. **Kalimutan mo na ang nangyari sa iyong pananim dahil sa baha. May kasabihan tayong: sisikat din ang araw**, *Try to forget what happened to your crops because of the flood. We have a saying: every cloud has a silver lining.*

Isukat mo nga (*ee-soo-kaht maw ngah*) Literal and true meaning *why don't you try it on?* Trying an article of clothing etc. something on in a shop.

Bahag-hari (*bah-hahg-haa-ree*) Literally, *the king's loin cloth*. This is the Tagalog word for rainbow!

ⓘ Cultural tip

Dress sense is very important in Filipino culture. Formal occasions require formal clothes. If you are unsure what to wear, don't be afraid to ask your Filipino friends for advice. If you are attending weddings, business meetings or baptisms, why not invest in a Filipino 'Barong Tagalog'. This is Filipino national dress and very acceptable as formal attire. Good-quality material is easily obtainable. There are many tailor shops where they can take your measurements and make the garment up for you. Made-to-measure suits and dresses are generally very good value for money in the Philippines.

13 | SA ISTASYON NG BUS
At the bus station

In this unit you will learn how to

■ ask about tickets, destinations, departures and arrivals
■ express days of the week, etc.
■ use **mag** and **ma** verbs

Asking about tickets, destinations and departures

Dialogue 1

The Cook family are going to the north of Luzon. They are at the ticket office enquiring about departures.

Bill	Magandang umaga. Gusto kong bumili ng tiket para sa tatlo papuntang Banaue.
Opisyal	Magandang umaga po naman. Ibig po ba ninyo tiket na papunta lamang doon o balikan?
Bill	Kung puwede balikan at sa Biyernes ika-lima ng Abril ang balik.
Opisyal	Kailan po ninyo ibig magbiyahe?
Bill	Kung puwede sa Martes.
Opisyal	*Sandali* lang po at titingnan ko.
Bill	OK lang, maghihintay ako.
Opisyal	Tatlo *po* ang biyahe sa Martes, ika-dalawa ng Abril. Ang una ay aalis sa alas 4.30 nang umaga, tapos alas 10.30, at alas 2.30 nang hapon. Mabuti *po* ang alas 4.30 nang umaga kung maaari kayong magbiyahe nang maaga.

Bill	Oo. Puwede ka**ming** magbiyahe nang maaga. Saan ka**mi** puwedeng mag-almusal?
Opisyal	**Hi**hinto *po* ang bus nang mga a**las** 7.30 sa Pam**pa**nga **up**ang maka**pag**-almusal ka**yo**.
Bill	Ma**but**i kung gano**on**.
Opisyal	**E**to *po* ang **t**iket nin**yo** **pa**ra sa tat**long** pasa**hero**. Mali**gay**ang **pag**la**lak**bay *po*!
Bill	Ma**ra**ming sa**la**mat.
Opisyal	*Wala* pong anu**man**.

Talasalitaan	*Vocabulary*
balikan	*return*
kung puwede sana	*if possible*
dating	*arrival*
gusto kong bumili	*I want to buy*
ng tiket	*tickets*
para sa tatlo	*for three*
papunta sa	*going to*
naman	*too, also*
hihinto	*will stop*
aalis	*will go* etc.
kung puwede sana	*if possible*
ang biyahe	*the trip*
sa araw	*during the day*
nang umaga	*in the morning*
tapos	*afterwards/ then*
nang hapon	*in the afternoon*
magbiyahe	*to travel*
maghintay	*to wait*
alis	*departure*
nang maaga	*early*
mag-almusal	*to have breakfast*
upang	*in order to/ so that*
makapag-almusal	*can have breakfast*
kung ganoon	*if that's the case*
eto po	*here sir*
tiket ninyo	*your tickets*
maligaya(ng)	*happy*
paglalakbay	*trip*

Translation

Bill	Good morning. I'd like to buy tickets for three (persons) to Banaue.
Official	Good morning sir. Do you want single tickets or return?
Bill	Return tickets, please if possible coming back on Friday April 5.
Official	When do you want to travel sir?
Bill	If possible, on Tuesday.
Official	Please wait sir while I check.
Bill	Yes. I'll wait.
Official	Sir, there are three trips on Tuesday April 2. The first is at 4.30 in the morning, then at 10.30 and at 2.30 in the afternoon. The 4.30 (departure) is the best (one) if you can travel early.
Bill	Sure. We can travel early. Where can we have breakfast?
Official	Sir, the bus is going to make a stop at 7.30 at Pampanga so that you can have your breakfast.
Bill	That's good.
Official	Sir, here are your tickets for three passengers. Have a good trip!
Bill	Thank you very much.
Official	You're welcome.

Other useful vocabulary for travelling can be found in the vocab box.

Talasalitaan	Vocabulary
pasahero	passenger
tiket	ticket
pamasahe	fare
biyahe	trip
pang-isa	single
sasakay	will board
bababa	will alight/get off
sukli	change
upuan	seat
bakante	vacant

parahin	*to stop* (a public vehicle)
konduktor	*conductor*
drayber	*driver*
umangkas	*to get a lift*
siksikan	*packed to capacity*
mama	term a passenger uses to call driver's attention
barya	*change*

✔ Exercise 1 Listening and understanding

Listen carefully once again to the conversation between Bill Cook and the clerk. Based on the dialogue, identify which of the following statements are true and which are false.

1. Gustong bumili ni Bill ng tiket papuntang Davao.
2. Kung puwede sana gustong umalis nang maaga ni Bill.
3. Sabi ng opisyal: 'Mag-almusal kayo at titingnan ko.'
4. Sabi ni Bill sa opisyal: 'Maghihintay ako.'
5. Tatlo ang biyahe sa araw.
6. May biyahe sa gabi at maaga ito.
7. Hindi puwedeng magbiyahe sina Bill nang maaga.
8. Maaari silang mag-almusal nang maaga.
9. Sa Pampanga hihinto ang bus.
10. Hindi sila mag-aalmusal sa Pampanga.

✔ Exercise 2

Can you say the following sentences in the negative?

1. Gusto kong bumili ng tiket.
2. Puwede bukas nang umaga.
3. Humihinto ang bus nang mga alas 7.30.
4. Malapit ang Babauae buhat sa Maynila.
5. Mabuti ang alas 4.30 nang umaga.

Days, months and dates

In Dialogue 1, Bill Cook mentions that he wants to travel on Tuesday April 2. To give the date in Tagalog, simply use **ika** +

Tagalog number. For example: **ika-apat ng Disyembre** = *December 4.*

Question: **Kailan ang kaarawan mo?** *When is your birthday?*
Answer: **Sa ika-apat ng Disyembre.** *On December 4.*

Here is a complete list of the days of the week and months of the year:

Days of the week		Months of the year	
Lunes	*Monday*	Enero	*January*
Martes	*Tuesday*	Pebrero	*February*
Miyerkoles	*Wednesday*	Marso	*March*
Huwebes	*Thursday*	Abril	*April*
Biyernes	*Friday*	Mayo	*May*
Sabado	*Saturday*	Hunyo	*June*
Linggo	*Sunday*	Hulyo	*July*
		Agosto	*August*
		Septyembre	*September*
		Oktubre	*October*
		Nobyembre	*November*
		Disyembre	*December*

Exercise 3

What comes after _____? Can you fill in the blank with the correct answer?

1. Miyerkoles _____
2. Agosto _____
3. Oktubre _____
4. Sabado _____
5. Martes _____
6. Mayo _____
7. Biyernes _____

Exercise 4

Can you translate the following into Tagalog? Use the vocabulary box provided to help you:

Example: July 4   Answer: Ika-apat ng Hulyo

1. His birthday is on August 30.
2. School begins on Monday.
3. We will be visiting you on Saturday, May 10.
4. The conference was last Tuesday, June 14.
5. We are going to the zoo on Sunday, September 3.
6. Are you leaving on Saturday?
7. Who is arriving on Thursday, January 5?

Talasalitaan	*Vocabulary*
simula	*start*
bibisita	*be visiting*
kumperensiya	*conference*
pupunta	*going*
aalis	*leaving*
darating	*arriving*
paaralan	*school*

🔊 Language skills

1 Mag *verbs*

Most Tagalog verbs begin with **mag**. Like the **um** verbs we met in Unit 12, **mag** verbs can also be transitive (with an object) or intransitive (without an object). You will remember that **um** verbs take either a prefix (an addition before the verb root), or an infix (an addition within the verb root). **Mag** verbs are easier in that they take only a prefix. **Mag** verbs also need an object. As with the **um** verbs, the connecting word 'ng' is used before the object. For example: **Magbili ng bigas**. *Sell rice.* **Mag** verbs need a subject, but they do not always need: 1) a time element; 2) a preposition; 3) an adverb.

The **mag** verb is very versatile in that while it forms both major transitive verbs (verbs with a direct object) and intransitive verbs (verbs without a direct object), it continues to carry the word that the verb suggests. For example: **magtennis** (*to play tennis*), **maglaba** (*to wash clothes*), **magbihis** (*to put clothes on*), **magdasal** (*to pray*) etc. Although most verb stems can be used with the **mag** prefix, it is important to remember that some verbs are **um** verbs only, while some verbs are **mag** verbs only. Listen carefully to how each verb is used by native Tagalog speakers. Through listening and repeating what you hear, you will soon be able to distinguish between the different verb types. If you are unsure, check out the verb list at the back of this book or check your Tagalog dictionary.

The versatility of the MAG verb becomes clear when we see the variety of ways in which it can be used:

1. **mag** + noun, e.g. mag + bus = magbus, *to go by bus*
2. **mag** + noun designating a member of a profession, e.g. abogado (*lawyer*) = mag-abogado, *to become a lawyer*
3. **mag** + article of clothing, e.g. mag + kamiseta = magkamiseta, *to wear a tee-shirt*
4. **mag** + language, e.g. mag + Tagalog = magTagalog, *to speak Tagalog*
5. **mag** + item designated by the noun, e.g. magbunga, *to bear fruit*
6. **mag** + noun expressing action involving two or more actors, mag + salubong (*greet one another*) = magsalubong, *to meet*
7. **mag** + adjective, e.g. mag + mabagal (*slow*) = magmabagal, *be slow in*, mag + mayaman = magmayaman, *to pretend to be rich*
8. **mag** + times of day, e.g. mag + madaling-araw (*dawn*) magmadaling-araw, *be dawn*

Changing the tense of the **mag** verb is easy. Take for example the verb stem **laba** (*wash clothes*):

mag + laba	=	maglaba	infinitive (used only in requests, commands and suggestions)
mag + la+laba	=	maglalaba	future
*nag + la+laba	=	naglalaba	present
*nag + laba	=	naglaba	past
kapag + la + laba	=	kapaglalaba	recent action

(***Note**: the prefix **mag** is used in the infinitive and future tenses and changes to **nag** in the present and past tense.)

Here are a few commonly occurring **mag** verbs. Listen to how they are pronounced on the tape:

mag-ayos	*to arrange*
mag-alis	*to remove*
mag-abang	*to wait for someone*
mag-aral	*to study*
magbantay	*to guard*
magbigay	*to give*
magbili	*to sell*
magbintang	*to accuse*
magdasal	*to pray*
maghain	*to serve food on the table*
maghugas	*to wash*
maglaba	*to wash clothes*
maglakad	*to walk*
maglaro	*to play*
maglinis	*to clean*
magluto	*to cook*
magmana	*to inherit*
magmasid	*to watch*

A further selection of **mag** verbs can be found at the back of this book.

Exercise 5

Look at the pictures and try to find the correct verb to describe each activity? Give your answers in the **mag** verb form:

3.

A guide to expanding the mag sentence:

A) Transitive verbs (with object)

Verb	+ actor	+ object
Nagbibili	si Jose	ng lumang alahas
Selling/sells	Jose	old jewellery

Jose is selling / sells old jewellery.

Verb	+ actor	+ object	+ place
Nagluto	kami	ng pansit	sa bahay ni Letty
Cooked	we	noodles	at Letty's home

We cooked some noodles at Letty's home.

Verb	+ particle	+ actor	+ object	+ place + time
Nagdala	pala	sila	ng pagkain	sa party kagabi
Brought	so	they some food	to the party	last night

So they brought some food to the party last night.

B) Intransitive verbs (without an object)

Verb	+ actor
Maglalaba	si Margaret
Will wash/ will be washing clothes	Margaret

Margaret will be washing clothes.

Qualifier/ Verb	+ actor	+ place and/or time
Hindi nagsalita	si Gener	sa pulong kahapon.
Did not talk/speak	Gener	at the meeting yesterday.

Gener didn't talk/speak at the meeting yesterday.

✔ Exercise 6

Using the verb, form and scenario provided, see if you can do the
following in Tagalog:

1. Suggest to a friend to play. (laro) (infinitive)
2. Say that you cleaned the car already. (linis) (past)
3. Say that Maria is washing the dishes. (hugas) (present)
4. Suggest to everyone you want to pray. (dasal) (infinitive)
5. Say that Lina and her friends will be cooking. (luto) (future)

Mag and recent action

Just to keep us on our toes, when using the recent action with
mag verbs, we must be careful to remember that **mag** changes
to **pag**. For example:

ka +	future	= recent action
ka +	maglalaro (will play)	= kapaglalaro
ka +	maglilinis (will clean)	= kapaglilinis
ka +	mag-aaral (will study)	= kapag-aaral

See Unit 12, page 169.

🔊 Enquiring about arrivals

📼 Dialogue 2

Jobert is enquiring about the arrival of the Cook family on the bus
from Banaue.

Jobert Anong oras ang dating ng bus ngayon galing sa
Baguio?
Manager Alas 7.45 *po* nang gabi.
Jobert Bakit, anong oras ba itong umalis buhat sa Baguio?
Manager Kanina pong alas 9.00 nang umaga.
Jobert Saang mga lugar ba ito hihinto?
Manager Sa Ilocos *po*, sa, Tarlac, Pampanga at Bulacan.
Jobert Ganoon ba? Maraming salamat.
Manager *Wala* pong anuman.

Talasalitaan	Vocabulary
ang dating	*the arrival*
ngayon	*today/now*
galing sa	*from*
mga lugar	*places*
bakit	*why*
umalis	*departed*

Translation

Jobert   What time will the bus from Baguio arrive?
Manager Sir, 7.45 in the evening.
Jobert   (Why) What time did it leave / depart from Baguio?
Manager A while ago at 9.00 this morning.
Jobert   What places will it make a stopover?
Manager At Ilocos, Tarlac, Pampanga and Bulacan
Jobert   Is that so? Thank you very much.
Manager You're welcome sir.

Exercise 7

Use Dialogue 2 to answer the following questions:

1. Ilang oras ang biyahe ng bus galing sa Baguio?
2. Hihinto ba ang bus sa Zambales?
3. Alin ang ikatatlong probinsiya na hihintuan ng bus?
4. Ilan lahat-lahat ang probinsiya?

Talasalitaan	Vocabulary
ilan(g)	*how many*
alin	*which one*
ikatatlo(ng)	*third*
lahat-lahat	*altogether*

✔ Exercise 8

Give a Tagalog summary of the schedule in Dialogue 2 in the second column.

English   Tagalog

1. Departure from Baguio: *9.00 a.m*
2. Arrival from Baguio: *7.45 p.m*
3. Stopover: *Ilocos, Pangasinan, Tarlac*
                                 Pampanga & Bulacan

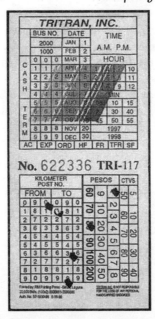

✔ Exercise 9

Look at the bus ticket. Can you answer the following questions?

1. Magkano ang halaga ng tiket?
2. Ang numero ng tiket ay: anim, dalawa, dalawa, apat, apat, anim.
3. May petsa ba ang tiket ng bus?
4. Ilang kilometro ang layo ng biyahe?
5. Sinasabi ba sa tiket kung anong oras ang alis?
6. Sinasabi ba sa tiket kung anong oras ang dating?

⧉ Language skills

2 Ma *verbs*

maligo	*to have a bath*
matulog	*to sleep*
maupo	*to sit down*
makinig	*to listen*
mahiga	*to lie down*

There are five special verb stems that are neither **um** verbs nor **mag** verbs. These verbs are known as **ma** verbs due to them taking the prefix **ma**. The five **ma** verbs are intransitive and their tenses cannot be formed by using **um** or **mag**. As there are so few **ma** verbs, the best approach is simply to try to memorise them. Like **um** and **mag** verbs, **ma** verbs can be used with pseudo-verbs. Example: **Gusto kong maligo** *I'd like to have a bath*.

Forming tenses with ma

Ma + ligo = maligo	=	infinitive (used with requests, suggestions and commands)
Ma + li + ligo	=	future
Na + li + ligo	=	present
Na + ligo	=	past

Example sentences:

Verb	+ actor	+ time
Naliligo	ako	araw-araw

I have a bath every day

Question marker + verb		+ direction
Sino	ang nakikinig	sa kaniya?

Who is listening to him / her?

Verb	+ actor	+ particle	+	preposition
Naupo	ka	ba		sa silyang ito?

Did you sit on this chair?

Exercise 10

Choose the correct form from the brackets:

1. Ayaw mo bang (maligo, naliligo, naligo) tayo sa dagat? (infinitive)
2. (Makikinig, nakikinig, nakinig) ako sa awitin niya. (present)
3. Maraming (naupo, nauupo, maupo) sa sahig kagabi sa awditoryum. (past)
4. Gusto po ba ninyong (mahiga, nahiga, mahihiga) sa kamang iyan? (infinitive)
5. Si Patricia yata ang (natutulog, natulog, matulog) sa bahay ni John kagabi. (past)

Finding out what your journey will be like

Dialogue 3

The Cook family are on the bus from Banaue to Manila. Bill Cook is talking to the conductor.

Bill	Anong oras tayo darating sa Maynila?
Konduktor	Mga alas-siyete y medya po nang gabi.
Bill	Saan tayo hihinto upang makapagbanat ng katawan?
Konduktor	Sa Pampanga po at meron ding kubeta at paliguan doon.
Bill	Magdadagdag ba kayo ng gasolina?
Konduktor	Opo.
Bill	May telepono ba doon para makatawag ako?
Konduktor	Meron po.
Bill	Salamat.
Konduktor	Wala pong anuman.

Talasalitaan	*Vocabulary*
magdadagdag	*will add*
darating	*will arrive*
mga alas siyete y medya	*around 7.30*
nang gabi	*at night*
makatawag	*be able to call*
makapagbanat	*to be able to stretch*
kubeta	*toilet*
paliguan	*shower/bathroom*
gasolina	*petrol*
telepono	*telephone*
para	*so that/ in order to*

Translation

Bill	What time are we arriving in Manila?
Conductor	Around 7.30 in the evening.
Bill	Is there any place where we can stop to stretch ourselves (lit, our body)?
Conductor	In Pampanga sir. There are also bathroom facilities there.
Bill	Are you going to top up your petrol?
Conductor	Yes sir.
Bill	Are there any telephones there for me to make a call?
Conductor	There are (telephones there) sir.
Bill	Thank you.
Conductor	You're welcome sir.

Exercise 11

Using the dialogue as your guide, can you do the following?

1. Ask the conductor what time the bus is stopping at Pampanga. (use Anong oras)
2. Ask him where else you will be stopping. (use pa)
3. Ask the conductor if there are bathroom facilities at the stop. (use Mayroon)
4. Tell the conductor you want to use the bathroom. (use Gusto kong)

Exercise 12 Understanding and speaking

Imagine that you are on a bus bound for Batangas, south of Manila.
Why not have a go at speaking with the conductor. Listen carefully
to the conductor's responses. Using the hints and the vocabulary
box to help you, write out your part of the dialogue and then
practice speaking it:

Ikaw	(greet the conductor, saying good morning)
Konduktor	Magandang umaga po. Didiretso po ba kayo sa Batangas?
Ikaw	(say yes, but that you are unsure about what time the bus returns to Manila)
Konduktor	Babalik po ba kayo pa-Maynila bukas?
Ikaw	(we will return tomorrow afternoon)
Konduktor	Ganoon po ba? Mayroon pong bus na paalis sa istasyon sa alas 3.00
Ikaw	(three o'clock, that's fine)
Konduktor	Ibig po ba ninyong bumili ng tiket na papunta lamang doon o balikan?
Ikaw	(just singles please. Three adults)
Konduktor	Iyan po ay tres siyentos treynta pesos.
Ikaw	(Say here you are / here's my payment)
Konduktor	Maraming salamat po. Marunong kayong managalog!
Ikaw	(say thank you very much, too)

Talasalitaan	*Vocabulary*
didiretso	*straight on*
babalik	*will return*
bukas	*tomorrow*
ganoon po ba?	*is that so ma'am/sir?*
paalis	*leaving*
istasyon	*station*
balikan	*return*
tres siyentos treynta	*330*
marunong	*know/knows how to*
managalog	*to speak Tagalog*

Language skills

3 Maka + um verb stem *To be able to, to happen to, to come to, to manage to* Makapag + mag verb stem *To be able to, to happen to, to come to, to manage to*

In Dialogue 3, Bill Cook used the words **makapagbanat** and **makatawag**. These verb forms seem new and in jargon are known as circumstantial verbs. These verb forms above all give us a glimpse into Filipino culture. According to Filipino beliefs, some actions are brought about purely by circumstance, by accident or by occurrences beyond the actor/s' control. The active verbs **um** and **mag** verbs have special prefixes to express the circumstantial or involuntary nature of these actions. With **um** verbs, use the prefix **maka**. For example: **makabili** *to be able to / to happen to / to come to / to manage to buy*. With **mag** verbs, the prefix is **makapag**. For example: **makapag** + **laro** = **makapaglaro** *to be able to / to happen to / to come to / to manage to play*. Look at the guide on how to use the **maka** and **makapag** prefixes in the active **um** and **mag** verbs:

um verbs

Maka = (prefix) + alis (verb stem)

Maka + alis =   makaalis = infinitive

> to be able to leave
> to happen to leave
> to manage to leave
> to come to leave

Maka + ka + alis = makakaalis = *will be able* etc. *to leave*   = future

Naka + ka + alis = nakakaalis = *is able* etc. *to leave*   = present

Naka + alis   =   nakaalis   = *was able* etc. *to leave*   = past

Some examples:

makakain	=	*to be able* etc. *to eat*
makabili	=	*to be able* etc. *to buy*
makabasa	=	*to be able* etc. *to read*
makasulat	=	*to be able* etc. *to write*
makakanta	=	*to be able* etc. *to sing*
makaalis	=	*to be able* etc. *to leave*

mag verbs

makapag + (prefix)   luto (verb stem)

makapag + luto = makapagluto = infinitive (used in requests, commands and suggestions)

to be able to cook
to happen to cook
to manage to cook
to come to cook

maka + ka + pag + luto = makakapagluto = *will be able* etc. *to cook* = future

naka + ka + pag + luto = nakakapagluto = *is able* etc. *to cook* = present

nakapag+ luto = nakapagluto = *was able* etc. *to cook* = past

Here are some examples:

Makapagsimba	=	*to be able to go to church*
Makapagsalita	=	*to be able to talk/speak*
Makapagbili	=	*to be able to sell*
Makapagluto	=	*to be able to cook*
Makapaglakad	=	*to be able to walk*
Makapaglinis	=	*to be able to clean*
Makapaglaba	=	*to be able to wash clothes*

Some variations of **maka** and **makapag** sentences:

Verb	+ actor	+ object	+ preposition
Nakabili	kami	ng magandang damit	sa palengke

We managed to buy a beautiful dress from the market.

Verb	+ actor	+ particle
Nakapagluto	ka	na ba?

Were you able to cook?/ Did you manage to cook?

Verb	+ particle	actor +	object	Prepostion
Nakagawa	na raw	ang mga bata	ng saranggola	kahapon.

Apparently, the children [already] managed to make a kite yesterday.

Exercise 13

Look at the following sentences. Can you supply the missing verb form?

1. Araw-araw, _____ kami sa palaruan. (laro)
2. Hindi _____ ang mga turista kanina dahil sa bagyo. (alis)
3. _____ ba tayo ng mga pasalubong bukas? (bili)
4. Sa Sabado, maraming _____ ng masasarap na pagkain. (luto)
5. Sino sa mga babae ang _____ sa bus noong linggo? (tulog)

One-minute phrases

Magmeryenda muna tayo (*mahg-mer-yen-dah moo-nah tah-yaw*) Literally, *to have a snack first let us.* (Please note that 'first' should not be given emphasis here.) An expression of casual but polite invitation meaning *Why don't we have a snack?* or *Could I invite you to have a snack?*

Mag-beer muna tayo/ mag-kape muna tayo (*mahg-bber-moo-nah tay-yaw/mahg-kah-pe moo-nah fay-yaw*) *Could I invite you to a beer?*, *Shall we have coffee?* etc. (These expressions have the same connotation as above except that **meryenda** is replaced with beer or coffee) 'Mag +___ muna tayo' has a potential to expand and can be used as a structure for other invitations.

Sa ibang araw na (*sah ee-bahng ah-rao nah*) Literally, *in other days already.* Meaning *Some other day/Next time.* **Sa ibang araw na** is a nice way of turning down an invitation.

Medyo tagilid (*mehd-yaw tah-gee-leed*) Literally, *somewhat tilted*. Similar in meaning to the English expression *The dice are loaded*. This phrase pertains to a situation the result of which is not positive. For example: **Sa palagay mo mananalo si Ginoong Santos sa eleksiyon?** *Do you reckon Mr Santos will win the election?* **Hindi yata. Medyo tagilid ang resulta.** *I don't think so. The results are not in his favour / the dice are loaded against him.*

May panahon ka ba? (*migh pah-nah-hawn kah bah?*) Literally, *Do you have time?* Meaning: *Are you available?, Do you have a moment?* etc. Students of the Tagalog language sometimes think that Filipinos are asking about the weather when they hear this question! Be careful not to mix up the two meanings of the word **panahon**.

ⓘ **Cultural tip**

It will not take you very long to recognise that the Philippines is a country where 'snacks' are an essential part of life. In the west, we speak of 'three square meals a day'. Filipinos tend to eat more frequently, but in smaller amounts. If you take a long trip by bus or jeep, it is not uncommon to stop off at a small town or even a sarisari store for a snack. Bus stations and Jeepney stands abound with hawkers selling everything from grilled fish to chewing gum. If you are travelling anywhere with Filipino friends, make sure you take a supply of snacks along with you. If you take nothing on a long journey, they may not complain but you can be sure that they will be hungry!

14 SA TABING-DAGAT
At the beach

In this unit you will learn how to

■ hire a boat and prepare for a picnic on the beach
■ use **mang** verbs and particles

Hiring a boat

Dialogue 1

Bill, Louise and Roy Cook are at a beach resort. The surrounding islands look beautiful and so they decide to hire a boat.

Bill   Maganda na ang panahon ngayon, magandang mamangka.

Louise Oo *nga*. Mamasyal *kaya* muna tayo tapos magtanong kung saan maaaring umarkila ng *bangka*. Roy, gusto mo bang sumama?

Roy   Gusto ko. Tena. (Namasyal sa tabing-dagat ang mag-anak)

Bill   Marami pang *mangingisda* sa laot. Nakikita ba ninyo?

Louise Oo. O, heto na pala ang pa-arkilahan ng *bangka*.

Bill   Magandang araw. Gusto naming umarkila ng *bangka* para sa tatlo. Magkano ba?

May-ari Dalawandaang piso *po* sa bawa't oras.

Bill   Sino naman ang tsuper namin?

May-ari Heto po siya. Les ang pangalan niya. (*Ngumiti* si Les)

Bill   Magbabayad na ba kami ngayon?

May-ari Pagbalik na *po* ninyo.

Bill   Maraming salamat.

May-ari *Wala* pong anuman.

Talasalitaan	Vocabulary
para sa tatlo	*for three* (persons)
magkano	*how much*
mamangka	*to go boating*
oo nga	*I agree*
mamasyal	*to take a stroll*
kaya muna tayo	*why don't we first*
tapos	*then*
magtanong	*enquire*
kung saan	*where*
magbabayad	*will pay*
umarkila ng bangka	*to hire a boat*
sumama	*to come/go with*
marami(ng)	*many*
bawa't oras	*each hour*
pa(ng)	*still*
tsuper	*(boat) driver*
mangingisda	*fishing*
laot	*sea*
ang pangalan	*the name*
ngumiti	*smiled*
paarkilahan	*a place to hire*
pagbalik	*when you return*

Translation

Bill The weather is lovely now, it would be nice to go boating.

Louise I agree. Why don't we take a stroll first then we can enquire where there are boats for hire. Roy, would you like to join us?

Roy I'd love to. Let's go. (The family go for a stroll on the beach)

Bill There are still many fishermen at sea. Can you see (them)?

Louise Yes. Look, here's the place to hire boats from.

Bill Good day. We would like to hire a boat for three people. How much will it cost us?

Owner Two hundred pesos an hour sir.

Bill	(And) who is the captain of our boat?
Owner	Here he is sir. His name is Les (Les smiles)
Bill	Do we have to pay now?
Owner	When you get back sir.
Bill	Thank you.
Owner	You're welcome.

Exercise 1

Answer the following questions with complete Tagalog sentences:

1. Bakit (why) sabi ni Bill 'magandang mamangka'?
2. Sila ba ay mamamangka muna (first) o mamamasyal muna?
3. Ano ang nakita nila sa dagat habang (while) namamasyal sila?
4. Sa palagay mo (in your opinion), mura ba ang pag-arkila ng bangka?
5. Nagbayad na ba kaagad (immediately) sila sa may-ari ng bangka?

Language skills

1 Mang *verbs*

We have already met the **um** and **mag** active verb forms. The third form of active verbs are known as the **mang** verbs. In Dialogue 1, you will have noticed a few **mang** verbs: **mamangka**, *to go boating*, **mamasyal**, *to go for a walk* and **mangisda**, *to go fishing*. **Mang** verbs form transitive (e.g. **mamili** – *to go shopping*) and intransitive (e.g. **mangawit**, *be tired*) sentences. Broadly speaking, **mang** verbs could be described as **um** verbs where the action has been pluralised. This may sound confusing at first to the native English speaker but it is in fact quite simple.

For example, if we were to say **bumili ako ng sapatos**, then this **um** verb sentence would be translated as *I bought some shoes*. The act of 'buying' shoes is a one-off event. However, if we pluralise the action described by the **um** verb, then we end up with a very different sentence – **namili ako ng sapatos**, *I shopped for shoes*. The **mang** verb form suggests that the action of 'buying' was broader than a one-off event. As such, **namili ako ng sapatos** would be translated as *I shopped for shoes*. As the verb 'to shop' implies the possibility of a process or more than one action (i.e. moving from shop to shop in order to buy more than one pair of shoes), Tagalog would therefore consider it as a plural action. Don't worry if this seems to be confusing. Listen carefully to how native Tagalog speakers use **mang** form verbs. You will soon become accustomed to them.

Apart from the pluralisation of action, a further characteristic of **mang** form verbs is that they can be used to express an action which is either 'deliberately harmful' (e.g. **mangain**, *to devour*) or an 'activity directed towards more than one object' (e.g., **manguha**, *to gather*). Another notable use of **mang** is to indicate an intensive or repeated activity directed toward a single object (e.g. a young man repeatedly dating a young woman = **mangibig**, *to date*).

Formation of mang verbs

1. Words that begin with p and b e.g. mang + pasyal (*take a stroll*), mang + buhay (life).
    Formula: Change **mang** to **mam**. Drop first letter of word (pasyal becomes asyal) (buhay becomes uhay).

    mam + asiyal = mamasyal *to go for a stroll* = infinitive
    mam + uhay = mamuhay *to live/conduct one's life* = infinitive

2. Words that begin with d = mang + dukot (*put one's hand into a pocket*).
    Formula: Change **mang** to **man**. Add the word to man.

    man + dukot = mandukot *to go pickpocketing* = infinitive
    man + daya = mandaya *to go cheating others* = infinitive

3. Words that begin with t and s = mang + takot (*afraid*), mang + saksak (*stab*).
    Formula: Change **mang** to **man**. Drop first letter of word (takot becomes akot), (sakit becomes akit).

    man + akot = manakot *to frighten* [several people]
    man + akit = manakit *to cause pain*

4. Words that begin with k = mang + kuha (*get*).
   Formula: Retain **mang**. Drop first letter of word (kuha becomes uha).

   mang + uha = manguha 'to get' = infinitive

5. Words that begin with a, i (and other vowels) = mang + anak (child).
   Formula: Merely add **mang** to word that begins with a vowel.

   mang + anak = manganak *to give birth to* = infinitive
   Mang + isda = mangisda *to go fishing* = infinitive
   Mang + agaw = mang-agaw *to go grabbing* = infinitive
   Mang + alok = mang-alok *to offer* = infinitive

Listen to the following verb forms on the tape. Can you see the difference between the underlying verb form and the **mang** verb form?

Underlying verb	Mang verb
bumili *to buy*	mamili *to go shopping*
kumain *to eat*	mangain *to devour*
dumukot *to put hand inside pocket*	mandukot *to go pickpocketing*
sumugat *to wound*	manugat *to wound* (deliberately)
tumaga *to cut*	managa *to slash* (with intent to hurt or destroy)
magwalis *to sweep*	mangwalis *to hit with a broom*
kumuha *to get*	manguha *to gather*
pumitas *to pick*	mamitas *to go a-picking*
tumahi *to sew*	manahi *to sew* (a number of things)
tumakot *to frighten*	manakot *to frighten* (a number of people)
dumikit *to get stuck to*	manikit *to get thoroughly stuck to*
sumuyo *to curry favour with*	manuyo *to curry favour with*
umibig *to love*	mangibig *to pay court to / to date*
pumasyal *to pay a visit/drop by*	mamasyal *to take a walk/stroll*

Forming *mang* verb tenses

Mang (prefix) + isda (fish) = mang + isda 'to go fishing' infinitive (used for requests, commands and suggestions).

    ma + ngi + ngisda = future
    na + ngi + ngisda = present
    na + ngis + da = past

Mang (prefix) + **buhay** (life) =

    mam + uhay = *to live* infinitive
    ma + mu + mu + hay = future
    na + mu + mu+ hay = present
    na + mu + hay = past

Variations of a *mang* sentence

Verb	+ actor
Mamimili	si Anne

Anne is going shopping

Verb	+ particle	+ actor
Namamalengke	kaya	+ si Elizabeth?

I wonder if Elizabeth is shopping at the market?

Qualifier	+ verb	+ actor	+ time
Hindi	mangingisda	ang mga lalaki	sa Biyernes.

The men are not going fishing on Friday

Question word	+ actor	+ object	+ place
Sino ang mamimitas		ng dalanghita	sa bukid?

Who will go picking oranges on the farm?

Qualifier	+ verb	+ place	+ time
Maraming	namamasyal	sa Luneta	tuwing Linggo.

Many (people) go strolling in Luneta every Sunday

Actor	+ verb	+ object	+ beneficiary
Si Edith	ang namili	ng mga aklat	para kay Manny.

It was Edith who shopped for books for Manny

Exercise 2

Can you translate the following?

1. I will go picking fruit tomorrow.
2. They will go fishing on Wednesday.
3. There are many people picking pockets in the market.
4. I will take a stroll tonight.
5. Let us go shopping!

Exercise 3

Can you supply the answer? (Use the explanations in this chapter to help you.)

1. Bukas, _____sila ng rosas at ibang bulaklak sa hardin. (pitas/pick) (future)
2. Sino ang gustong _____? (isda / fish) (infinitive)
3. Walang _____ ngayon sa palengke kasi may baha. (bili/shop) (present)
4. Meron bang _____ sa bayan? (dukot / pickpockets) (present)
5. _____ siya ng blusa noong bakasyon (tahi / sew) (past)

Mang verbs and recent action

Remember that when using the recent action with **mang** verbs, the same rules apply as outlined above except that **mang** changes to **pang**. For example:

ka +	Future	= Recent action
ka +	mamalengke (*will go marketing*)	= kapapamalengke
ka +	mamamaril (*will go shooting*)	= kapapamaril
ka +	mamimili (*will go shopping*)	= kapapamili

(See also Unit 12, page 169.)

◙ Language skills

2 Particles

You may remember coming across small words such as **po** (a sign of respect), **pa** (*still*), **naman** (*on the other hand*) and **na** (*already*) in previous units. In spite of their small size, these words are important elements in Tagalog sentence construction. Their function is to highlight or add impact to a statement, question or exclamation. In English these small words are known as adverbs, while in Tagalog they are known as particles. They occur in certain fixed places in Tagalog sentences.

As a rule, a particle is located 'sandwiched' in between the comment on the left and the subject on the right. For example, **Superbisor si Edith**. *Edith is a supervisor*. (without particle) becomes: **Superbisor** (comment) **pala si Edith** (subject). *So, Edith is a supervisor*, or **Superbisor na si Edith**, *Edith is already a supervisor*. However, it is possible to use more than one particle. How then do we decide the correct order of usage? Where two particles are used together, then the basic rule of thumb is this: the shorter particles (one syllable) go before the longer (two syllable) particles. For example: **Superbisor na pala si Edith**. *So, Edith is already a supervisor*!' In some instances, you may find anything up to four or five particles in a single sentence! Due to the many possible combinations, it would be unfair to try to suggest a single rule of usage. In such cases, the trick is to ask one of your Filipino friends how to 'string' the particles together, then memorise a few of the combinations that will be of use to you.

Let's take a closer look at how two of these particles **na** (*already*) and **pa** (*still*) are used:

Explanation of na and pa

Na denotes immediate performance of an action. It also means *already* or *now*.

Examples:

Bumili ka na	*(You) buy now*
Arkitekto na si Manny	*Manny is already an architect*

Bukas na ang binyag	*The baptism will now be tomorrow*
Ayoko na	*I don't like it anymore*
Malaki na ang anak ni Tessie	*Tessie's child is big now*

Pa is used to mean continuation or resumption of an action.

Examples:

Bumili ka pa	*(You) buy some more*
Hilaw pa ang mga saging	*The bananas are still unripe*
Tulog pa ba si Father Fred?	*Is Father Fred still asleep?*
Bata pa ang bagong meyor	*The new mayor is still young*
Nagluluto pa ako	*I'm still cooking*

Example sentences:

1 Malalaki na ang mga anak ni Ginoong de Leon
   Mr de Leon's children are grown up now

2 Wala pa sila
   They (are not here) haven't arrived yet

3 Bukas na ako mamamalantsa
   I'm going to do my ironing tomorrow

4 Bukas na ang palabas
   The show will be (held) tomorrow

5 Kumain pa po kayo
   Please eat some more sir

Exercise 4

Look at the pictures. Each one is accompanied by two statements (one **na** and one **pa** statement). Can you decide which statement is appropriate to each picture?

Tulog pa si Erwin
Gising na si Erwin

Gising na si Ardin
Tulog pa si Ardin

Nagluluto pa si Fe
Kumakain na si Fe

✔ Exercise 5

Place the following jumbled-up sentences into their correct word order. Be careful to place the particle in the correct position.

1. pasko / malapit / ang / na
2. pa / nakakakain / hindi / ako
3. ba / sa / na / Sabado / ng / binyag / ang / anak mo
4. sa / sagot / na / tanong / alam / ba / ang / mo
5. sila / pa / kumakain / ba

Going swimming

Dialogue 2

The Cook family are back on the beach after their boating trip.

Bill   Ma**b**uti at naka-arki**la ta**yo ng *bangka*.
Louise   **O**o *nga*. Nakapamasi**yal** tu**loy ta**yo.
Roy   Naka**k**ita a**ko** ng malala**k**ing *isda* sa **tu**big.
Louise   Na**k**ita ba nin**yo** ang mga *mangingisda*?
Bill   Oo. Nag**ta**taka a**ko** kung **b**akit naka**ka**kapangisda si**la**
             kahit may mga na**mam**angka.
Roy   Nasi**ya**han a**ko** at *nakapamangka* **ta**yo.
Louise   Ako **rin**.
Bill   **Gus**to kong luma**ngoy** na na**man**.
Louise   Masa**rap** ang **tu**big. **Si**ge, luma**ngoy ta**yo.
Roy   **Te**na.

Talasalitaan	*Vocabulary*
tahimik	*calm*
naka-arkila	*was able to hire*
bangka	*boat (canoe)*
nakapamangka	*was able to go boating*
nakapamasyal	*managed to take a stroll*
tuloy	*as a result*
nakakita	*happened to see*
malalaking isda	*big fish*
nakita ba ninyo	*did you see*
mangingisda	*fisherman*
nakakapangisda	*are able/manage to catch fish*
masyado(ng)	*so*
namamangka	*boating*
nasiyahan	*was pleased*
kung bakit	*why*
lumangoy	*to swim*
nagtataka	*wondering*
tena	*let's go*

Translation

Bill	It was good that we were able to hire a boat.
Louise	I agree. And the sea was so calm.
Roy	I could see big fish in the water.
Bill	Did you see the fishermen?
Louise	Yes. I was wondering how they are able to fish while there are boats (around them).
Roy	I am pleased that we were able to go boating.
Louise	I am too.
Bill	I'd like to go swimming again.
Louise	The water is nice. Come on let's swim.
Roy	Let's go.

Exercise 6

Answer the following questions in complete Tagalog sentences:

1. Sino ang nasiyahan noong makaarkila sila ng bangka?
2. Ano ang nakita nila noong sila'y namamangka?
3. Ano ang nagagawa ng mga mangingisda kahit maraming bangka sa paligid?
4. Nasiyahan ba ang pamilya Cook sa kanilang pamamangka?
5. Pagkatapos, ano ang ginawa nilang tatlo?

Exercise 7

The following pictures are based on Dialogue 2. Can you find the correct verb to describe each action? Can you make up a simple sentence to describe each picture?

For example:

Verb: mangisda
Sentence: Nangingisda si Roy Cook

Language skills

3 Makapang *To be able to, to happen to, to manage to, to come to*

In Dialogue 2, you will no doubt have noticed some new verb types: **nakapamasyal** (*managed to go strolling*), **nakapangisda** (*was able to go fishing*) and **nakapamangka** (*was able to go boating*). These verb types represent the circumstantial form of the **mang** verbs. The actions represented by these verb forms are based on 1) circumstances; 2) ability; 3) involuntary actions. For example 1) **makapang + palengke = makapamalengke**, *to be able to go shopping in the market.* **Makakapamalengke na si Jayne kasi dumating na si John.** *Jayne will be able to go to the market because John has arrived.* 2) **makapang + tahi = makapanahi** *to be able to sew.* **Nakakapanahi na si Tina kasi ibinili siya ng makina ni Philip,** *Tina is able to do some sewing now because Philip bought her a sewing machine.* 3) **Makapang + pasyal = makapamasyal,** *to be able to go for a walk/stroll.* **Nakapamasiyal si Bernard at si Gary pagkatapos ng hapunan.** *Bernard and Gary managed to go for a stroll after supper.* Look at some comparisons:

Simple Mang Verb	Makapang Verb
mangisda *to go fishing*	Makapangisda *to be able to go fishing*
mamaril *to go shooting*	Makapamaril *to be able to go shooting*
mamili *to go shopping*	Makapamili *to be able to go shopping*
mamalengke *to go to the market*	Makapamalengke *to manage to go to the market*

How to form the makapang tense:

Prefix: Makapang,   infinitive: mamili, *to go shopping*
Formula: Change makapang to makapa. Change mamili to **mili** = **makapamili**.

= Makapamili	=infinitive, *to be able to go shopping*
makakapamili	= future
nakakapamili	= present
nakapamili	= past

Prefix: makapang,   infinitive: mangisda *to go fishing*
Formula: Retain **makapang**. Merely add makapang to **isda** = **makapangisda**

makapangisda	= infinitive, *to be able to go fishing*
makakapangisda	= future, *will be able to go fishing*
nakakapangisda	= present, *able to go fishing*
nakapangisda	= past *was able to go fishing*

Sentence variation in makapang

Verb	+	actor	+ time
Nakakapamalengke		si Rosie	araw-araw

Rosie can go to the market every day.

Qualifier/verb +		actor	+ place
Hindi nakakapamasyal		ang mga bata	sa tabing-dagat

The children are not able to take a walk on the seashore

Verb	+ particle/s	+ actor	+ time
Nakakapamaril	na ba	ang mga lalaki	kung Linggo?

Are the men [already] *able to go shooting on Sundays?*

More sentences

1. Ang lalaki ay nakapandukot sa palengke
   The man was able to go pickpocketing in the market

2. Nakakapamalengke ka ba kung Huwebes?
   Are you able to go to the market on Thursdays?

3. Parang makakapangisda ang mga mangingisda ngayon
   It looks like the fishermen can go fishing today

Exercise 8

Fill in the blanks with the correct circumstantial verb form **maka** for **um**, **makapag** for **mag** and **makapang** for **mang**).

1. I wonder if they were able to buy some coke? (bili / past)
   _____ kaya sila ng coke?

2. The children managed to play at night. (laro / past)
   _____ ang mga bata sa gabi.

3. I happened to borrow a book from the library. (hiram / past)
   _____ ako ng libro sa silid aklatan.

4. He can leave early. (alis / present)
   _____ siya nang maaga.

5. I want to be able to return tomorrow. (balik / infinitive)
   Ibig kong _____ bukas.

Exercise 9

The following sentences are wrong because of the verb tense. Can you correct the mistake?

1. Nakapangisda sila bukas.
2. Makabili ako ng pasalubong mamaya.
3. Hindi kami nakakakain sa party kahapon.
4. Sino ang makakabisita sa iyo noong isang linggo?
5. Makakain na po ba kayo?

Exercise 10 Speaking, listening and understanding

Imagine that you have just returned from a boat trip with your Filipino friends. You go to pay the owner who engages you in friendly conversation. Translate your part of the dialogue into

Tagalog before practising the conversation with the help of the tape. Use the vocabulary box to help you.

Owner   Maligayang pagdating! Kumusta ang biyahe mo?
You   Thank you. It was a very relaxing afternoon. We were able to go fishing too.
Owner   Nangisda? Aba, mabuti naman! May nahuli ba naman kayo?
You   Yes. We were able to catch a big tuna fish and two lapulapu [red snapper].
Owner   O, eh di may maluluto kang panghapunan mo.
You   Yes! I hope we will be able to return here next year and catch more fish.
Owner   Bukas ang bahay namin sa iyo!
You   Here's my payment for the boat hire.
Owner   Maraming salamat sa iyo.
You   Thank you very much too.

Talasalitaan	Vocabulary
pagdating	arrival
nangisda	went fishing
nahuli	caught
makahuli	be able to catch
maluluto	able to be cooked
panghapunan	for supper
makabalik	be able to return
bukas	open
pag-arkila	hire

One-minute phrases

Sa madaling salita (*sah mahdah-leeng sah-lee-tah*) Literally, *in quick words*. Similar in meaning to the English expression 'to cut a long story short'. For example: **Marami pa akong ikukuwento sa iyo, pero sa madaling salita, wala na akong panahon**, *I have a lot more to tell you but to cut a long story short, I have ran out of time.*

Pagka-alis na pagka-alis (*pahg-kah-ah-lees nah pahg-kah-ah-lees*) Literally, *upon leaving, upon leaving*. Meaning immediately after leaving. For example **Pagka-alis na pagka-alis ng eroplano, umuwi na kami**. *Once the aeroplane left, we went home immediately.*

Mangyari pa (*mahng-yah-ree pah*) Literally, *happening still*. This Tagalog phrase is equivalent in meaning to the English expression 'of course'. For example: **Umalis si Boy nang walang paalam sa magulang niya, mangyari pa, nagalit ang mga ito sa kaniya**. *Boy left without saying goodbye to his parents, of course they were upset with him.*

Masarap maligo (*mah-sah-rahp mah-lee-gaw*) Literally, *delicious to take a bath/to swim* **Masarap** (*delicious*) is a word we would not ordinarily associate in English with anything other than food. The word has a much broader usage in Tagalog, hence it can be applied to an assortment of pleasurable activities. in this case, the meaning is 'It's nice to take a bath'. For example: **Laging masarap maligo sa dagat**, *It's always nice to take a bath (swim) in the sea.*

Lipas na sa moda (*lee-pahs nah sa maw-dah*) Literally, *past the fashion*. Similar to the English phrase 'out of fashion'. For example: **Hindi ba lipas na sa moda ang malaking kuwelyo at bell bottoms?**, *Aren't wide collars and bell bottoms out of fashion now?*

Cultural tip

A beach picnic is a popular form of relaxation for Filipinos. Why not suggest a trip to the beach with your Filipino friends? Filipino culture places very high value on 'harmony' in relationships. What better way to deepen your friendships and promote harmony than opting for a relaxing outing in a restful environment? There are many bamboo beach houses available for short-term rental and boats for short excursions. Even if you feel confident in your Tagalog, it's a good idea to get your Filipino friends to agree on a price with the boat or beach house owner. Chances are that you would end up paying significantly more. Even if you are paying, let your friends do the talking. They will feel much happier and you will probably save money!

15 | SA SIMBAHAN
At church

In this unit you will learn

■ more about the passive
■ 'in' verbs
■ more on particles

Becoming a godparent

Dialogue 1

Beth and Edwin have asked Roy to be a godfather at the baptism of their baby.

Beth	Maaari bang gawin ka naming ninong sa binyag ng aming anak?
Roy	Talaga? Aba, oo – isang malaking karangalan ito.
Edwin	Dalawa kayong ninong at dalawa rin ang ninang.
Roy	Kailan ba gaganapin ang binyag?
Beth	Sa Sabado, ika-4 ng Disyembre sa simbahan sa baryo.
Roy	Anu-ano ang dapat kong gawin?
Edwin	*Madali* lang. *Tatayo* lang kayo sa tabi ng magulang habang nagseseremonya ang pari.
Roy	Ganoon lang pala. Anong oras sa Sabado?
Beth	Alas 9:30 nang umaga. Pagkatapos, may salu-salo sa aming bahay.
Edwin	O, sige hihintayin ka namin kasama ni Jobert. Tumawag ka lang kung meron kang itatanong.

Talasalitaan	*Vocabulary*
maaari	*can*
gawin	*be made*
ninong	*godfather*
ang pari	*the priest*
binyag	*baptism*
aming anak	*our child*
pala	*so*
ninang	*godmother*
kailan	*when*
gaganapin	*will be held*
pagkatapos	*afterwards*
anu-ano	*what are*
dapat	*must/should*
ko(ng)	*I*
hihintayin	*will wait for*
madali lang	*just easy*
tatayo	*will stand*
sa tabi	*next/beside*
kasama	*together with/companion*
habang	*while*
nagseseremonya	*officiating*
ganoon	*like that*
sa baryo	*at the barrio*
salu-salo	*party*
tumawag	*call* (on the telephone)
kung	*if*
itatanong	*something to ask*

Translation

Beth   Would you like to be a godfather to our child ? (*at the baptism of our child*)

Roy   Really? Of course - this is a big honour.

Edwin   There will be two godfathers and also two godmothers.

Roy   When will the baptism be held?

Beth   On Saturday December 4 at the barrio chapel.

Roy   What will I have to do?

Edwin   (It's) Easy. You will just stand next to the parents while the priest performs the ceremony.

Roy   So that's it. What time on Saturday?

Beth   9.30 in the morning. Afterwards, a reception follows at our house.

Edwin   All right. We'll be waiting for you with Jobert. Please call if you have anything to ask.

☑ Exercise 1 Mga Tanong: (Questions)

Using Dialogue 1 to help you, answer the following questions in Tagalog:

1. Ano ang paanyaya (*invitation*) ni Beth at Edwin kay Roy?
2. Ilan ang magiging (*become*) ninong at ninang?
3. Saan gaganapin (*will be held*) ang binyag at salu-salo?
4. Tinanggap (*accept*) ba ni Roy ang paanyaya?
5. Sino ang kasama (*companion*) ni Roy papunta (*going to*) sa simbahan?

Language skills

1. 'IN' Passive verbs

In Units 12, 13 and 14 we were introduced to the Tagalog active verb types (**um**, **mag**, **mang**). Dialogue 1 introduces us to a number of passive verbs (**gawin**, *to make*, **gaganapin**, *will be held*, **hihintayin**, *will wait for*). Whereas the active verbs we have looked at lay emphasis on the actor ('doer' of the action), passive verb sentences lay emphasis on the object. With just a glance at the comparison table, you will quickly see that both active and passive verbs use different actors (see table). These different actors are necessary in as far as they inform the listener as to where the emphasis of the sentence lies: on the object or on the actor. In Tagalog, active verbs take the **ang** form actors while passive verbs use **ng** form actors. The basic rule of thumb is this: in passive verb sentences, the actor you use is from the **ng** group (**ni, nina, ko, mo, niya, namin, natin, nila,** etc.), while in active verb sentences the actor is from the **ang** group (**si, sina, ako, ka, ikaw, siya, kami, tayo, kayo, sila,** etc.) Stick to this rule and you won't get lost.

The first of the Tagalog passive verbs is the **in** verb. This verb type is recognised by the suffix 'in' added after the verb root. For example: kain + in = **kainin** (*be eaten*). Like the active verbs, you can expand passive sentences by adding an adverb, a particle, a preposition, or a time element and so on. It is also important to note that some **in** verbs are directional verbs. For example: **Sasabihin ko sa kanila ang kailangan mo**, *I'll tell them what you need*. This sentence has a verb, an actor, a receiver of the action (the **sa**) and a goal (the object).

Passive and active verb actors: a comparison table

Um/mag/mang	Object	In/i/an	Object
A	Any of B	B	Any of A
Si		Ni	
Sina		Nina	
ako		ko	
ka/ikaw		mo	
siya		niya	
kami		namin	
tayo		natin	
ito		nito	
iyan		niyan	
iyon		noon	
ang		ng	

Don't forget: ko + ka = kita

Look at the following sentences to compare active and passive verbs:

From active verb		to passive verb	
um verb	to	**in** verb	
Verb	bumili	Verb	binili
Actor	ako	Actor	ko
Object	ng magasin	Object	ang magasin
Time element	kahapon	Time element	kahapon
*I bought **a** magazine yesterday*		*I bought **the** magazine yesterday*	

mag verb	to	**in** verb	
Verb	magluto	Verb	lutuin
Actor	tayo	Actor	natin
Object	ng pansit	Object	ang pansit
Time element	para sa party	Time element	para sa party
	ni Caroline		ni Caroline

*Let us cook **some** noodles for*   *Let us cook **the** noodles for*
  Caroline's party   *Caroline's party*

mang verb	to	**in** verb	
Verb	naninigarilyo	Verb	sinisigarilyo
Actor	si Ambo	Actor	ni Ambo
Object	ng Marlboro	Object	ang Marlboro
Time element	lagi	Time element	lagi

Ambo always smokes   *Ambo always smokes **the***
  Marlboro   *Marlboro*

In these sentences you can see that the **in** verbs are followed by a definite article.

Exercise 2

Here are some **um**, **mag** and **mang** sentences. Rewrite them as **in** sentences, using the guide to help you:

> Example: Bumasa tayo ng nobela. (Um)
>   Basahin natin ang nobela.

1. Bukas ba kayo bibili ng bagong stereo?
2. Gumagawa siya ng bulaklak na papel.
3. Tumatahi ka ba nito?
4. Tumutugtog siya ng kundiman sa piyano.
5. Naglilinis pa ako ng kuwarto ko.
6. Pumili ka ng sariwang gulay.

Attending a baptism

Dialogue 2

After the baptism, Roy wants to take a few pictures of the group outside the church.

Roy	Kukunan ko ng retrato ang aking inaanak sa binyag.
Beth	Puwede ba kunan mo rin ng retrato ang mga ninong at ninang?
Roy	Aba oo. Kasama rin ang mga magulang ng sanggol.
Edwin	Eto pala si Father Rex. Isama natin siya.
Beth	Father Rex, sumama po kayo sa amin.
Father Rex	O sige. Salamat. Maganda ang binyagang ito.
Edwin	Salamat po, Father.
Father Rex	Walang anuman.

Talasalitaan	*Vocabulary*
kukunan	*will take*
retrato	*picture*
aking inaanak	*my godchild*
sumama	*to join*
kunan	*to take*
aba oo	*of course*
sanggol	*baby*
eto pala	*so here is*
isama	*to include*
o sige	*all right*
binyagang ito	*this baptism*

Translation

Roy	I want to take some pictures of my godchild.
Beth	Can you take a picture of the godparents too?
Roy	Of course. Including the parents of the baby.
Edwin	Here comes Father Rex. Let's ask him to join us.
Beth	Father Rex, Please join us.
Father Rex	All right. Thank you. This is a good baptism.
Edwin	Thank you Father.
Father Rex	You're welcome.

✔ Exercise 3

Using complete Tagalog sentences, what do you say when:

1. You want to take a picture of your friends?
2. You are asking your friend to take your picture?
3. You want to make a nice comment about someone's dress?
4. You want to ask someone to join you?

⬚ Language skills

2. Changing the tense of in verbs:

The **in** infinitive is used for requests, commands and suggestions.

kuha	=	stem *get/take*		
kuha + in	=	kuhain (becomes kunin)	=	infinitive
ku + kunin	=	kukunin	=	future
k + in +ukuha	=	kinukuha	=	present
k+ in + uha	=	kinuha	=	past

alis = stem *remove*

alis + in	=	alisin	=	infinitive
a+ alis + in	=	aalisin	=	future
in + a + alis	=	inaalis	=	present
in+ alis	=	inalis	=	past

✔ Exercise 4

Supply the appropriate tense forms of the following **in** verbs. Use the examples to guide you:

Infinitive			Future	Present	Past
1. ibig =	stem *love*	=			
2. kain =	stem *eat*	=			
3. linis =	stem *clean*	=			
4. sulat =	stem *write*	=			
5. tapos =	stem *finish*	=			

More on **in** verbs:

As object, focus **in** verbs typically denote actions 'radically' affecting the goal, such as those causing change in its structure. For example:

Infinitive	Stem	
gawin	gawa	*to make, do*
lutuin	luto	*to cook*
tapusin	tapos	*to finish*
tadtarin	tadtad	*to chop*

Sometimes used with a directional, focus **in** verbs may express motion in relation to a goal (in which case there is usually some element of contact with the goal). For example:

Infinitive	Stem	
panhikin	panhik	*to go up into*
pasukin	pasok	*to enter*
pukulin	pukol	*to throw something at*
salpukin	salpok	*to strike against*
sampalin	sampal	*to slap one's face*

Most cooking terms fall under **in**:

Infinitive	Stem	
saingin	saing	*to cook* (as in rice)
lagain	laga	*to boil*
prituhin	prito	*to fry* (in deep oil)
sangagin	sangag	*to fry* (with very little oil, as in rice)
putulin	putol	*to cut*
hiwain	hiwa	*to slice*
tadtarin	tadtad	*to chop*

Most cleaning terms fall under **in**:

linisin	linis	*to clean*
kuskusin	kuskos	*to scrub*
ayusin	ayos	*to arrange/tidy up*

Most stative actions (actions describing a state of being) are **in**:

gulatin	gulat	*to surprise*
takutin	takot	*to scare*
hiyain	hiya	*to embarrass*
gutumin	gutom	*to make hungry*
biguin	bigo	*to disappoint*

Illnesses can be verbalised under **in**: Here, there is no actor, just a goal:

lagnatin	lagnat	*to have a fever*
sipunin	sipon	*to suffer from cold*
malaryahin	malarya	*to suffer from malaria*

To be infested by insects fall under **in** when verbalised. Here again, there is no actor, just a goal.

anayin	anay	*to be infested with termites*
langgamin	langgam	*to be infested with ants*
lamukin	lamok	*to be swarmed with mosquitoes*
surutin	surot	*to be infested with bedbugs*

For example:

1. Nilalanggam ang cake.
   The cake is swarming with ants.
2. Sinisipon ka ba?
   Are you suffering from cold?
3. Minalarya ang mga sundalo.
   The soldiers suffered from malaria.
4. Nilalagnat si Mario.
   Mario has a fever.

Sentence variations

Verb +	actor +	object:
Hiwain	ninyo	ang sibuyas at kamatis.

You slice the onions and tomatoes

Qualifier +	actor +	verb +	object:
Huwag	ninyong	kainin	ang pagkain nila

Don't you eat their food!

Qualifier +	particle +	actor +	object:
Binabago	talaga	ng araw	ang kulay ng ating balat.

Indeed, the sun changes the colour of our skin

Question marker +	actor +	object (directional):
Sino	ang gumulat	sa kaniya?

Who surprised him/her?

Qualifier +	actor +	object +	verb:
Hindi	ko	siya	pipilitin

I won't force her

Note: There are irregular **in** verbs that change when forming the infinitive. For example: **bili**, *buy* becomes **bilhin**, **sunod**, *follow* becomes *sundin*, **kuha**, *get/take* becomes **kunin**, **dala**, *carry* becomes **dalhin**, **sabi**, *say* becomes sabihin.

Exercise 5

Choose the correct verb from the brackets and translate the sentence into English:

1. (Hinuhuli/hulihin/hinuli) ng pulis ang mga sidewalk vendors araw-araw. (present)
2. Alam mo ba kung ilang mangga ang (kinain/kakainin/kainin) ni Bosyo kanina? (past)
3. Kailan mo (tinahi/ tatahiin/ tinatahi) ang aking bestida? (future)
4. Huwag mong (sasabihin/ sinabi/ sinasabi) kay Rex ang sagot mo. (future)
5. Kahapon, (nilinis/ lilinisin/ linisin) na niya ang bagong kotse. (past)

☑ Exercise 6

Look at the three pictures. From the accompanying word box, see if you can match up two appropriate **in** verbs to each picture:

linisin	*to clean*
inumin	*to drink*
bilhin	*to buy*
kainin	*to eat*
sirain	*to destroy*
sipunin	*to have a cold*
gulatin	*to surprise*
lutuin	*to cook*
lagnatin	*to have a fever*
kunin	*to get*
biruin	*to tease/joke*
kilalanin	*to know*
sabihin	*to tell*

Dialogue 3

After the baptism the priest is seen speaking to Roy.

Pari Ku**mus**ta ka Roy.

Roy Ma**bu**ti *po* na**man**. At ka**yo** *po*?

Pari Ma**bu**ti rin na**man** salamat. Isa ka pa**la** sa mga **ni**nong ng **ba**gong bin**yag**.

Roy **O**po. Ti**nan**ong ni**la ako** kung pu**we**de a**ko** at tinang**gap** ko na**man** ang paan**ya**ya.

Pari Ma**bu**ti. Ang mga ma**gu**lang mo, **da**rating ba?

Roy *Hindi po.*

Pari **Pu**punta ka ba sa salu-**sa**lo?

Roy **O**po.

Pari O, **si**ge mag-enjoy ka.

Roy Sa**la**mat *po*.

Talasalitaan	*Vocabulary*
isa ka sa mga	*you're one of the*
pupunta	*will go*
salu-salo	*party*
bago(ng) binyag	*newly baptised*
tinanong	*was asked*
puwede ako	*I'm available*
tinanggap	*accepted*
paanyaya	*invitation*
magulang mo	*your parents*
darating	*will arrive*
mag-enjoy	*to enjoy*

Translation

Priest How are you, Roy.

Roy I'm fine sir. And you?

Priest I'm fine too, thank you. So you're one of the godfathers of the newly baptised?

Roy Yes I am. They asked if I was available and I accepted the invitation.

Priest Good. Your parents, are they coming?

Roy No sir.

Priest	Are you going to (attend) the party?
Roy	Yes sir.
Priest	All right. You enjoy yourself.
Roy	Thank you sir.

✔ Exercise 7

Here are the answers, but can you supply the questions?

1. Oo. Ninong din ako.
   Question:
2. Dalawa kaming ninong.
   Question:
3. Wala rito ang mga magulang ko.
   Question:
4. Pupunta siguro ako sa salu-salo.
   Question:

✔ Exercise 8

Look at the following pictures and listen to the tape. You will notice that the pictures are out of sequence with the story. After listening to the story, number the pictures in their correct order:

After replaying the tape and listening to the story several times, why not have fun by retelling the story in Tagalog to some of your Filipino friends.

Language skills

3. More on particles

In Unit 14 we looked at the particles (adverbs) **pa** and **na**. A fuller list of common Tagalog particles and their uses follows. The ability to learn and use particles in your spoken Tagalog will not only add 'polish' to your sentences but will no doubt impress your Filipino friends too! Look at the table and study the examples that follow:

Particle	When and how it is used
naman	*on the other hand* (also used as a form of reply meaning too/as well/ in fact)
po	used out of respect in answering or addressing an elder or superior or person of rank
ba	interrogative particle answerable by yes or no
pala	*so!*
nga	*indeed, truly*
raw/daw	*according to them/ they say/ apparently/ she/he said* etc.(raw is used with a word after a final vowel)
kaya	used idiomatically to express doubt *I wonder/ do you think*
yata	*I think, maybe, it seems*
rin/din	*also,too, as well* (rin is used with a word after a final vowel)
na naman	*again*

Example sentences

1. Naupo si Phil at tumayo naman si Harry.
   Phil sat down and on the other hand, Harry stood up.
2. Umuulan na naman!
   It's raining again.
3. Kumusta po kayo?
   How are you sir/madam? (very formal)
4. Nagbabakasyon rin kami taun-taon.
   We also go on holiday every year.
5. Mandurukot kaya ang taong ito?
   I wonder if this man is a pickpocket.
6. Ito pala ang istasyon ng pulisya.
   So this is the police station.
7. Ginagamit mo ba ito?
   Are you using this?
8. Hindi raw niya kailangan ang pasaporte natin.
   Apparently he/she doesn't need our passport.

✔ Exercise 9

Here are some sentences. Fill in the blank space with an appropriate particle, then translate the sentence into English. Use the clues to help you:

Example: Kumakain ka ba ng balut?
         Translation: *Do you eat balut?*

1. Hindi _____ sila Pilipino. (so!)
   Translation:
2. Magaganda _____ ang mga bulaklak sa hardin ninyo. (indeed)
   Translation:
3. Sino _____ ang mga bagong bisita nila? (I wonder)
   Translation:
4. Tinatawag ka _____ ng mga kaibigan mo. (I think)
   Translation:
5. Narito _____ ang mga kailangan ko? (?)
   Translation:

Use of ba

The particle **ba** cannot be translated directly into English. Its purpose is to indicate that a sentence is in fact a question. Use of **ba** is optional, except in question formulas such as **hindi ba**, etc. In the more sophisticated Manila Tagalog, it is often missed out altogether.

As a particle, **ba** is normally found sandwiched between the comment and the subject of a sentence. For example, **Turista** (comment) **ba si Ginoong Abbott** (subject)?, *Is Mr Abbott a tourist?* When more than one particle is used in a sentence, as a permanent rule, **ba** comes after **na (na ba), pa (pa ba), rin (rin ba), raw (raw ba)** and **na naman (na naman ba)**. When a long string of particles is used, **ba** can be found at the end of a sentence, thus **Namili ka rin daw ba?**, *Did they say you also went shopping?*

Occasionally the subject is omitted altogether, such as when the speaker raises his / her voice tone clearly indicating that they want to ask a question. For example, **Malinis na ba ang mesa?**, *Is the table clean already* becomes **Malinis na ba?** (ang mesa), *Is it* [the table] *clean already?*

An amusing word of warning to the Tagalog learner: Be careful when using the particle **ba** in connection with the second person singular **ka** (informal). In this case, **ka** precedes **ba**, i.e. **ka ba** (instead of **ba ka** which translates into English as *cow*! For example, **Guro ka ba?**, *Are you a teacher?*, not **Guro ba ka?**, which would translate as *teacher cow!*

One-minute phrases

> **Kunan mo ako** (*koo-nahn maw ah-kaw*) Literally, *take/get (something) from me*. Meaning take my picture/photograph!! For example: **Gene, kunan mo naman ako sa camera ko,***Gene, would you be kind enough to take my picture with my camera?*
>
> **Ikaw ang masusunod** (*ee-kao ahng mah-saw-saw-nawd*) Literally, *you're the one to be followed*. Meaning as you like it/ You're the boss! For example: **Kung gusto mong umalis tayo nang maaga, ikaw ang masusunod**. *If you want us to leave early, then you're the boss.*

Dahan-dahan ang pagsasalita (*dah-hahn dah-hahn ahng pahg-sah-sah-lee-tah*) Literally, *slow-slow the talking*. Meaning could you speak a little more slowly. For example: **Dahan-dahan lang ang pagsasalita para maintindihan ko ang sinasabi mo**, *Please speak slowly so that I'd be able to understand you.*

Anuman ang mangyari (*ah-noo-mahn ahng mahng-yah-ree*) Literally, *whatever the happening*. Similar in meaning to the English expression 'come what may'. For example: **Darating daw sila anuman ang mangyari**, *They said they would arrive come what may.*

Tumingin-tingin (*too-mee-ngeen tee-ngeen*) Literally, *to have a look/see*. Meaning to have a look around/ to see. For example: **Kapag namalengke ka, tumingin-tingin ka nga kung may sariwang lapulapu**, *If you go to the market, would you have a look if there are fresh lapulapu.*

(i) **Cultural Tip**

Relationship bonds are high on the agenda in Filipino culture. Filipinos are deeply loyal to their families and are prepared to sacrifice their own confort and personal happiness in order to improve the lot of their loved ones. Where no blood ties exist, Filipino culture finds other ways to forge connections. One such way is the **kumpare** or **kumare** system. These words can be translated literally as 'co-father' or 'co-mother'. Here, a respected person is invited by a family to become a godparent at the baptism of one of their children. If you are invited to be a godparent remember that it is considered to be an honour. You are then no longer just a visitor or an outsider, but a 'co-mother' or a 'co-father' to the child. You are now 'connected' to the family at a deeper level. Of course, it is good to be aware that such connection may carry certain financial expectations or even obligations. Saying 'yes' to such an invitation may have consequences, but saying 'no' is potentially just as complicated.

16 | MAAARI BANG GAWIN MO ITO?
Could I ask a favour of you?

In this unit you will learn how to

■ make requests and suggestions
■ give a command
■ give instructions

Making requests and suggestions

Dialogue 1

At the Abiva residence, Louise Cook is asking Lily to do something for her.

Louise   Maaari bang ipakihulog mo ang mga sulat ko?

Lily   Aba opo. Ibigay *po* ninyo sa akin at ihuhulog ko kaagad.

Louise   Heto. Labindalawa ang mga iyan. *Wala* akong selyo. Ibili mo na tuloy ako ng selyo at ipakilagay mo ang mga selyo sa sulat.

Lily   Sige *po*. Ako *po* ang bahala. Pupunta ako sa post office.

Louise   Maraming salamat ha? Heto ang pera.

Lily   *Wala* pong anuman, Ginang Cook.

Talasalitaan	*Vocabulary*
ipakihulog mo	*could you post*
tuloy	*as well*
aba opo	*of course* (formal)
ibigay	*to give*
sa akin	*to me*
ihuhulog	*will post*
kaagad	*immediately*
ibili	*to buy for*
pakilagay	*please put*
ang bahala	*will look after*

Translation

Louise   Could you kindly post my letters?

Lily   Sure ma'am. If you give them to me I'll post them immediately.

Louise   Here. There are twelve there. I don't have stamps. If you could also buy some stamps for me and put them on the letters.

Lily   All right ma'am. I'll look after them. I'm going to go to the post office.

Louise   Thank you very much indeed. Here is the money.

Lily   You're welcome, Mrs Cook.

☑ Exercise 1

Listen to the dialogue again and then answer the following questions.

1. Ano ang sinabi ni Louise Cook kay Lily?
   Answer:
2. Ilan ang sulat na ihuhulog ni Lily?
   Answer:
3. Bakit bibili si Lily ng selyo?
   Answer:
4. Saan bibili ng selyo si Lily?
   Answer:

🗗 Language skills

1. Passive 'i' verbs

A second passive verb form is known as the **i** type verb. Dialogue 1 gives us a few examples: **ibigay**, *to give*, **ihuhulog**, *will post*, **ibili**, *to buy for*. As with all passive verb forms, it always takes a **ng** form actor (either **ni, nina, ko, mo, niya, namin, natin, ninyo, nila, ninyo, niyan, noon,** or **ng**), while the object or goal is always an **ang** form word (either **si, sina, ako, ka/ikaw, siya, kami, tayo, kayo, sila, ito, iyan, iyon, ang mga ito, ang mga iyan, ang mga iyon,** or **ang**). For example: **Ibinalik ni Elvira** (actor) ang libro (object), *Elvira returned the book*. The infinitive of the **i** verb is easily recognised by the prefix **i** before the root word. For example: **i** + hulog = **ihulog**, *to post or to drop*, i + tapon = **itapon**, *to throw* and so on.

The **i** verb is unique in that it is object focused, meaning that we lay more emphasis on the object rather than on the doer of the action. For example: **Isinara ko ang bintana**, *The window* (object) *was closed by me.* or *I closed the window.* If this same sentence uses an active verb, the focus would then be on the doer of the action: **Nagsara ako ng bintana**, *I closed a window.* Some **i** verbs are also used as beneficiary words, meaning that an action is performed for the benefit of another person. For example: **ibili**, *to buy for* (someone), **ikuha**, *to get for* (someone) **igawa**, *to make for* (someone), **isama**, *to take someone along* (for someone). In all of these cases, the recipient (or beneficiary) of these verbs is represented with an **ang** form word.

For example: **Ibinili ko si Eileen ng sapatos**, *I bought (a pair of) shoes for Eileen.* **Igagawa ko si Neneng ng manyika**, *I'll make a doll for Neneng.* The **i** verb is also directional, that is, it uses **sa** as a goal. Example: **Ibigay natin ito sa kanila**, *Let us give this to them.* **Ipinasok ni Larry ang mga silya sa loob**, *Larry took the chairs in/inside/indoors.*

Compare the um and i Beneficiary

Bumili ako ng sorbetes para kay Tess	*I bought some ice cream for Tess*
Ibinili ko ng sorbetes si Tess	*I bought Tess some ice cream*
Gumawa sila ng saranggola para sa akin	*They made a kite for me*
Iginawa nila ako ng saranggola	*They made me a kite*
Sumama ako sa kanila sa sine	*I went to the cinema with them*
Isinama nila ako sa sine	*They took me to the cinema*

Compare the mag and i forms

Mag-aakyat siya ng panggatong	*He/she will bring/take up some firewood*
Iaakyat niya ang panggatong	*He/she will bring/take up the firewood*
Nagprito ba kayo ng itlog?	*Did you fry some eggs?*
Iprinito ba ninyo ang itlog?	*Did you fry the eggs?*

| Naglalabas na sila ng mga silya | *They are taking out some chairs now* |
| Inilalabas na nila ang mga silya | *They are taking out the chairs now* |

Some example sentences:

1. Ibinigay ni Bernie ang bolpen kay Elizabeth
   Bernie gave the pen to Elizabeth
2. Isasama mo ba si Stephen sa sine?
   Are you going to take Stephen to the cinema?
3. Isasampay ko muna ang mga damit
   I'll hang the clothes first
4. Ano ang inilagay mo sa sopas?
   What did you put in the soup?
5. Isasara ko na po ba ang mga bintana?
   Shall I close the windows now?
6. Itinahi ako ni Letty ng magandang blusa
   Letty has sewn a lovely blouse for me
7. Igagawa mo ba siya ng laruan?
   Are you going to make a toy for him/her?

Changing the tense of the i verb

Prefix	I		
Stem	tapon *throw*		
Infinitive	I + tapon	=	itapon *to be thrown*
Future	I + ta + tapon	=	itatapon *will be thrown*
Present	I + t + in + a_ tapon	=	itinatapon *is being thrown*
Past	I + t + in + a + pon	=	itinapon *was thrown*

 ### Some familiar i verbs – Listen and repeat

Listen to the correct pronunciation on the tape. Listen carefully to the slight variations in pronunciation of each tense and then try to repeat without the help of the tape.

Infinitive	Translation	Future	Present	Past
ibigay	*to give*	ibibigay	ibinibigay	ibinigay
ilagay	*to put/place*	ilalagay	inilalagay	inilagay
itapon	*to throw*	itatapon	itinatapon	itinapon
itago	*to keep in a safe place*	itatago	itinatago	itinago
itabi	*to keep aside*	itatabi	itinatabi	itinabi
ibagsak	*to drop with force*	ibabagsak	ibinabagsak	ibinagsak
itaas	*to take up/raise*	itataas	itinataas	itinaas
isabit	*to hang on a hook*	isasabit	isinasabit	isinabit
isampay	*to hang on a line*	isasampay	isinasampay	isinampay
itulak	*to push*	itutulak	itinutulak	itinulak
isukat	*to try something on*	isusukat	isinusukat	isinukat
isara	*to close*	isasara	isinasara	isinara
ipasok	*to take inside*	ipapasok	ipinapasok	ipinasok
ilabas	*to take outside*	ilalabas	inilalabas	inilabas
ipasa	*to pass*	ipapasa	ipinapasa	ipinasa
ibili	*to buy for*	ibibili	ibinibili	ibinili
ikain	*to eat for*	ikakain	ikinakain	ikinain
ikuha	*to get for*	ikukuha	ikinukuha	ikinuha
igawa	*to make for*	igagawa	iginagawa	iginawa
isama	*to take someone with*	isasama	isinasama	isinama
itahi	*to sew for*	itatahi	itinatahi	itinahi
isakay	*to take aboard*	isasakay	isinasakay	isinakay

Some i verbs are used in connection with activities of a social nature (beneficiary):

Stem	Meaning	
ikumusta	kumusta	*to say hello for*
idalo	dalo	*to attend for*
ihalik	halik	*to kiss for*
iyakap	yakap	*to embrace for*
ibalita	balita	*to send news for*

Ikumusta mo kami sa kanila	*Say hello to them from us*
Ihalik mo ako sa nanay	*Kiss Mother for me*

Some **i** verbs denote actions affecting the position of the **ang**, without causing a change in its structure. They often correspond to **mag** verbs.

Stem	Meaning	
iakyat	akyat	*to bring/take up*
ialok	alok	*to offer*
itapon	tapon	*to throw*
iuwi	uwi	*to take home*

Inialok ni Peter ang kotse niya sa akin — *Peter offered his car to me*

Bakit mo iuuwi iyan? — *Why are you taking that home?*

In their passive form, **mag** verbs denoting ways of preparing food are represented as *i* verbs:

iluto	luto	*to cook*
iihaw	ihaw	*to broil/grill*
iprito	prito	*to fry*
ipaksiw	paksiw	*to make paksiw*

Ipinirito mo ba ang isda?	*Did you fry the fish?*
Iniluto ko na ang bangus	*I have cooked the milkfish already*

Exercise 2

Look at the cartoons. Can you say what actions are being performed? Write your answer in the space provided. A noun has been provided to help you.

Example: Itinatapon ang basura (ang basura)

aklat

bola

bestida

Sentence variations using **i** form verbs:

Verb	+	actor	+	beneficiar	+	object	+	adverb
Ikukuha		ko		siya		ng tubig		

I will get him/her (a glass of) water.

Igagawa	namin	sila		ng laruan

We will make a toy for them.

Isinasama	nila	ako		sa parke	lagi.

They always take me along with them to the park

Ibili	mo	kami		ng sandwich

Buy some sandwiches for us

Pseudo-Verb + particle +verb + actor + receiver of the action + object

Maaari	bang	ibili	mo	kami		ng sandwich?

Could you buy some sandwiches for us?/ Could you buy us some sandwiches?

verb	actor	object
Ilalabas	ni Tessie	ang mga panindang gulay

Tessie will take the vegetable goods outside/outdoors

adverb	particle	actor	verb	object
Mamaya	na	namin	itatapon	ang basura

We will throw out the rubbish later on

Question word	+	object	+	actor	+	place	+	time
Ano		ang itinulak		nila		sa kalsada		kahapon?

What was it that they pushed on the street yesterday?

Exercise 3 Listening and Speaking

Listen to the tape. You will hear the speaker mention different times of the day. Each time of day is accompanied by a verb in the infinitive form. Using your skill and knowledge of **i** verbs, provide the correct tense to accompany the time element.

Dialogue 2

Jobert has been a great help to the Cook family. Bill is speaking to him.

Bill   Jobert, masyado yatang pinapagod ka namin. *Nahihiya kami* sa *ginagawa* mo *para* sa *am*in.

Jobert	*Hindi* na**man**. **Kon**ting **ba**gay lang i**to**. No**ong nas**a London **ako** tinu**lun**gan ni**nyo ako**. Ma**laki** ang **ut**ang na lo**ob** ko sa in**yo**.
Bill	I**kaw** na**man**. **Ba**le *wala* iyon. Kali**mut**an mo na i**yon**.
Jobert	**Aba**, isi**nama** ninyo **ako** sa mga lu**gar** na *hindi* ko ma**aa**bot kung *hindi* sa in**yo**. Ibin**ili** ni**nyo ako** ng mga kai**lang**an ko. Iniha**tid** ni**nyo ako** sa pali**par**an.
Bill	Ma**raming** sa**lamat** Jobert sa pag-a**laa**la mo **pero** *hindi* ka **da**pat mag-i**sip** ng gani**yan**.
Jobert	**Walang** anu**man**. Ma**raming** sa**lamat** na *muli*.

Talasalitaan	*Vocabulary*
isinama	*accompanied*
pinapagod ka	*tiring you*
nahihiya	*embarrassed*
ginagawa	*doing*
para sa amin	*for us*
hindi naman	*not so*
bagay	*thing*
noong	*when*
tinulungan	*helped*
muli	*again*
utang na loob	*debt of gratitude*
bale wala	*means nothing*
kalimutan	*forget*
maaabot	*won't be able to reach*
kung hindi	*had not been*
ibinili	*bought for*
kailangan	*needs*
inihatid	*took to*
pag-alaala	*concern*
mag-isip	*to worry*
ganiyan	*like that*

Translation

Bill	Jobert, I think we are tiring you a lot. We are feeling (a little) embarrassed by what you're doing for us.
Jobert	Not at all. This is only a small thing. When I was in London you helped me. I owe you a lot.
Bill	Oh, you. That's nothing. Please forget about that.
Jobert	Well, you took me to places that I would not have reached had it not been for you. You bought me things I needed. You took me to the airport.
Bill	Thank you Jobert for your concern but you shouldn't think like that.
Jobert	Don't mention it. Thank you very much again.

☑ Exercise 4

Can you answer the following questions?

1. Bakit nahihiya si Bill kay Jobert?
2. Bakit nag-aalaala si Jobert?
3. Magbigay ng dalawang bagay na ginawa nina Bill para kay Jobert sa London.
4. Kung ikaw, mag-aalaala ka rin ba katulad ni Jobert?

⚙ Language skills

2. Mag = verb
Walang + verb

May + active verb or **mayroong** + Active verb	= *someone, somebody*
May + passive verb or **mayroong** + Passive verb	= *something*
Walang + active verb	= *no one, nobody*
Walang + passive verb	= *nothing*
Marami + active or Passive	= *a lot of/ lots of*

We have already met the words **may**, **mayroon** *has/have*, **mayroon** *there is/there are* and **marami** *many*.

These words are used not only to express possession but may also be used as **may** phrases expressing 1) presence; 2) something indefinite. Simply speaking, a **may** phrase expresses presence when there is no subject in the sentence and **may** (or **mayroon**) is followed by a noun. This is in fact less complicated than it sounds. Look at this example: **May pagkain sa mesa**. *There is food on the table (food is present on the table).*

In indefinite phrases, **may** (or **mayroon**) is followed by a verb. For example: **May bibili ba ng Coke bukas?**, *Will someone buy Coke tomorrow?*, **May bumibili ng coke.** *Someone is buying Coke.* **May naglilinis dito araw-araw**, *Someone cleans here everyday.* **Mayroong* kumatok kagabi**, *Someone knocked on the door last night.* **Maraming* namimili sa palengke kung Sabado**, *Many (people) go to the market on Saturdays.* (* **Note**: as a general rule, **mayroon** and **marami** become **mayroong** and **maraming** when followed by a noun). No doubt you will have noticed that each of these sentences has no subject. When the verb in an indefinite **may** phrase is an active verb (**um, mag, mang**), then the sentence has no subject. However, if the verb in an indefinite **may** phrase is a passive verb (**in, i, an**) then there is a subject. For example: **May kinuha ako sa kaniya**, *I took something from him/her.* **Mayroong itinapon si Stephen sa sahig**, *Stephen threw something on the floor.* **Maraming inalis sa trabaho noong bago mag-pasko**, *Many (employees) were made redundant before Christmas.*

You will remember that the opposite to **may** is **wala**. **Wala + ng** not only expresses absence or non-possession of something, but like **may**, **mayroon** and **marami**, it can be used to express the indefinite. As with may, mayroon and marami, if the verb used with **wala** is an active verb (**um, mag, mang**), then there is no subject. For example: **Walang kumakain ng luto ko**, *No one is eating what I've cooked*, **Walang naglalaro ng tennis ngayon.** *Nobody is playing tennis today.* **Wala bang mamimili bukas?** *Isn't anyone going shopping tomorrow?* Again, if the verb used with **wala** is a passive verb, (**in, i** or **an**) then there is a subject. For example: **Walang binili si Roy sa duty free**, *Roy didn't buy anything from the duty free.* **Wala ka bang ibibigay kay Sophie?** *Aren't you giving anything to Sophie?*, **Walang tinawagan si Amy kagabi**, *Amy didn't call anyone* (on the telephone) *last night.*

Reference table			
Active verb (**um, mag, mang**)		No Subject +	Time etc.
may	kumakain		kagabi
mayroong	kumakain		kagabi
maraming	kumakain		kagabi
walang	kumakain		kagabi
Passive verb (**in, i, an**)		Subject +	Time etc.
may	kinain	si Patricia	kanina
mayroong	kinain	si Patricia	kanina
maraming	kinain	si Patricia	kanina
walang	kinain	si Patricia	kanina

Sample sentences:

May sumigaw sa klase kanina
Someone shouted in class a while ago

Maraming nagbabasketball sa kalye hapon-hapon
Many play basketball in the street every afternoon

May tumawag raw sa akin kagabi
Apparently someone called me (on the telephone) *last night*

Walang kumain ng luto ni Bennie
Nobody ate Bennie's cooking

May nagdarasal sa simbahan sa umaga
Someone prays in church in the morning

May nangyari sa kaniya
Something happened to her/him

May kumakatok yata
I think someone is knocking on the door

May sinabi ka ba sa kaniya?
Did you tell him/her anything?

Walang ginagawa ang mga empleyado dito
The employees here are not doing anything

Maraming binili si Ginang de los Reyes sa tindahan
Mrs. de los Reyes bought a lot of things from the store

Exercise 5:

The following sentences are jumbled up. Can you put them back into their correct order?

1. dito marami(ng) araw-araw bumibili ng libro.
2. sa pinto may kumakatok yata.
3. ako kahapon may kinuha sa kaniya.
4. walang noong Linggo sa akin sa ospital sumama.
5. sa kabila ng tennis na naman may naglalaro.

Language Skills

3. Requests, commands and suggestions

To make a simple request in Tagalog, just use **maaari bang/ puwede bang** followed by the infinitive form of an active or a passive verb! What could be simpler? Look at these examples:

Maaari bang maupo kayo?   *Would you mind sitting down?*
Puwede po bang huwag   *Would you mind not smoking?*
  tayong manigarilyo.

Exercise 6

Try making your own command, request or suggestion:

Example: **pumirma**. (Request): Maaari bang pumirma kayo dito? *Sir/madam, could you please sign here?*

1. Command: tumayo (*to stand up*)
   Sentence:
2. Request: maupo (*to sit down*)
   Sentence:
3. Suggestion: matulog (*to sleep*)
   Sentence:
4. Request: manigarilyo (*to smoke*)
   Sentence:
5. Suggestion: mamasyal (*to go for a walk*)
   Sentence:

✔ Exercise 7

You are on the telephone to your local hardware store. You have decided to help your Filipino friend make some improvements to her house but first of all, you will need a few supplies. Complete the following dialogue, using the vocabulary box to help you:

Ikaw *Say good morning*
Store Magandang umaga. Ano po ang maipaglilingkod ko sa inyo?
Ikaw *Ask if they have any cement*
Store Marami po kami niyan.
Ikaw *Say you would like to reserve ten bags*
Store Aba opo. Mayroon pa po ba kayong nais (bilhin)?
Ikaw *Ask if they have any marine plywood*
Store Wala po. Ordinaryong plywood lamang.
Ikaw *Ask if they have any aluminium roofing sheets*
Store Opo. Mayroon po. Kararating lang po ng bagong delivery ngayong umaga.
Ikaw *Good. Ask him to reserve twelve sheets for you*
Store O, eh iyon pong pampako sa pambubong na aluminum?
Ikaw *Yes. Two kilos please*
Store Mayroon pa po ba kayong kailangan?
Ikaw *No, that's all thank you. I will drop by at midday*
Store Ayos lang po, sir. Paalam na po.
Ikaw *Goodbye*

Ask one of your Filipino friends to help you practise this dialogue aloud.

One-minute phrases

Ikumusta mo ako (*ee-koo-moos-tah maw ah-kaw*) Literally, *Say hello you me*. Similar to its English equivalent ('say hello for me'), this Tagalog expression is used when sending greetings to a third person.

Ipagpaumanhin po ninyo (*ee-pahg-pah-oo-mahn-heen paw neen-yaw*) Literally, *Please bear with/excuse* (formal) *you*. Meaning 'to make something appear less serious/ to excuse'. This is a very polite and commonly used expression acknowledging any form of inconvenience caused to another person. For example: **Ipagpaumahin po ninyo ang sagabal na ito sa inyong kalsada**, *We apologise for this obstruction on your street.*

Unti-untiin (*oon-tee oon-tee-een*) Meaning 'to do something little by little/slowly'. A useful phrase used in the same way as its English equivalent. For example, **Sabi ni Nanay, unti-untiin daw natin ang pagkain ng sorbetes**, *Mother said that we have to eat the ice-cream little by little.*

Labag sa batas (*lah-bahg sah bah-tahs*) Meaning 'against the law'. For example: **Labag sa batas ang magpasok sa ating bansa ng anumang drugs**, *It is against the law to bring into our country any drugs.*

Pagdating na pagdating (*pag-dah-ting nah pag-dah-ting*) Literally, *upon arrival, upon arrival.* Meaning immediately upon arrival. For example: **Sabihin mo kay Pedro na pumunta sa opisina ko pagdating na pagdating niya**, *Tell Pedro to come straight to my office the moment he arrives.*

Cultural tip

As a people who consider smooth and harmonious relationships to be one of life's essentials, Filipinos have developed ways and means of engendering favour and good standing with one another. One such way is the **utang na loob** or debt of gratitude system. Very simply, it is understood that any favours received or favours granted do, indeed, have to be returned. To help another person out places that person in your debt, and one day they must find a way of repaying you. Local politicians have been known to use this cultural value to their benefit, particularly around election time. Relationship ties are commonly strengthened by **utang na loob** which underlines the Filipino cultural value of inter-dependence. Don't be surprised to be on the receiving end of a favour. It is culturally understood that favours will strengthen ties with you which may come on useful one day!

17 | **ISANG KASALAN**
A wedding

In this unit you will learn how to

■ understand Filipino customs and traditions: a wedding
■ use reflexive verbs

🔊 Understanding Filipino customs and 📖 traditions: a wedding

Dialogue 1

It is Pinky Abiva's wedding day. The bride and groom are talking to their guests.

Louise Kay ganda ng damit-pangkasal mo Pinky.

Pinky Salamat Louise. Mahusay ang modista namin.

Roy Maligayang bati, Pinky. Narito na pala ang mga ninong, ninang sa kasal, mga abay sa kasal, mga cord sponsors at mga tagapagdala ng singsing.

Pinky Oo, tinulungan nila akong *maghanda* para sa araw ng kasal ko.

Louise Maraming matatapos na gawain kung marami ang *gagawa, hindi ba?*

Roy Naayos na rin ba ang problema tungkol sa retratista?

Pinky Aba, oo. Inayos na ni Jobert.

Louise Ang tungkol sa pulot-*gata*?

Pinky *Hindi* pa namin naiisip, kasi marami kaming inasikaso. *Sandali* lang ha? Maraming dumarating na mga bisita.

Louise Okay lang.

Talasalitaan	*Vocabulary*
kay ganda	*how beautiful*
damit-pangkasal	*wedding dress*
modista	*dressmaker*
narito na	*here now*
mga ninong at ninang	*witnesses*
sa kasal	*wedding*
mga abay sa kasal	*wedding assistants*
tagapagdala ng singsing	*ring bearer*
tinulungan ako	*helped me*
maghanda	*to prepare*
para sa araw ng kasal ko	*for my wedding day*
matatapos na gawain	*jobs will be finished*
dumarating	*arriving*
ang gagawa	*will do*
naayos	*managed to arrange*
problema	*problem*
tungkol sa	*about*
retratista	*photographer*
inayos	*fixed/arranged*
pulot-gata	*honeymoon*
hindi pa	*not yet*
naiisip	*able to think about*
inasikaso	*dealt with*
sandali lang	*wait a moment*

Translation

Louise Your wedding dress is so beautiful, Pinky.
Pinky Thank you Louise. Our dressmaker is very good.
Roy Congratulations, Pinky. So the witnesses are here now, the cord sponsors and the ring bearers.
Pinky Yes, they (all) helped me prepare for my wedding day.
Louise Things can be done if there are many (hands) to help, isn't that so?
Roy Was the problem concerning the photographer solved?
Pinky Oh, yes, thanks to Jobert. (Jobert helped fix it)
Louise How about your honeymoon?

Pinky   We haven't (yet) thought about it, we have so many (other) things to attend to.

Louise   That can be sorted out later. (lit:, that's all right)

✔ Exercise 1

True or false? If the answer is false, try to give the correct one:

Example: Kasama sa mga abay sa kasal ang pari.

Answer: Mali. Hindi isa sa mga abay sa kasal ang pari. Ang pari ang nagbibigay ng seremonya.

1. Maaaring walang ninong at ninang ang ikinakasal.
    Sagot:
2. Kailangang maghanda maraming buwan bago ikasal.
    Sagot:
3. Laging puti ang damit-pangkasal ng babaeng ikinakasal.
    Sagot:
4. Sa Pilipinas, laging may handaan kung may kasalan.
    Sagot:

✔ Exercise 2

Improving your vocabulary. Look at the puzzle. Find as many wedding-related words as you can:

N	I	N	O	N	G	S	O	L	S
P	A	I	L	I	R	O	K	O	I
A	M	N	O	R	I	F	I	B	M
G	P	A	R	I	L	M	B	I	B
K	A	N	A	N	G	D	U	S	A
A	R	G	A	L	U	M	L	I	H
I	P	U	L	O	T	G	A	T	A
N	O	S	O	T	I	M	K	A	N
S	I	N	G	S	I	N	G	R	O
R	E	T	R	A	T	I	S	T	A
T	R	A	C	O	R	D	M	H	M

Language skills

1. Passive an verbs

Dialogue 1 introduced us to a third type of passive verb known as the **an** verb. Like the **in** and the **i** passive verb forms, the 'doer' of the action (actor) in the **an** verb form is identified by a **ng** word (**ni, nina, ko, mo, niya, namin, natin, ninyo, nila** etc.). The **an** verb is easily recognised by the addition of **an** (as a suffix) to the root verb. For example: hugas + **an** = **hugasan**, *to be washed*. In a passive **an** verb sentence, the **ang** form (**si, sina, ako, ka, siya** etc.) indicates the goal of the sentence while another **ng** word indicates the object. For example: **Bigyan natin ng pagkain ang bata**, *Let's give the child some food.*

The **an** form verb differs from other verb forms in that: 1) the goal (or **ang**) is the receiver of the action. For example, if we were to say: **Binigyan ko si Alan ng mainit na kape**, *I gave Alan* (a cup of) *hot coffee*, then Alan is clearly identified as the receiver of the act **binigyan** because he has received the coffee. Any action therefore that the **an** verb suggests is received by the goal. In English, we would express this by using the words from, at, with, to etc. For example: **Tinapunan ko si Lewis ng bola**, *I threw a ball at Lewis*.

2) The goal (or ang) is treated as a 'space'. For example: **Winawalisan ni Patricia ang balkonahe**, *Patricia is sweeping the porch*. For the 'info-holics' among us, it is interesting to note that most **an** verbs are derived from transitive **um** or **mag** verbs. For example, the **um** verb **Bumili siya ng saging sa matandang babae**, *He/she bought some bananas from the old woman* becomes **binilhan niya ng saging ang matandang babae**, *from the old woman he bought bananas*, when expressed in the **an** form. Here, the emphasis is on the goal or **matandang babae**. In the same way, **Nagbigay kami ng damit sa pulubi**, *We gave some clothes to the beggar*, becomes **Binigyan namin ng damit ang pulubi**, *the beggar was given some clothes by us*, with emphasis on **pulubi** as the goal. When **in** and **i** verb roots are used as **an** verbs, the meaning of the verb changes. Look at the examples.

How to form an verb tenses

Verb root: punas + suffix: an = punasan = *to wipe* (*to be wiped*) infinitive (can be used in requests, command & suggestions)

pu + punas + an = pupunasan = *will be wiped* = future
p + in + u + punas + an = pinupunasan = *being wiped* = present
p + in + u + nas + an = pinunasan = *was wiped* = past

In some instances, **an** verbs change to **han** when forming the infinitive. This depends on whether the accent on the second syllable is hard or soft:

For example:

Verb root: sama + suffix: han = samahan = *to be accompanied* infinitive

sa + sama + han = sasamahan = *will be accompanied* = future

s + in +a + sama + han = sinasamahan = *being accompanied* = present

s + in + a + ma + han = sinamahan = *was accompanied* = past

Listen carefully to native Tagalog speakers and you will soon pick up the difference between hard and soft accented words. Here are a few examples:

tira +	an	= tirahan/tirhan
pila +	an	= pilahan
para +	an	= parahan
sara +	an	= sarahan/sarhan
asa +	an	= asahan
bili +	an	= bilihan
basa +	an	= basahan
ganda +	an	= gandahan
dami +	an	= damihan
dumi +	an	= dumihan
pinta +	an	= pintahan
punta +	an	= puntahan

A brief comparison between **in**, **i** and **an** verbs.

in	**an**
kain (*eat*)	
Kakainin nila iyan	Kakainan nila iyan
They will eat that	*They will eat from that*
alis (*remove*)	
Inalis ni Joe ang plato sa mesa	Inalisan ni Joe ng plato ang mesa
Joe removed the plate from the table	*A plate was removed by Joe from the table*
punit (*tear off*)	
Pinupunit ni Sarah ang papel	Pinupunitan ni Sarah ang papel
Sarah is tearing the paper (into pieces)	*Sarah is tearing off from the paper*

You will remember that the receiver of the action in **i** verbs is always indicated by **sa**. In the **an** verb form, the receiver of the action is indicated by an **ang** form word. Compare the following examples:

I	**An**
Ibibigay ni Alan kay Lina ang pera	Bibigyan ni Alan si Lina ng pera
Alan will give Lina the money	*Alan will give Lina some money*
Itatapon ko ang sirang silya sa basurahan	Tatapunan ko ng sirang silya ang basurahan
I will throw the broken chair into the bin	*I will throw a broken chair in the bin*
Isinara ni Mario ang pinto	Sinarhan ni Mario ang pintuan.
Mario shut the door	*Mario closed the door*

An verb sentence variations:

Verb +		actor +	object/goal
Dinumihan		ni Charlotte	ang kaniyang damit.

Charlotte soiled her clothes

Verb +	particle +	actor +	Receiver of the action/goal
Sinulatan	ba	ni Louisa	ang kaibigan niya?

Did Louisa write to his/her friend?

Qualifier + actor + particle + verb +   object +   goal
Hindi   mo   raw   binigyan + ng pera   si Viv.
Apparently, you didn't give Viv (any) money.

Question word +   receiver of the action +   actor +   time
Sino   ang nginitian   ni Tim   kanina?
Who did Tim smile at a while ago?

Pseudo-verb + verb +   actor +   Object +   Receiver/goal
Gustong   bigyan ni Lucy   ng bibingka   ang bata.
Lucy would like to give the child some rice cakes.

Exercise 3

Using the examples to guide you, change the following sentences into **an** form sentences:

1. Kakainin ko ang pansit sa plato.
   Answer:
2. Tumutulong ako sa kaniya.
   Answer:
3. Maglalagay kami ng rosas na halaman dito.
   Answer:
4. Gusto kong ibigay kay Larry ito.
   Answer:
5. Ilalagay ba natin ito doon?
   Answer:
6. Huwag mong aalisin ang libro sa mesa.
   Answer:

Exercise 4

Fill in the blank spaces with the correct verb form:

1. Bukas _____ (tulong) namin sila. (future)
2. Kailan ninyo _____ (laki) ang inyong kusina? (past)
3. _____ (sukli) ka na ba ng tsuper? (past)
4. Si Wills at si Ruth ang _____ (sama) niya bukas. (future)
5. Mahusay sumayaw ang _____ (bigay) nila ng premyo sa disco.(past)
6. _____ (halik) ng bata ang lolo niya. (present)
7. _____ (sarap) ng tagapagluto ang handa sa parti. (future)
8. Ayokong _____ (palit) ang aking maleta. (infinitive)

Exercise 5:

When arranged in the correct sequence, the following sentences will tell a story. Arrange the sentences into the correct order and then translate the story into English. Use the vocabulary box to help you.

Sa kasalan

Napagod sa pagsayaw ng Tinikling ang pamilya Cook subali't nasiyahan sila.

Habang kumakain ang ilan sa mga bisita, tumugtog ang maliit na banda.

Isa sa mga tugtugin ay Tinikling.

Tumulong sa paghahain at pagsisilbi ang mga kaibigan ni Pinky.

May tugtugin at ang mga panauhin ay sumayaw.

Tuwang-tuwa ang lahat dahil sa marunong mag-Tinikling si Bill at si Louise.

Maraming kumuha ng retrato sa bagong kasal paglabas nila ng simbahan.

Dumating ang bagong kasal kasunod ang mga panauhin.

Isa-isang nagpaalam ang mga panauhin.

Nagbigay din ng speech ang 'best man'.

Inihanda ng mga tagapagluto ang pagkain at inumin dahil sa darating na ang mga panauhin.

Maraming sasakyan ang umalis sa simbahan papunta sa bahay ng bagong kasal.

Ang mga nagluluto sa kusina ay abala.

Paglabas nila sa simbahan, sinabugan ng bigas ang bagong kasal.

Inanyayahan ng mga panauhin na sumayaw ng Tinikling si Bill, Louise at Roy. Maraming pagkain at marami ring inumin.

Sa dulang, nagbigay ng maikling speech ang mga bagong kasal.

Talasalitaan	*Vocabulary*
napagod	*got tired*
pagsayaw	*dancing*
subali't	*but*
bagong-kasal	*newly wed*
paglabas	*upon leaving*
tumugtog	*played* (a musical instrument)
banda	*band*
inihanda	*prepared*
tugtugin	*music*
tumulong	*helped*
paghahain	*offering*
pagsisilbi	*serving*
panauhin	*guests*
sumayaw	*danced*
tuwang-tuwa	*happy*
lahat	*everybody*
sinabugan	*sprinkled with/showered with*
marunong	*know*
kumuha	*took*
nagpaalam	*said goodbye*
nagbigay	*gave*
tagapagluto	*cook*
sasakyan	*cars etc.*
nagluluto	*cooking*
inanyayahan	*invited*
dulang	*table*

 ## Exercise 6 Listening

 Here are some commonly used **an** verbs. Listen to the correct pronunciation on the tape. After listening to the pronunciation a few times, try to repeat what you heard without the help of the tape:

Infinitive	Meaning	Verb root
awitan	*to sing*	awit
ayusan	*to arrange*	ayos
asahan	*to rely upon*	asa
alalayan	*to assist/guide*	alalay
basahan	*to read to*	basa

bigyan	*to give to*	bigay
bihisan	*to clothe*	bihis
damitan	*to clothe*	damit
damihan	*to make many*	dami
dumihan	*to soil / dirty*	dumi
gandahan	*to make beautiful*	ganda
halikan	*to kiss*	halik
habaan	*to lengthen*	haba
sundan	*to follow*	sunod
tularan	*to copy/imitate*	tulad
puntahan	*to go to*	punta
pintahan	*to paint*	pinta

Language skills

2. Expressing the circumstantial in passive verbs

Ma, Mai, Ma-an   *To be able to, to happen to, to come to, to manage to*

The three passive verbs **in**, **i** and **an** form the circumstantial as follows:

■ by adding the prefix **ma** to **in** verb roots. For example: **ma + kain = makain** (*to be able to be eaten*)

■ by adding the prefix **mai** to **i** verb roots. For example: **mai + tapon = maitapon** (*to be able to be thrown*)

■ by adding the prefix **ma** and suffix an to **an** verb roots. For example: **ma + hugas + an = mahugasan** (*to be able to be washed*).

As in active verbs, some actions are brought about purely by circumstance, by accident or by occurrences beyond the actor's control.

Here is a guide on how to use the **ma**, **mai** and **ma-an** prefixes with the passive **in**, **I** and **an** verbs.

In verbs

Ma = (prefix) + **kain** (verb root)
ma + kain =   makain   =   infinitive
                to be able to be eaten
                to happen to be eaten
                to manage to be eaten
                to come to be eaten

ma + ka + kain = makakain = *will be able etc. to be eaten* = future
na + ka + kain = nakakain = *able etc.to be eaten* = present
na + kain = nakain = *was able* etc. *to be eaten* = past

I verbs

Mai = (prefix) + **bigay** (verb root)
Mai + bigay = maibigay = infinitive
  to be able to be given
  to happen to be given
  to manage to be given
  to come to be given

mai + bi + bigay = maibibigay = *will be able etc. to be given* = future
nai + bi + bigay= naibibigay = *able* etc. *to be given* = present
nai + bigay = naibigay = *was able* etc. *to be given* = past

An verbs

Ma (prefix) + **hugas** (verb root) + **an** (suffix)

Ma + hugas + an = mahugasan = infinitive
  to be able to be washed
  to happen to be washed
  to manage to be washed
  to come to be washed

ma + hu + hugas + an = mahuhugasan = *will be able* etc. *to be washed* = future
na + hu + hugas + an = nahuhugasan = *able* etc. *to be washed* = present
na + hugas + an= nahugasan = *was able* etc.*to be washed* = past

Some examples of the circumstantial in passive verbs

In verbs

mabili	*to be able* etc. *to be bought*
makain	*to be able* etc. *to be eaten*
madala	*to be able* etc. *to be brought*
malinis	*to be able* etc. *to be cleaned*
maluto	*to be able* etc. *to be cooked*
masulat	*to be able* etc. *to be written*

I verbs

maitapon	*to be able* etc. *to be thrown*
maibigay	*to be able* etc. *to be given*
maisama	*to be able* etc. *to be taken with*
maituro	*to be able* etc. *to be taught*
maigawa	*to be able* etc. *to be bought for*
maisakay	*to be able* etc. *to be given a lift*

An verbs

mahugasan	*to be able* etc. *to be washed*
malinisan	*to be able* etc. *to be cleaned*
mahalikan	*to be able* etc. *to be kissed*
masulatan	*to be able* etc. *to be written to*
masamahan	*to be able* etc. *to be accompanied*
mabayaran	*to be able* etc. *to be paid*

Exercise 7

Read each of the following sentences carefully. Using the alternative tense given in the brackets, rewrite each sentence. Don't forget to adjust the time-element, if any is given.

Example: Gusto kong malinisan ang mesa. (present)
Answer: Nalilinisan ko ang mesa.

1. Nasulatan mo na ba si Sophie? (present)
   Answer:
2. Naitatapon ni Harry ang basura lagi. (future)
   Answer:
3. May nabuksan siyang kabinet kanina. (present)
   Answer:
4. Hindi nasamahan ni Caroline si Phil sa bayan kagabi. (future)
   Answer:
5. Sino ang naisasakay mo sa kotse araw-araw? (past)
   Answer:

🔊 Talking about customs

📼 Dialogue 3

At the party following the marriage ceremony, Bill Cook witnesses
some traditional Filipino wedding customs for the first time. He
strikes up a conversation with Peter, Pinky's uncle.

Peter Kumusta kayo, si Peter ako. Tiyo ni Pinky. Sana
nagustuhan ninyo ang aming handaan.

Bill Aba oo. Masaya ang kasalang ito. Ngayon lang ako
nakakita ng pera na ikinakabit sa damit ng bagong kasal.

Peter Isa iyan sa mga tradisyong Pilipino.

Bill Napansin ko rin na nagmamano ang bagong kasal sa mga
lolo at lola at ang lola ay bumubulong sa babae at ang lolo
naman ay bumubulong sa lalaki.

Peter Oo *nga*. *Hindi* lang iyon. Mamaya, may ibibigay ang
matatanda sa kanila. Nakabalot ito sa *panyo*. Kadalasan
ito'y pera upang gawing puhunan ng bagong mag-asawa.

Bill Magandang kaugalian iyan. Bakit naman tumatakbo ang
bagong kasal na parang nag-uunahan sila?

Peter Ah kasi, may kasabihan ang mga Pilipino na kung sino sa
dalawang bagong kasal ang unang umakyat sa bahay,
siya ang masusunod.

Bill Ganoon ba?

Talasalitaan	*Vocabulary*
tiyo	*uncle*
sana	*I hope*
nagustuhan	*liked*
handaan	*reception*
ibibigay	*will be given*
ngayon lang	*just now*
nakakita	*was able to see*
ikinasal	*married*
kinakabitan	*being attached*
tradisyon(g)	*tradition*

napansin	*noticed*
nagmamano	*kissing the hand*
bagong kasal	*newly wed*
masusunod	*will be followed*
lolo at lola	*grandpa and grandma*
bumubulong	*whispering*
babae at lalaki	*man and woman*
oo nga	*indeed*
matatanda	*the old ones*
nakabalot	*wrapped*
kadalasan	*often times*
puhunan	*capital*
tumatakbo	*running*
nag-uunahan	*beating each other*
kasabihan	*saying*
umakyat	*climb up*

Translation

Peter How are you, I'm Peter, Pinky's uncle. I hope you like our party.

Bill Oh, yes. This wedding celebration is good. This was my first time to see (paper) money being pinned to the clothes of the newly weds.

Peter That's a Filipino tradition.

Bill I also noticed that the newly weds kissed the hands of the (their) grandparents and that the grandmother whispered (something) to the girl (while) the grandfather whispered (something) to the boy.

Pete Indeed. That's not all. Later on, the old people will give (something) to them wrapped in a handkerchief. Usually this is money to be used by the newly weds as capital.

Bill That's an interesting custom. Why are the newly weds chasing one another?

Peter Oh, that's because we have a Filipino saying that whoever (between them) manages to climb up (the stairs) to the house first will be the 'boss'.

Bill Really?

✔ Exercise 8

Answer in complete Tagalog sentences:

1. Ano ang unang tradisyon na binanggit (mentioned) ng tiyo ni Pinky?
2. Sino ang humahalik sa bagong kasal na babae?
3. Bakit binibigyan ng nakabalot na pera ang bagong kasal?
4. Ano ang dahilan (reason) kung bakit tumatakbo ang mag-asawa?

📻 Language skills

3. Sarili ko/aking sarili etc. Reflexive Mismo Intensive

'I myself will do the painting.' 'Letty will feed herself.' 'Liam overworks himself.' All of these examples indicate an action done to or on behalf of the self. The subject is the beneficiary of the action. These are reflexive expressions. The Tagalog word used to express the reflexive is **sarili** (*self, own*). The Tagalog reflexive is used either in connection with a **ng** form personal pronoun (**ko, mo, niya, namin, natin, ninyo** and **nila**) or a **sa** form personal pronoun (**akin, iyo, kaniya, amin, atin, inyo** or **kanila**) plus a **ng** ending. The **sa** form personal pronouns then become: **aking, iyong, kaniyang, aming, ating, inyong** and **kanilang**. Both **ng** and **sa** form personal pronouns can be used interchangeably. There is no hard and fast rule suggesting when **sa** or **ng** can or cannot be used. Look at the following examples given in both forms: **sarili ko/ aking sarili** = *myself* , **sarili mo / iyong sarili**, *yourself* etc. Here are some example sentences: **Sinaktan niya ang sarili niya**, *He hurt himself.* **Huwag mong saktan ang sarili mo**, *Don't hurt yourself.* However, the word **sarili** may also be used on its own. For example: **Sarili ko ito**. *This is my own.* **Sarili ni Steve ang bahay na ito**, *This house is Steve's own.* When a reflexive phrase is used as a describing word, a **ng** word may be used. For example: **Tumitingin si Mamerta ng sarili niyang retrato**, *Mamerta is looking at a picture of herself.*

Another way of expressing the reflexive in Tagalog is through the word **mismo**. **Mismo** is a stronger word than **sarili** and so serves to further stress the personal pronoun that accompanies it. **Mismo** takes a **ng** ending when following a pronoun. For example: **Mismong ako**, *I myself*, **mismong sila**, *they themselves*, **mismong kami**, *we ourselves* and so on. When a personal pronoun precedes mismo, then **ng** is not used. For example: **Ako mismo**, *I myself*. **Siya mismo**, *he himself*. **Sila mismo**, *they themselves* and so on. **Mismo** can also be used with a **sa** form word. For example: **Mismong sa Cubao siya nakatira**, *It's in Cubao itself that he/she lives*.

Some example sentences:

1. Kinuha niya mismo ang pera sa bangko
   He took the money himself from the bank
2. Ako mismo ang sumalubong kay Paul sa paliparan
   I myself went to meet Paul at the airport
   (or *I went to meet Paul at the airport myself*)
3. Sinaktan niya ang sarili niya
   He hurt himself
4. Siya mismo ang tumingin sa akin
   It was he himself who examined me

Exercise 9

Supply **mismong** + noun/ pronoun or a pronoun + **mismo** in the blank space: Don't forget the linker **ng** if one is necessary.

1. Sumulat _____ sa akin. (he/she)
2. _____ ang bumili ng pagkain para sa party. (we)
3. Nilinisan _____ ang kotse namin. (they)
4. _____ ba _____ ang nagdala ng mga maleta? (you)
5. _____ ang pumunta sa kasal ni Pinky. (Fred and friends)

Exercise 10

Look at the pictures below while listening to your tape. Can you match the verb with the correct picture?

One-minute phrases

Saan ang punta mo? (*sah-ahn ahng poon-tah moo?*) Meaning where are you going? A very common question in Tagalog. It is not meant to be taken literally, requiring an explanation of where you are going. Rather, it is just another way of saying 'hello' or acknowledging you. It is just another way of making small talk.

Diyan lang (*dyan lahng*) Literally, just there. This phrase is usually used as a polite answer to the question: **Saan ang punta mo?**, *Where are you going?* As **Saan ang punta mo?** it is only a form of saying 'hello' it commonly elicits a simple reply such as **D'yan lang**, *just there*.

Wala nang oras (*wah-lah nahng aw-rahs*) Literally, *no more time*. Meaning *we've run out of time/time is short*. This short phrase can also mean: **Wala nang panahon**, *time has run out*. For example: **Wala nang oras ang mga bisita upang matulog**, *The guests have no time left to go to sleep*.

Maghintayan tayo (*mahg-heen-tah-yahn tah-yaw*) Meaning let's wait for one another. When two people agree to meet one another at an agreed location. For example: **Maghintayan tayo sa harap ng McDonald's sa Kalye Lorenzo,** *Let's wait for one another in front of* [the] *McDonald's in Lorenzo Street.*

Nag-uurong-sulong (*nahg-oo-oo-rawng soo-lawng*) Literally, *moving backward, moving forward.* Meaning 'hesitating'/ 'cannot make one's mind up'. For example: **Nag-uurong-sulong si Maria kung pupunta siya sa Palawan bukas,** *Maria cannot make her mind up/ is hesitating as to whether she will go to Palawan tomorrow.*

Cultural Tip

Filipino weddings are formal occasions and so require formal attire. If invited to be a sponsor at a wedding, remember that it is an honour which carries responsibilities beyond the wedding day itself. The bride and groom look to their sponsors as dependable figures in whom they can rely for advice and other forms of concrete support throughout their married lives. Although Filipino weddings are formal, they are also very festive occasions steeped in many fascinating traditions. Relax, enjoy the experience and remember to make yourself at home!

18 | SA ISANG PISTANG BAYAN
At a town fiesta

In this unit you will learn how to
■ celebrate the Filipino fiesta
■ use the gerund
■ handle a water buffalo!

Celebrating the Filipino fiesta

Dialogue 1

Bill, Louise and Roy have been invited to a barrio fiesta.

Bill Napakaraming tao sa pistang ito. Maraming dekorasyong palawit sa kalye, sarisaring bandera at talagang makulay ang buong lugar.

Louise Oo nga. Apat raw ang banda at maraming paputok mamayang gabi kapag nagkoronasyon ng reyna ng pistang bayan.

Roy Nagpunta ako sa kabayanan at maraming mga may puwesto. Karamihan ay mga tindang damit at laruan.

Louise Sang-ayon sa meyor mayroon daw reyna ng pistang bayan. Siya ang nanalo sa 'popularity contest.' Mayaman siguro.

Roy Sa parke ay may tsubibo at mga labanan sa basketbol. Meron ding iba't ibang *palaro* para sa mga bata katulad ng pag-akyat sa kawayan, pagsungkit ng laso, pagsakay sa kalabaw, pagtakbo sa sako, pagkain ng murang niyog at iba pa. Gusto kong manood.

Louise Manood din tayo ng parada. May karosa at ililigid daw ang reyna at ang kaniyang mga abay. Gusto kong makita ang mga kasuotan.

Bill **Ta**yo ay kumbi**da**do sa **ba**hay ng kapi**tan** kasi *naghanda* raw si**la pa**ra sa **at**in. **Me**ron daw litso**ng ba**boy.

Roy O **si**ge, pumun**ta tay**o. **Gus**to kong makakita ng nag**li**litson.

Bill **O**o nga.

Talasalitaan	Vocabulary
napakarami(ng)	*so many*
pista(ng)	*feast day*
dekorasyon(g)	*decoration*
palawit	*bunting*
sarisari(ng)	*assorted*
talagang makulay	*really colourful*
buong lugar	*whole place*
kawayan	*bamboo*
pagsungkit	*hooking with a pole*
paputok	*fireworks*
mamayang gabi	*tonight*
kapag	*when/during*
nagkoronasyon	*crowned*
nagpunta	*went*
kabayanan	*town*
puwesto	*stalls*
karamihan	*many of*
tinda(ng) damit	*clothes for sale*
ililigid	*will be driven around*
sang-ayon	*according to*
reyna	*queen*
nanalo	*won*
mayaman	*rich*
para sa atin	*for us*
pistang bayan	*town fiesta*
parke	*park*
tsubibo	*ferris wheel*
labanan	*contest*
palaro	*games*
katulad ng	*like*
pag-akyat	*climbing*
pagsakay	*riding*
pagtakbo	*running*

sako	*sack*
pagkain	*eating*
murang niyog	*young coconut*
manood	*watch*
parada	*parade*
karosa	*procession cart*
kaniya(ng)	*her*
mga abay	*consorts*
kumbidado	*invited*
kapitan	*captain*
naghanda	*prepared food*
pumunta	*go*

Translation

Bill   The (town) fiesta is packed with people. The streets are decorated with different kinds of flags and the whole place is really colourful.

Louise   I agree. I heard that there are four bands and there will be plenty of fireworks tonight during the coronation (of the fiesta queen).

Roy   I went to the town centre and there are many stalls. Most (of them) are of clothes and toys.

Louise   According to the mayor there will be a fiesta 'queen'. So she won the popularity contest! Perhaps she's rich.

Roy   There is a ferris wheel at the park and a basketball contest. There are also children's games like bamboo climbing, hooking the ribbon, riding the water buffalo, sack racing and eating young coconut. I'd like to go and watch.

Louise   Let's also watch the parade. There is a decorated cart and the 'queen' and her consorts will be driven around (the town). I'd like to see their costumes.

Bill   We have been invited to the Barrio Captain's house. They have made some preparations (for us). Apparently they are preparing *lechon.**

Roy   Okay, let's go. I'd like to be able to see how to cook lechon.

Bill   I agree.

> *_Lechon_: a traditional Filipino delicacy
>
> _Cooking lechon_: A pole is pushed through a freshly slaughtered and cleaned suckling pig. The pig is then roasted on a spit over an open fire. The process takes between four and five hours during which the carcass is regularly turned and periodically daubed with oil to give it a crispy skin.

Exercise 1 Mga tanong: (Questions)

1. Anong uri ng pagdiriwang ang pinuntahan nina Bill?
2. Kailan kokoronahan ang 'reyna'?
3. Anu-ano ang mga tinda sa kabayanan?
4. Sa palagay mo, ano ang mahalaga sa isang popularity contest?
5. Magbigay ng tatlong palaro para sa mga bata.
6. Bakit isasakay sa karosa ang reyna at mga abay?
7. Sino ang nag-imbita sa pamilyang Cook?

Language skills

1. Pag + verb root
Ka + verb root + an
Ang + verb

No doubt you are familiar with stories from your childhood where frogs were transformed into handsome princes (or was it the other way round?) at the wave of a magic wand. The Tagalog language cannot endow you with magical powers but it too has its own form of magic wand with the ability of transforming verbs into nouns. This process is known as nominalisation, and the resulting word a gerund. This process of transforming verbs into nouns may at first sound rather complex, but is in fact quite simple. Notwithstanding a few exceptions in English, a gerund is basically a nominalised verb ending in 'ing' (i.e. cooking, singing, dancing etc.). In Tagalog, the prefix **pag** is added to a verb stem to produce a gerund. The gerund is commonly used in response to the question word 'how', expressing the manner in which a word is performed. For example: **pag + kanta = pagkanta** (_singing_). **Gusto ko ang**

pagkanta mo, *I like your singing*, **pag + sayaw = pagsayaw** (*dancing*). **Ang pagsayaw ang paborito kong libangan**, *Dancing is my favourite pastime*.

Another method of forming a noun from a verb stem is by using the prefix ka together with the suffix **an**. **Ka** and **an** sandwich the verb resulting in a nominalised verb. For example: **Ka + galing + an = kagalingan**, *goodness*, **ka + ibig + an = kaibigan**, 'friend' etc. Occasionally, the suffix **an** may become **han** if this makes the word easier to pronounce. For example: **ka + ligaya + han = kaligayahan**, *happiness*. **Ka + ganda + han = kagandahan**, *beauty*. When a verb stem ends with the letter 'd', this letter becomes an 'r' when forming a gerund with **ka + an**. For example: **tamad**, *lazy* = **ka + tamad + an = katamaran**, *laziness*. More examples follow.

Another way of transforming a verb into a noun in Tagalog is simply by placing the word **ang** before the verb (in any tense)! For example: 1) **ang nagsasalita** (the person talking) or *speaker*. **Sino ang nagsasalita?**, *Who is the speaker?*; **ang maglalaba ko** (the person washing clothes for me) *my laundry person*, **Narito na ang maglalaba ko**, *My laundry person is already here*.

Further example sentences:

1. Kami ang mag-aayos ng mga gamit mo
   We will be the ones to tidy up your things
2. Maraming kaibigan si Larry
   Larry has many friends
3. Kumusta ang pagtulog mo?
   How's your sleeping? [how did you sleep?]
4. Gusto ng mga guro ang pagtula ni Doming
   The teachers liked Doming's poem recitation
5. Kilala mo ba ang nagsasalita?
   Do you know the person talking?
6. Ayaw ni Nanay ang pagsama ni Stephen sa barkada niya
   Mother doesn't like Stephen going out [with his gang]
7. Gabi na ang kaniyang pagsimba
   His/her churchgoing is/was quite late already
8. Ano ang ipinagbili mo?
   What (goods) did you sell?

Exercise 2

Give the **ka + an** form of the following words (remember the rule about verb stems ending with the letter 'd'):

1. palad (*palm*)
   Answer:
2. tamad (*lazy*)
   Answer:
3. wala (*none*)
   Answer:
4. yaman (*rich*)
   Answer:
5. bahay (*house*)
   Answer:
6. mali (*wrong*)
   Answer:

Some commonly nominalised verbs

Pag prefix:

pagkain	*eating*
pag-alis	*leaving*
pagtawa	*laughing*
pagsalita	*talking/speaking*
paglapit	*coming nearer*
paglayo	*going away*
pag-ibig	*love*

Ka prefix + **an** suffix:

kahinaan	*weakness*
kabaitan	*kindness*
kabutihan	*goodness*
karapatan	*right*
karunungan	*knowledge*
kasinungalingan	*lies*
katindihan	*intensity*
kalimitan	*frequency*
kalalakihan	*menfolk*
kababaihan	*womanhood*
katauhan	*personality*
katarungan	*justice*
kakayahan	*ability*

Exercise 3

Fill in the blanks with an appropriate noun from the two preceding lists.

1. _____ ay lakas.
2. Puro _____ daw ang sinasabi ng mga politiko.
3. Dalawa ang pila. Isa sa mga _____ at isa sa mga _____.
4. Lahat tayo ay may _____ sa mundong ito.
5. Ano ang _____ mo sa trabahong ito?

Exercise 4 Listening and recognising

Listen to the conversation on the tape. You will hear a number of nominalised **pag** and **ka + an** words used. Can you pick out the words used from those listed here?

karapatan	pagngiti
kaligayahan	kasabihan
paglabas	kasunduan
pagpunta	kalimitan
pag-alis	kasalanan
pagsama	pagtawa
kaayusan	pagsulat
kasamaan	pagtalima
pagkain	pagpasok

Dialogue 2

The Cook family continue to enjoy their day out at the barrio Fiesta. Bill is in conversation with one of the guests at the Barrio Captain's house.

Rudy Kumusta *po* kayo? Si Rudy *po* ako. Sana nag-eenjoy kayo sa aming pistang bayan.

Bill Oo. Nagtataka lang ako. Parang gumagastos ang mga tao kapag may pistang bayan. Kahit saan ako tumingin, may pagkain at may inumin.

Rudy Ganoon *nga po*. Nag-iipon ng pera ang mga tao sa loob ng isang taon upang *makapaghanda* sa pista.

Bill *Hindi* yata tama iyan kasi magpapagod ka sa trabaho sa loob ng isang taon pagkatapos gagastusin mo ng minsanan. Bi**glang** mawawala ang i**ni**pon mong **pe**ra **da**hil lang sa pis**ta**.

Rudy Totoo iyan su**bali**'t kaugalian na ng mga Pili**pi**no i**yan**. Ka**pag** nau**bos** na ang **pe**ra, ba**ha**la na!

Bill Gano**on** ba?

Rudy O**po**. Kada**la**san pa *nga* ang iba nangu**ngu**tang **pa**ra *makapaghanda* lang.

Bill Ma**hi**rap din pa**la** ang kaugaliang ito, ano?

Rudy Tala**ga** – **pe**ro sinasabi lang **na**min – 'ba**ha**la na!'

Talasalitaan	Vocabulary
pagkatapos	*afterwards*
gagastusin	*will be spent*
nag-eenjoy	*enjoying*
bigla(ng)	*suddenly*
pistang bayan	*town fiesta*
kahit saan	*anywhere*
tumingin	*look*
may pagkain	*there is food*
totoo	*true*
ganoon nga	*really like that*
nag-iipon ng pera	*saving money*
kapag	*if/when*
sa loob ng	*in(side)*
isang taon	*one year*
upang	*in order to*
makapaghanda	*be able to prepare*
magpapagod	*to become tired*
sa trabaho	*at work*
minsanan	*in one go*
mawawala	*will disappear*
ang inipon	*the savings*
dahil lang	*just because of*
subali't	*but*
kaugalian	*custom*
naubos	*finished*
bahala na	*come what may*
kung minsan	*sometime*
nangungutang	*borrow money*
sinasabi lang	*just say*

Translation

Rudy　How are you sir? I'm Rudy. I hope you're enjoying our town fiesta.

Bill　Yes (I am). I'm just wondering. It looks as though people like to spend money when there is a fiesta. Everywhere I look there is food and drink.

Rudy　It's really like that. People save money all year in order to enjoy the fiesta.

Bill　I'm not sure that's a good idea because people work very hard at work all year just to spend (their earnings) in one go. Their savings suddenly disappear just because of the fiesta.

Rudy　That's true but that's already a Filipino custom. When the money happens to run out, leave it to destiny!

Bill　Is that so?

Rudy　Yes. Often times others even borrow money just to prepare.

Bill　This custom is rather difficult, isn't it?

Rudy　Indeed – but we just say '*bahala na*'. (see cultural tip)

Exercise 5

Which of the following statements are true? If the statement is false, can you give the correct answer in Tagalog?

1. Ayaw gumastos ng mga tao kapag may pistang bayan.
2. Nag-iipon ang mga tao ng pera upang bumili ng kalabaw.
3. Unti-unti nilang ginagastos ang perang inipon nila.
4. Mabuting kaugalian ang magdiwang ng pista.
5. Mabuti para sa lahat ng tao ang pista.

Exercise 6: Listening & Speaking

On your way to a fiesta, you meet some friends on the road. You stop to have a chat before continuing. Use the suggestions to help you fill out your part of the dialogue. Use the tape to practise the dialogue:

Nonoy　Kaibigan, kumusta ba? Dadalo ka ba sa pista?

Ikaw　(*Say yes, we are going to the fiesta*)

Nonoy	Marami nang tao doon. Mahilig ka bang sumayaw?
Ikaw	*(Tell him you like dancing very much)*
Nonoy	Mabuti!! Maganda ang tugtog at may pagkain din.
Ikaw	*(Ask him where the food and drinks are being sold)*
Nonoy	Doon, malapit sa Munisipyo.
Ikaw	*(Thank him and invite him to join you)*
Nonoy	Hindi na, salamat. Busog na ako.
	Magkita na lang tayo mamaya, sa sayawan.
Ikaw	*(Tell him that you will look for him)*
Nonoy	O, sige. Paalam na kaibigan!
Ikaw	*(Goodbye)*

Language skills

2. Maki, Makipag, Makipang
Participational verb forms in active verbs

Tagalog reserves a special group of verb forms to express actions done collectively or requiring the participation of others. These verb forms are known as participational or social verbs. Social verbs are characterised by the prefix **maki** for **um** and **ma** verbs, by **makipag** for **mag** verbs, and finally by **makipang** for **mang** verbs. Since participational verbs are actor focused (i.e., with the emphasis on the 'doer' of the action), it follows logically that they only take active verbs. For example: **Makiupo tayo doon**, *Let's share the seat over there*. **Nakikipaglaro ka ba sa mga bagong kapitbahay?**, *Do you play with the new neighbours?*. **Kahapon, nakipamaril sina John**, *Yesterday, John went shooting* (with others). In some cases, when the 'doer' of the action takes part in an activity previously initiated by another person, this is expressed by means of the **sa** form. For example: **Nag-swimming sila sa ilog**; (prior action) **nakipagswimming ako sa kanila**, *They went swimming in the river; I went swimming with them*. **Kumakain sila ng pansit**; **nakikain ako sa kanila**. *They were eating noodles; I ate with them*.

How to form participational verbs

Maki (source um verbs)

Maki (prefix) + bili (verb root) *buy*
maki + bili = makibili *to buy with* = infinitive
maki + ki + bili = makikibili *will buy with* = future
naki + ki + bili = nakikibili *buying with* = present
naki + bili = nakibili *bought with* = past

Makipag (source mag verbs)

Makipag (prefix) + laro (verb root) *to play with* = infinitive
maki + ki + pag + laro = makikipaglaro *will play with* = future
naki + ki + pag + laro = nakikipaglaro *playing with* = present
naki + pag + laro = nakipaglaro *played with* = past

Makipang (source mang verbs)

Makipang becomes makipam (prefix)   + balita (drop b) = alita
makipam + alita = makipamalita *to share news with* = infinitive
makiki + pa + ma + lita = makikipamalita *will share news with*
= future
nakiki + pa + ma + lita = nakikipamalita *sharing news with*
= present
naki + pa + ma + lita = nakipamalita *shared news with* = past

Sentence variations

Verb   +   actor   +   social counterpart
Nakikipag-away   si Joselito   kay Toto
Joselito is quarrelling/ fighting with Toto.

Pseudo-verb +   verb +   actor +   social counterpart
Ayaw   makipag-usap   ni Will   kay Gladys.
Will doesn't want to talk to Gladys.

Question word +   verb + Social counterpart + Time
Sino   ang makikipagsayaw   sa akin   mamaya?
Who will dance with me later on?

Exercise 7

Translate the following into Tagalog:

1. Auntie Marge will be eating with them tonight. (kumain)
2. Where did you ask for a seat? (maupo)
3. Are you going shopping with Auntie Dot? (mamili)
4. Jose is getting into a fight again. (mag-away)
5. I'm still talking with Janet. (mag-usap)

A few participational verbs indicate a request to use other people's facilities:

makikain	*to ask to share some food with*
makiinom	*to request a drink*
makisindi	*to request a light*
makitulog	*to request to share sleeping facilities of*
makihiga	*to request to share resting facilities of*
makisuyo	*to request to do something for*
makipagluto	*to request to use cooking facilities of*
makitawag	*to request to use the telephone of*
makisakay	*to request to use other people's transport*
makiangkas	*to request a lift*

Sentences in **maki** (remember that requests and suggestions use the infinitive form):

1. Maaari po ba kaming makiinom?
   Could we ask for a drink?
2. Puwede bang makiupo si Kim dito?
   Could Kim sit here?
3. Puwede bang makipamasyal kami sa inyo?
   Could we take a stroll with you?
4. Maaari bang makisakay kami hanggang sa bayan?
   Could we kindly have a lift to the town?
5. Puwede bang huwag kang manigarilyo dito?
   Could you not smoke here?
6. Makisindi ka sa lalaking iyon.
   Ask for a light from that man.

Some reciprocal social verbs:

makipag-away	*to fight with*
makipagtalo	*to argue with*
makipaglaban	*to fight with*
makipag-usap	*to converse with*
makipagkamay	*to shake hands with*
makipaghiwalay	*to separate from*

Example sentences:

1. Nakikipag-away na naman si Matthew
   Matthew is fighting again
2. Nakipagtalo si Sue sa opisyal
   Sue argued with the official
3. Gusto kong makipag-usap sa iyo nang masinsinan
   I want to talk to you seriously
4. Nakipagkamay si Lennard sa kaniyang kalaban
   Lennard shook hands with his opponent
5. Ayaw makipaghiwalay ni Anto sa asawa niya
   Anto doesn't like to separate from his wife

✔ Exercise 8

Change the following sentences into either a request or suggestion (remember to change the actor or the time element):

Example: Makikitawag ako sa telepono bukas.
Request form: Maaari bang makitawag ako sa telepono bukas?

1. Nakipag-usap kami kay Ginoong Reyes.
2. Nakitulog ako sa kanila.
3. Nakikipag-away kayo sa mga bata.
4. Makikisakay kami kina Baby.
5. Nakikipagluto ang mga bisita dito.

Handling a water buffalo!

Dialogue 3

Bill, Louise and Roy are visiting a farm in the barrio. Roy is learning how to handle the carabao (water buffalo).

Roy Ganito ba ang paghawak sa renda ng kalabaw? *Baka* suwagin ako nito.

Kiko Puwede na sa unang beses. *Hindi*, mabait iyan. Hindi ka susuwagin niyan. Hawakan mo nang maluwag. Ganiyan *nga*. Tapos medyo kausapin mo siya. Sabihin mo rin sa kaniya 'Tsk...Tsk...Tsk' kung gusto mo siyang lumakad.

Roy Ganoon lang pala. Uulitin ko. Ganito ba? 'Tsk...Tsk...Tsk...'

Kiko Oo, ganiyan. Magaling ka palang humawak ng kalabaw. Kung gusto mo, sumakay ka.

Roy May kaunti akong karanasan noong nagtrabaho ako sa isang sabsaban ng kabayo sa Inglaterra.

Kiko Ganoon ba, kaya pala *madali* kang matuto!

Roy *Hindi* ba higit na mahirap ang humawak ng kabayo.

Kiko *Hindi naman*.

Roy Sasabihin ko sa mga kaibigan ko na nakahawak ako ng kalabaw. Puwede mo ba akong kunan ng retrato?

Kiko Bakit *hindi*?

Roy Salamat. Teka, kukunin ko lang ang kamera ko sa bahay.

Kiko O, sige.

Talasalitaan	*Vocabulary*
ganito	*like this*
ang paghawak	*how to hold*
renda	*reins*
baka	*might*
suwagin	*gore* (bull)
nito	*this* (**ng** form)
higit	*more*
sa unang beses	*for a first time*

ang paghawak	*handling*
hawakan	*hold*
niyan	*that* (**ng** form)
karanasan	*experience*
nagtrabaho	*worked*
sabsaban	*stable*
kabayo	*horse*
kaya pala	*no wonder*
madali(ng)	*easily*
matuto	*to learn*
mahirap	*difficult*
sasabihin	*will tell*
nang maluwag	*loosely*
ganiyan	*like that*
medyo	*sort of*
kung gusto mo(ng)	*if you want*
lumakad	*to walk/ move*
kausapin	*talk to*
sabihin	*tell/ say*
sa kaniya	*to him/ her*
uulitin	*will repeat*
magaling	*good at/ clever*
nakahawak	*managed to handle*
kunan	*take*
bakit hindi	*why not*
teka	*just a moment*
kukunin	*will get/ fetch*
sumakay	*ride*

Translation

Roy Kiko, is this how to hold the reins of the carabao? He won't try to swipe me, will he?

Kiko Not bad for a first timer. No, he's a good-natured carabao. He won't charge you. (Just) Hold him loosely. Yes, just like that. Talk to him too. Just say 'Tsk... Tsk... Tsk' if you want him to move.

Roy Ah ! So it's that easy. Let me try: Like this? 'Tsk...Tsk...Tsk...'

Kiko Yes! Just like that. You're very good at handling a carabao. If you like, you can even ride him.

Roy   I've got a little bit of experience from when I used to work at a stable back in England.

Kiko   Is that so? No wonder you are learning so quickly !

Exercise 9

Answer the following questions:

1. Ano ang ginagawa ni Roy?
2. Ano ang dapat (should) niyang gawin (do) upang (so that) hindi siya suwagin ng kalabaw?
3. Maari bang sumakay si Roy sa kalabaw?
4. Ano ang dahilan (reason) at magaling si Roy sumakay ng kalabaw?

Language skills

3. Ganito   Like this
Ganiyan   Like that
Ganoon   Like that (over there)

In our dialogue, Roy Cook was learning how to handle a water buffalo or carabao. He asked Kiko to comment on how well he was doing. You may have noticed the words: **ganito**, *like this*, **ganiyan**, *like that*, **ganoon**, *like that* (over there). These words are commonly used in Tagalog in connection with the demonstration of an action. On most occasions, **ganito**, **ganiyan** and **ganoon** are used together with a gerund. For example: **Ganito ba ang paghiwa ng sibuyas?**, *Is this how onions are cut?* **Ganiyan ang pagpinta ng dingding**, *That's (the way) to paint the wall.* **Ganoon ang sinabi ni Dave**, *Dave said something like that.* The words **ganito**, **ganiyan** and **ganoon** may also be used in situations where two objects are compared. When this happens, then the stem of the adjective is prefixed by the letters **ka**. For example: **ka** + **layo** (from **malayo** *far* = **kalayo**) **Ganito ba kahaba ang tali ng kahon?**, *Is the string of the box as long as this?* **Ganiyan kaganda ang bulaklak na rosas**. *The rose is as beautiful as that.* **Ganoon kalaki ang mapa ng Cebu**, *The map of Cebu is as big as that.*

Sentence variations in the use of ganito, ganiyan, and ganoon.

Qualifier	+	ganiyan	+	gerund	+	object
Hindi		ganiyan		ang pagsulat		ng abakada

That's not how to write the ABC / Writing the ABC is not like that

Ganito	+	particle	+	comparison	+	subject/topic
Ganito		pala		kalayo		ang baryo ninyo

So your barrio is as far as this

Qualifier	ganoon	comparison	subject/topic
Walang	ganoon	kasarap	ang luto ni Aling Puring

Nothing like that is as tasty as Aling Puring's cooking

✔ Exercise 10

Reorganise the following into coherent Tagalog sentences:

1. sa amin kabait ganoon si Ginoong Cruz.
2. ba ng silyang rattan ganito ang paggawa?
3. ang pagsara paano ng kahong ito?
4. ang pagluto hindi ng adobo ba ganito?
5. sa akin mo ang pagtugtog sabihin ng himig (piece) na ito.

✔ Exercise 11

Look at the picture. Which of the words best describes the articles listed beneath it? Use **ganito**, **ganiyan** or **ganoon** as your answer.

apoy   _____
aso   _____
bata   _____
kaldero   _____
barko   _____
kutsara   _____
bola   _____
ulap   _____
tinidor   _____
punong niyog   _____
bahay   _____
pinggan   _____

One-minute phrases

Saka na lang (*sah-kah nah lahng*) Literally, *later already just*. Meaning later on. This phrase is commonly used to indicate that something has been postponed. For example: **Saka na lang tayo mamasyal**, *Why don't we just take* [our] *stroll later on*.

Baka sakali (*bah-kah sah-kah-lee*) Literally, *might perhaps*. This Tagalog phrase is similar in meaning to the English expression 'just in case'. It denotes the need to be prepared. For example, **Maghanda tayo at baka sakaling dumating ang mga bisita**, *Let us make some preparations in case the visitors arrive*.

At sa wakas (*aht sah wah-kahs*) Literally, *and at the end*. Similar to the English exclamation 'At last !'. For example: **At sa wakas, dumating din ang lolo at lola**, *At last, grandfather and grandmother* [have finally] *arrived!*

Ako ang bahala (*ah-kaw ahng bah-hah-lah*) Meaning, *I will take responsibility*. This Tagalog phrase is similar in meaning to the English expression 'Don't worry, leave it all to me'.

Masyadong magulo (*mahs-yah-dawng mah-goo-law*) Meaning, very messy/ entangled. This expression is used to express lack of clarity in another person's words or explanations. Sometimes it is used in connection with a troublemaker. For example: **Masyadong magulo ang usapan ng mga politiko sa Congress**, *The conversation of the politicians in Congress is rather messy*.

(i) **Cultural Tip**

Certain Filipino traits may sometimes be open to misinterpretation by the foreigner. One such trait is the common Filipino attitude of bahala na * (literally, *it's up to God*). At first glance, this could be understood as an attitude of fatalism or resignation in the face of difficulties or decisions. The Filipino could be accused of giving up too quickly. While this may be valid interpretation in some circumstances, it is not always necessarily the case. Filipino society is an intricate web of inter-dependent relationships which carry mutual obligations. Within these relationships, when expectations are not fulfilled or realised, the frustration experienced may result in the bahala na attitude surfacing. Rather than confront the source of the frustration, the Filipino shrugs his or her shoulders and says 'just let it be'. Avoidance may seem to be wiser move than open or direct confrontation of circumstances beyond his or her control. (* **Bathala** is an ancient Filipino name for god, pre-dating the Christian era.)

19 ANG BUHAY SA BARYO
Life in the barrio

In this unit you will learn how to

■ live in the barrio
■ help on the farm
■ use causative verbs

Living in the barrio

Dialogue 1

Bill, Louise and Roy Cook are enjoying their stay with Kiko and his family.

Louise   **Ting**nan mo ang mga **pu**nong-**ka**hoy. Nag**pa**pagaganda ang mga i**to** sa pa**li**gid ng **ba**hay.

Bill   Oo nga. Gano**on** din ang mga iba't i**bang** ha**la**man. **Me**ron si**lang** sampagi**ta**, ro**sal** at mala**king pu**no ng ilan**gi**lang. Nag**pa**pabango ang mga i**to** sa kapali**gi**ran.

Roy   A**lam** ba ni**nyo** na may mali**it** na palais**da**an si **Ki**ko? Nag**pa**papalaki si**ya** ng **ba**ngus. Sumu**nod** ka**yo** sa **a**kin, itu**tu**ro ko sa in**yo**.

Louise   *Madali* lang **ta**yo kasi nagpalu**to** ng mga kaka**nin** si **Ki**ko at ang a**sa**wa ni**ya**. Nagpa-ak**yat** din si**la** ng **mu**rang ni**yog pa**ra sa i**nu**min.

Bill   Anu-a**nong** mga kaka**nin**?

Louise   Bibobi**lo**, bibing**ka**, *kutsinta* at dila**di**la.

Roy   Masa**rap** ang bilobi**lo** *lalo* na kung may pan**sit**.

Bill   Tala**ga**! I**to** ang **bu**hay.

Talasalitaan	*Vocabulary*
tingnan	*look*
mga punong-kahoy	*fruit trees*
nagpapaganda	*making* (something) *pretty*
paligid	*around*
kakanin	*rice cakes*
nagpapa-akyat	*asking someone to climb*
mura(ng) niyog	*young coconut*
iba't iba(ng)	*different kinds*
halaman	*plants*
Sampagita	*sampagita* (the national flower)
rosal	*gardenia*
ilangilang	*ilangilang*
nagpapabango	*making* (something) *fragrant*
kapaligiran	*surroundings*
alam	*know*
palaisdaan	*fish pond*
nagpapalaki	*making* (something) *grow*
bangus	*milkfish*
sumunod sa akin	*follow me*
ituturo	*will show/point*
madali	*easy*
lang	*only*
nagpaluto	*caused someone to cook*
anu-ano(ng)	*what* (plural)
kakanin	*rice cakes* (local delicacies)
bilobilo	*a delicacy* (marble-shaped)
bibingka	*a delicacy* (see page 112)
kutsinta	*a delicacy*
dila-dila	*a delicacy* (tongue-shaped)

Translation

Louise Look at the fruit trees. They make a beautiful sight around the house.

Bill Oh yes. It's the same with the different types of plants. They even have sampaguita, rosal and a very large ilang-ilang tree. They make the surrounding (area) smell fragrant.

Roy   Did you know that Kiko also has a small fish pond? He is trying to raise milkfish. Why not come along with me and I'll show you (the fishpond).

Louise   We have to be quick because Kiko and his wife have cooked some delicacies (for us). He's also asked someone to pick some young coconuts for us to drink.

Bill   What kind of rice cakes are they?

Louise   Bilobilo, bibingka, kutsinta and dila-dila.

Roy   Bilobilo is delicious, especially with noodles.

Bill   I agree! This is the life!

Exercise 1

Using Dialogue 1, answer the following questions in Tagalog:

1. Ano ang nagpapaganda sa paligid ng bahay?
2. Magbigay ng mababangong halaman na alam mo.
3. Ano ang ginawa ni Kiko upang magpalaki ng isda?
4. Bakit kailangang magmadali ang pamilya Cook?
5. Ipaliwanag kung bakit sinabi ni Bill 'Ito ang buhay'!

🔊 Language skills:

1. Magpa + Active *To cause, to let, to have, to permit to ask, to make* etc.

'Tessie is *letting* the corn dry'. 'I will *allow* Elvira to cook tonight'. 'Bob will *let* the tomatoes grow in his garden.' ' I'll *ask* Lagring to sew a dress for me.' 'Why don't you *make* Erwin clean your car? 'Amado *permitted* me to walk'. All of the italicised words in these sentences are examples of indirect action verbs, also known as causatives. Tagalog uses causative verbs to point to an action performed by another person. In active verb sentences the causative is preceded by an **ang** form word. For example, **Nagpadala si Samantha ng regalo sa akin**, *Samantha sent some gifts to me.* **Nagpagawa sina Kim at Sue ng garahe**, *Kim and Sue had a garage built.* **Magpapasama ako kina Rosie at Aida sa ospital**, *I'll ask Rosie and Aida to accompany me to the hospital.* Notice that the **ang** form does not indicate the identity of the person actually performing the action, but rather, it indicates the identity of the one causing, letting, having, asking, making or permitting the action to be performed. The action is therefore said to be indirect or 'caused' by the other .

Dialogue 1 offers us a few examples: **nagpapaganda** (from **ganda**, *beautiful*) meaning 'making something beautiful', **nagpapabango** (from **bango**, *fragrant*) meaning 'making something fragrant', **nagpaluto** (from **luto**, *cook*) had someone cook something, **nagpapa-akyat** (from **akyat**, *climb*) having someone climb (in this case, a tree). With active verbs, the causative is easily recognised by the prefix **magpa** followed by the verb. In **magpa** causatives, the causer is identified in the **ang** form (**si, sina, ako, ka, siya, kami, tayo, kayo, sila** etc.) while the caused (i.e., the person caused/asked/led to perform the action) is identified in the **sa** form (**kay, kina, sa akin, sa iyo, sa kaniya, sa amin, sa atin, sa inyo, sa kanila** etc.) The object (which may be optional) is the **ng** form.

In order to avoid confusion, it is worth noting that some **mag** form verbs beginning with the letters **pa** may be mistakenly identified as causatives, even though they don't carry a causative meaning.

These verbs are commonly known as dead **pa** verbs. For example: **paalam** (*goodbye*), **magpaalam**, *to say goodbye*. **Nagpaalam ka ba kay Jayne?**; *Did you say goodbye to Jayne?*, **parusa** (*punishment*) **magparusa**, *to punish*. **Sino ang nagparusa sa magnanakaw?**, *Who punished the burglar?*, **palabas** (*show*) **magpalabas**, *to give a show*. **Nagpapalabas na sila sa oras na ito**, *They have already started the show at this time*, **pakana** (*plan*) **magpakana**, *to plan*. **Nagpapakana na ang meyor ng programa para sa pista**, *The mayor is already planning the programme for the fiesta*.

Three important rules in the **magpa** causative form:

1. The causer is in the **ang** form.
2. The caused is in the **sa** form.
3. The object (optional) is in the **ng** form.

Some example sentences

Nagpapabili **ako** (causer) kay Stewart (caused) ng kamatis at sibuyas (object) sa palengke (place) I *had Stewart buy some tomatoes and onions for me*.

Changing the tense of the Magpa verb:

magpa (prefix) + **um** verb root:
Magpa + bili = magpabili *to have* etc. *someone buy* = infinitive
Magpa + pa + bili = magpapabili will have etc. *someone buy* = future
Nagpa + pa + bili = *nagpapabili having* etc. *someone to buy* = present
Nagpa + bili = nagpabili *had* etc. *someone to buy* = past

magpa (prefix) + **mag** verb root:
Magpa + luto = magpaluto *to cause* etc. *to cook* = infinitive
Magpa + pa + luto = magpapaluto *will cause* etc. *to cook* = future
Nagpa + pa + luto = nagpapaluto *causing* etc. *to cook* = present
Nagpa + luto = nagpaluto *caused* etc. *to cook* = past

Some sentence variations in magpa causative:

Verb +	causer +	caused +	object +	time etc.
Magpapaluto	ako	kay Jamie	ng pansit	bukas.

I will ask Jamie to cook Filipino noodles tomorrow

Verb	+	particle	+	causer	+	caused
Nagpapaganda		raw		ang make-up		sa mukha ng babae.

It is said that make-up makes a woman's face beautiful

Question word	causer	+	verb	+	object	+	caused
Bakit	kayo		nagpapabili		ng pagkain		sa kanila?

Why are you asking them to buy food?

Verb	+	actor	+	time
Nagpalabas		sila		kagabi

They put on a show last night

Exercise 2

Can you change the following into **magpa** sentences?

1. Kumukuha ako ng libro sa kanila.
2. Maglalabas ba tayo ng silya?
3. Nagpasok ba si Henry ng mga maleta kanina?
4. Saan ka bumibili ng gulay at prutas?
5. Bumasa siya ng aklat sa klase.

Exercise 3 *Listening, speaking and understanding*

Your friend Edgar has invited you to attend his birthday party. It is the first time you have attended a Filipino birthday party and you are keen to watch and see what happens. Listen to the tape. Imagine that it is you who are speaking.

1. How many **magpa** causative verbs can you recognise?
2. Your friend arrives late and wants to know what has been happening. Listen again to the tape and respond to each of your friend's questions.

Helping on the farm

Dialogue 2

The Cook family are giving their hosts a hand on the farm.

Bill Anong oras sa umaga ninyo pinakakain ang inyong baboy? Ako na lang ang magpapakain, Kiko.

Kiko	O sige, bahala ka. Pinakakain ko sila sa mga alas siyete nang umaga. Kasabay ng aming almusal. Ako kadalasan ang nagpapakain sa kanila.
Bill	Gusto mo bang pakainin ko rin ang mga manok?
Roy	Ako na lang ang magpapakain sa mga manok.
Kiko	Kumain muna tayo ng almusal. Pinagluto ko na si Misis ng ating aalmusalin.
Bill	Okey lang.

Talasalitaan	*Vocabulary*
ang mga manok	*the chickens*
sa umaga	*in the morning*
pinakakain	*give food/feed*
magpapakain	*will feed*
pinagluto	*asked to cook*
aalmusalin	*what someone's having for breakfast*
kasabay	*at the same time*
aming almusal	*our breakfast*
kadalasan	*often*
nagpapakain	*give them food*
gusto mo ba(ng)	*would you like*
pakainin	*to serve/feed*
magpapakain	*will cause to eat*

Translation

Bill	What time in the morning do you have to feed your pigs? Could I feed them?
Kiko	Well all right, it's up to you. I feed them at around 7.00 in the morning, at [about] the same time [as] we have our breakfast. Usually I feed them myself.
Bill	Would you like me feed the chickens too?
Roy	Could I feed the chickens?
Kiko	Let's eat our breakfast first. I've already asked my wife to prepare our breakfast.
Bill	That's OK by me.

✔ Exercise 4

Answer the following questions:

1. Ano ang gustong gawin ni Bill?
2. Sino ang madalas nagpapakain sa mga baboy?
3. Ano ang gustong pakainin ni Roy?
4. Bakit kailangan muna nilang kumain ng almusal?

✔ Exercise 5

Following the English as closely as possible, translate the following into Tagalog:

1. … will have someone write a letter…
2. … had someone clean the car…
3. … asking someone to sew a dress…
4. … having someone to cut [my] hair…
5. … making yourself beautiful…

✔ Exercise 6

Look at the picture of a typical rural Filipino. Using **magpa** and **pa-in**, **pag-in** and **pang-in** words, create a present tense sentence to describe each of the actions you can see. For example: **Nagpapaligo si Mang Kiko ng kalabaw sa ilog**. 'Mang Kiko is washing the carabao in the river.' Use the word stems provided to help you.

| ligo | lipad | kain | alis | tuyo |

Language skills

2. Pa-in (ma/um verb roots), papag-in (mag verb roots), papang-in (mang verb roots)

Having managed to digest the basics of **magpa** causative verbs (causer = **ang** form, caused = **sa** form), you will be delighted to hear that there are other variations and forms of causative verbs, too! Look at the simple explanation that follows. You will soon notice that in these causative variations, the person permitting or causing the action is identified in the **ng** form (**ni, nina, ko, mo, niya, namin, natin, ninyo, nila**) while the person caused to act (the 'doer' of the action) is in the **ang** form (**si sina, ako, ka/ikaw, siya, kami, tayo, kayo, sila**). Note also that these variations are used in connection with active verbs.

Other causative forms

Ma and *um* verbs

Prefix **pa** + verb root + suffix **in**.

For example **pa** + **tulug** + in = **patulugin**, *to cause someone to sleep*
Patutulugin(verb) ni Tessie (causer) ang bata (caused)
Tessie will put the child to sleep

Mag verbs

Prefix **papag** + verb root + suffix **in**.
For example **papag** + **lutu** + **in** = **papaglutuin** *to have someone cook*
Pinapagluto (verb) kami (caused) ng guro (causer) sa klase namin
Our teacher had us cook in our class

Mang verbs

Prefix **papang** + verb root + suffix **in**.
For example **papang** + **ibig** + **in** = papangibigin *to cause/permit to pay court to*
Pinapangibig (verb)ng Lola (causer) si Ian (caused) kay Karen
Lola is permitting Ian to pay court to Karen

Four important rules to remember in the **pa-in**, **papag-in**, **papang-in** causative form:

1. The causer is the **ng** form.
2. The caused is the **ang** form.
3. The object (which can be optional) is another **ng** form.
4. There may be a receiver of the action which is a **sa** form.

Example sentences

pa-in   Pinabili (verb) ng guro (causer) ang mga estudyante (caused) ng aklat (object) *The teacher asked/had/caused the student to buy a book.*

papag-in Papaglabahin (verb) natin (causer) sila (caused) mamaya (time). *We will have/make them wash clothes later.*

papang-in Papamamalantsahin (verb) mo (causer) ba (particle) si Dorothy (caused)? *Will you have/ask Dorothy to iron clothes?*

Changing the tense of the pa-in, papag-in, papang-in verb:

Pa (prefix) + verb root + **in** (suffix) Origin: **ma/um** verbs

pa + higa + in = pahigain *to make* etc. *someone lie down* = infinitive

pa + hi + higa + in = pahihigain *will make* etc. *someone lie down* = future

p + in + a + hi + higa = pinahihiga *making* etc. *someone lie down* = present

p + in + a + higa = pinahiga *made* etc. *someone lie down* = past

Papag (prefix) + verb root + **in** (suffix) Origin: **mag** verbs

Papag + linis + in = papaglinisin *to make* etc. *someone to clean* = infinitive

Papag + li + linis + in= papaglilinisin *will make* etc. *someone to clean* = future

P+ in+a +pa+pag+linis = pinapapaglinis *making* etc. *someone to clean* = present

P + in + a + pag + linis = pinapapaglinis *made* etc. *someone to clean* = past

Papang (prefix) + verb root + **in** (suffix) Origin: **mang** verbs

Papang+isda+in = papangisdain *to permit* etc. *someone to fish* = infinitive

Papangi+ngisda+in = papangingisdain *will permit* etc. *someone to fish* = future

P+in+a+pa+pang+isda = pinapapangisda *permitting* etc. *someone to fish* = present

P+in+a+pang+isda = pinapangisda *permitted* etc. *someone to fish* = past

Some sentence variations in pa-in, papag-in, papang-in causative

Verb	+	causer	+	caused	+	object
Pabibilhin		ni Tony		si Mario		ng aklat

Tony will ask Mario to buy a book

Question marker	+	caused	+	causer	+	object	+	time
Sino		ang pinaglaba		ni Rene		ng kumot		kahapon?

Whom did Rene ask to wash the bedsheets yesterday?

Verb	+	causer	+	caused	+	place
Pinapapangisda		ng gobyerno		ang mga mangingisda		sa lugar na ito.

The government allows the fishermen to fish in this area

Exercise 7 *Listening, speaking and understanding*

Listen to the tape. You will hear a number of statements, each read out three times. Two of the statements use the incorrect verb form while one of the statements uses correct verb form (**pa-in, papag-in, papang-in**). Which of the statements is correct? Repeat the correct verb form aloud, then translate into English.

Dialogue 3

Roy and Bill are giving Kiko more help on the farm.

Bill   Kiko, tutulungan ka namin sa pagtatanim. Narito rin si Roy.

Kiko   Salamat. Ipalalagay ko kay Roy ang damo sa sako.

Bill   Gusto mo bang ipatapon ko ang mga damo?

Kiko   Mabuti. Ipapipitas ko rin sa kaniya ang mga hinog na guyabano. At *saka*, maaari bang palagyan ko kay Roy ng tubig ang mga *banga*? Kailangan ang tubig para sa inumin ng mga hayop.

Bill   Sige lang. Mabuti at makatutulong siya dito. Pinagamasan mo ba ang iyong palayan? Mukhang malinis ito.

Kiko   Oo. Oo *nga* pala, uminom muna tayo ng sabaw ng murang niyog.

Bill   Mabuting ideya. O, heto na si Roy.

Talasalitaan	*Vocabulary*
tutulungan	*will help*
pagtatanim	*planting*
narito	*here*
ipalalagay	*will cause to put*
makatutulong	*will be able to help*
ipatapon	*to cause to throw*
damo	*grass*
mukhang malinis	*looks quite clean*
ipapipitas	*will have something picked*
hinog	*ripe*
guyabano	*sour sap*
at saka	*and*
maaari	*can/possible*
palagyan	*to ask to be put*
banga	*earthen pot*
hayop	*animal*
pinagamasan	*had it cleaned*
palayan	*rice field*
oo nga pala	*by the way*
sabaw	*thin soup*
mura(ng)	*young*
niyog	*coconut*
ideya	*idea*

Translation

Bill   Kiko, we're going to help you with the planting. Roy is coming as well.

Kiko   Thank you. I'm going to ask Roy to put the grass in the sacks.

Bill   Shall I get Roy to throw the grass away?

Kiko   Yes, that's a good idea. I will have him pick the ripe guyabanos too. Can I ask Roy to put some water into the earthen pots? The animals need water to drink.

Bill   All right. (It's) Good that he'll be able to help here. Did you have the field cleaned up? It looks quite clean.

Kiko   Yes. By the way, let's have some coconut juice to drink.

Bill   Good idea. Thank you. Here comes Roy.

Exercise 8 Sagutin

1. Ano ang ipalalagay ni Kiko sa sako?
2. Sino ang magtatapon ng damo?
3. Bakit kailangang pitasin na ang guyabano?
4. Bakit sila naglalagay ng tubig sa banga?
5. Saan kinukuha ang sabaw ng niyog?

Exercise 9

Here are some familiar daily activities. Can you identify the causative verb?

📷 Languages skills

3. Ipa (in and i verbs), pa-an (an verbs) *To cause, to let, to let, to make, to allow to have, to permit*

The causative in passive verb sentences is easily recognised by the prefix **ipa** for **in** and **i** verbs, and the prefix / suffix **pa-an** for **an** verbs. The **ipa** and **pa-an** causatives both take the **ng** form when identifying the causer while using the **sa** form to identify the person caused to perform the action. In **ipa** and **pa-an** sentences, the object is identified by the **ang** form. Let's look at some example sentences:

> ipa +**tapon** = **ipatapon**, *to cause to be thrown*
> Ipatatapon ni Ginang Cruz kay Henry ang mga lumang kahon
> *Mrs Cruz will have Henry throw out the old boxes*
>
> **ipa** + **bili** = **ipabili**, *to cause to be bought*
> Ipabibili ko kay Abner ang mga kailangan ko sa pagtuturo
> *I will have Abner buy my teaching materials*

Three important rules to remember in the **ipa** and **pa-an** causatives forms:

1. The causer is the **ng** form.
2. The caused is the **sa** form.
3. The object (optional) is the **ang** form.

Some example sentences:

Ipasasara (verb) namin (causer) kina Bebot (caused) ang mga bintana (object) dito (place). *We will have Bebot and her friends shut the windows here.*

Ipinalalagay (verb) po (particle) ito (object) ni Ginoong Castillo (causer) sa mesa (place). *Sir/madam, Mr. Castillo wants this placed on the table.*

Ipapabuhat (verb) na lang (particles) namin (causer) ang mga maleta (object) sa kargador (caused) mamaya (time). *We will just have the porter carry the suitcases later on.*

Pinasasarhan (verb) ng gobyerno (causer) ang tambakan ng basura (object). *The Government is having the rubbish dump closed.*

Gusto (pseudo-verb) mo (causer) ba[ng] (particle) palagyan (verb) ng asukal (object) ang kape (receiver of the action)? *Would you like some sugar (to be put) in the coffee?*

*Note: The **an** verb takes a **ng** object as well as actor.

Changing the tense of the Ipa and Pa-an causatives:

Ipa (prefix) + (**in** and **i** verb root)
ipa + tapon = ipatapon *to cause* etc. *to be thrown* = infinitive
ipa + ta + tapon ipatatapon *will cause* etc. *to be thrown* = future
ipi +na+ta+tapon ipinatatapon *causing* etc. *to be thrown* = present
ipi + na + tapon inpinatapon *was caused* etc. *to be thrown* = past

Pa (prefix) + (verb root) + **an** (suffix)
pa + hugas + an pahugasan *to cause* etc. *to be washed* = infinitive
pa+hu + hugas+ an pahuhugasan *will cause* etc. *to be washed* = future
pina + hu + hugas + an pinahuhugasan *causing* etc. *to be washed* = present
pina + hugas + an pinahugasan *caused* etc. *to be washed* = past

Some sentence variations in the ipa and pa-an causative forms

Verb +	causer +	caused +	object
Pinapalitan	ko	kay Citta	ang binili kong pantalon

I had Citta exchange the (pair of) trousers I bought

Qualifier +	causer +	verb +	object
Hindi	nila	ipinatapos	ang bakod

They didn't have the fence finished

Question word + verb +		causer	place
Sino	ang ipinadala	ng eskuwelahan	sa paligsahan?

Who did the school send to the contest?

Question word + causer +		verb +	object
Kailan	mo	pinaputulan	ang buhok mo?

When did you have a haircut?

Example sentences:

1. Pinalakihan ni Ely ang kanyang kusina
   Ely had her kitchen made bigger
2. Pasasamahan kita kay Manny
   I'll ask Manny to accompany you
3. Pinatawagan niya sa akin si Citta
   He/she had me call Citta
4. Ipatutulak namin sa mga lalaki ang malaking mesa
   We'll have the men push the big table
5. Ipinasara ng Ate ang mga bintana kay Al
   Ate had the windows closed by Al

Exercise 10

Choose the appropriate causative verb form from the brackets, then translate the sentence:

1. Bukas, (ipinalagay, ipalalagay, ipinalalagay) ko kay Sarah ang mga halaman sa paso. (future)
2. Kailangan bang (ipapasok, ipasok, ipinasok) na ngayon ang mga damit sa sampayan? (infinitive)
3. Kailan natin (ipamimigay, ipamigay, ipinamimigay) ang mga lumang damit?' (future)
4. Noong isang taon (ipinaaayos, ipaaayos, ipinaayos) ni Binibining Zapanta ang kaniyang bahay. (past)
5. Ayaw nilang (papintahan, pinapintahan, papipintahan) ang kanilang bahay. (infinitive)

One-minute phrases

Hindi na bale (*heen-dee nah bah-leh*) Meaning 'It doesn't matter/never mind'. For example: **Hindi na bale kung hindi sila dumating sa miting**, *It doesn't matter if they don't/didn't arrive at the meeting.*

Pang-araw-araw (*pahng ah-rao ah-rao*) Meaning 'For daily use'. For example: **Pang-araw-araw ko ang lumang jeans na ito**, *I wear this old pair of jeans daily.*

Tamang-tama lang (*tah-mahng tah-mah lahng*) Literally, just enough only. Meaning something fits perfectly (like a glove). For example: **Tamang-tama lang sa iyo ang bagong sapatos mo**, *Your new pair of shoes fit you perfectly well.*

Mahirap na lang magsalita (*mah-hee-rahp nah lahng mahg-sah-lee-tah*) Literally, (it's) difficuly already just to speak/talk. This is a common Tagalog phrase used to suggest that it may be difficult or inappropriate to offer comment. For example: **Mahirap na lang magsalita pero kailangang pagsabihan mo ang anak mo**, *It's rather difficult to make any comments but you should talk to your child.*

Gawan ng paraan (*gah-wahn nahng pah-rah-ahn*) Similar in meaning to the English expression 'I'll do anything I can to make sure it works'. For example: **Gagawan ko ng paraan upang makabili ka ng uniporme mo**, *I'll do everything I can to make sure you can buy your uniform.*

Cultural tip

The **barrio** or **barangay** is the traditional Filipino village or settlement and lies at the very heart of the cultural, political and religious life of the Philippines. A quick glance around almost every **barrio** will reveal the existence of a small chapel and a meeting hall. There is a strong sense of 'togetherness' (**pakikisama**) among **barrio** folk. The people draw much of their identity from this sense of 'togetherness'. This attitude becomes a pattern of living wherever the Filipino finds him/herself.

20 | PAALAM
Goodbye

In this unit you will learn how to
■ make comparisons
■ express embarrassment
■ do last-minute shopping
■ say your last goodbyes

Expressing embarrassment

Dialogue 1

Bill, Louise and Roy Cook have enjoyed their stay with Kiko and his family in the barrio. They are preparing to leave.

Roy   Ting**nan** ni**nyo**! Binig**yan** a**ko** ni **Ki**ko ng re**ga**lo.

Louise   A**nong** ibini**gay** ni**ya** sa i**yo**? Ga**ano** kala**ki**?

Roy   I**sang** kala**baw** na i**nu**kit sa **ka**hoy. Hu**wag** kay**ong mag**-ala**la**. *Hindi* i**to** mas mala**ki** sa ma**le**ta ko.

Bill   Napakagan**da** ni**to**. *Mahiya* ka na**man**. *Wala* **ta**yong ibini**gay** na pasa**lu**bong sa kani**la** *kundi* mga pag**ka**in lang. Mala**king** aba**la** rin ang naibi**gay na**tin sa kani**la**.

Louise   Naka**ka**hiya na**man**. **Nag**pasalamat ka ba?

Roy   O**po**. *Nahihiya* nga a**ko** nang ibi**gay** ni**ya** i**to** sa **a**kin **pe**ro mag**dar**amdam daw si**la** ka**pag** *hindi* ko tinang**gap** ang re**ga**lo.

Bill   Gano**on** ba?

Talasalitaan	Vocabulary
binigyan	*was given*
abala	*disturbance*
ibinigay	*handed/gave*
gaano kalaki	*how big*
huwag	*don't*
mag-alala	*worry*
hindi mas malaki	*not as big as*
ng maleta ko	*of my suitcase*
magdaramdam	*will feel bad*
inukit	*carved*
kahoy	*wood / wooden*
napakaganda	*how beautiful*
mahiya ka naman	*are you without shame, don't you feel a little ashamed?*
ibinigay	*gave*
nakakahiya	*embarrassing*
nagpasalamat	*gave thanks*
nang ibigay	*when (it) was given*
kundi	*instead*
tinanggap	*received*

Translation

Roy Look! Kiko gave me a (parting) gift.

Louise What did he give you? How big is it?

Roy A wooden carving of a water buffalo. Don't worry. It's not too big for my suitcase.

Bill It's really beautiful. Don't you feel a little ashamed? We didn't bring any gifts for them other than a little foodstuff. We were a bit of a disturbance to them, too.

Louise Shame on you. Did you at least thank them?

Roy Yes, I did. Actually I was embarrassed when (the gift) was handed to me but (he) said he'd feel bad if I declined it.

Bill Is that so?

✔ Exercise 1

Answer the following questions in complete Tagalog sentences:
1. Ano ang regalo ni Kiko sa pamilya Cook?
2. Ano ang mangyayari kapag hindi tinanggap ni Roy ang regalo?
3. Anong uri ng regalo ang ibinigay ng mga Cook kina Kiko?
4. Bakit nag-alala ang mga Cook?

🔊 Language skills

1. Kasing/sing As... as

'As old as the hills', 'as white as snow', 'as sweet as honey', 'as strong as an ox'. These short sentences are examples of comparatives, expressed in English by means of an as... as construction. Tagalog expresses comparatives by the prefix **(ka)sing** before the root of a **ma**-adjective. The actor is expressed by a **ng** phrase (**ni, nina, ko, mo, niya, namin, natin, nila** etc.) and the complement (to which the comparison is being made) is in the **ang** form (namely **si, sina, ako, ka, siya, kami, tayo, kayo, sila** etc.). For example: **Kasinghaba/singhaba ng kalye namin ang kalye ninyo**, *Your street is as long as our street*. **Kasinlaki ng Pilipinas ang Inglaterra**, *England is as big as the Philippines*. Some speakers use **kasing** only and other speakers use both **sing** and **kasing** interchangeably in ordinary conversation. Both are correct.

It is worth remembering that certain adjectives can stand alone and are known as unaffixed adjectives. Any unaffixed adjective that corresponds to a noun (i.e. **tulog** (noun) *sleep*, **tulog** (adjective) *asleep*) do not occur with **(ka)sing**; whereas most other unaffixed adjectives (i.e. **pula**, *red*, **tanga**, *dumb*) do occur with **(ka)sing**. Here are some examples of the (ka)sing construction: **(Ka)singtangkad ni Samantha si Sally**, *Sally is as tall as Samantha*. **Kasingyaman ni Ginoong Ramos si Ginoong Cruz**. *Mr Cruz is as rich as Mr Ramos*. The prefix **(ka)sing** changes to **(ka)sim** when the preceeding adjective root begins with b and p. However, when **(ka)sing** is followed by an adjective beginning with the letters d or t, then it becomes **kasin**. For example: **(ka)singbait to kasimbait**, *as kind as*; **(ka)singpula to**

(ka)simpula, *as red as*; **(ka)singdami,** *as many as*; **to (ka)sindami, (ka)singtamad to (ka)sintamad** and so on.

Comparison of inequality is expressed in English by simply using the negative of the 'as… as' formula. For example: Bobby is not as noisy as Fred. This is not as sweet as that (one). In Tagalog, the same basic rules used in comparison of equality apply to comparison of inequality. For example: **Hindi kasingganda ng sampagita ang gumamela,** *(The) gumamela (flower) is not as beautiful as sampagita.* **Hindi kasinsariwa nito iyan,** *That is not as fresh as this (one).*

It is also possible to verbalise both the comparison of equality and the comparison of inequality through the simple addition of the prefix **mag**. If this happens, then the prefix **mag** is understood to mean 'equally' or 'equal in'. For example: **mag + (ka)sing**. The resulting formation expresses a quality shared equally by exactly two people, things, places, etc. For example: **Mag(ka)singtalino sina Jonathan at Manny,** *Jonathan and Manny are equal in intelligence.* **Magkasintaas si Joe at si Anne,** *Anne and Joe are equally tall.* Look at the example sentences that follow. Practice reading them aloud in order to familiarise yourself with the word order.

Example sentences:

1. Kasimbango ng rosal ang camia
   (The) camia (flower) is as fragrant as rosal
2. Kasimbaho ng bagoong ang tuyong isda
   Dried fish is as smelly as fish sauce
3. Kasinlinis ng mesa ang silya
   The chair is as clean as the table
4. Magkasintangkad sina Erwin at Ardin
   Erwin and Ardin are equally tall
5. Magkasinlayo ang Australia at New Zealand buhat sa Inglaterra
   Australia and New Zealand are equally far from England
6. Hindi magkasinlapit ang Maynila at Makati buhat sa Paliparang Ninoy Aquino
   Manila and Makati are not equally close to Ninoy Aquino airport

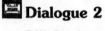 **Exercise 2**

Look at the following adjectives together with their **(ka)sing** prefixes. Build a Tagalog sentence around each adjective ((**ka**)**sing** + adjective) and then translate into English.

Example: (ka)sintanda: as old as
Kasintanda ni Joanna si Amy *Amy is as old as Joanna*

1. (ka) simbait: as kind as
2. (ka) simputi: as white as
3. (ka) sintaas: as high as (as tall as)
4. (ka) sinluwang: as wide as
5. (ka) singkipot: as narrow as
6. hindi (ka) singganda: not as pretty as
7. mag(ka)simbuti: equally good

Doing last minute shopping

Dialogue 2

Bill, Louise and Roy Cook have to do some last minute shopping for their pasalubong (gifts).

Louise Kailangan kong bumili pa ng mga **pam**pasalubong. Al**am** kong nakabili na a**ko** no**on pe**ro may nakalimutan yata a**ko**.

Bill Naiintindihan ko. **He**to na ang Priscilla's Gift Shop. Kung mga pamigay lang ang **bi**bilhin **na**tin, **na**pakarami **na**ting mapagpipilian dito.

Roy O, sige gusto ko ring humanap ng laruang jeepney. Ibibigay ko ito kay Stewart.

Louise Aba, maganda ito – kawayang tumutunog sa hangin para kina Viv at Tim. Ito namang mga nilalang handbag ay pangshopping nina Consuelo at Clarita.

Bill Marami yata tayong pamimilihin *kaya* credit card na lang ang ipambayad natin sa halip na cash.

Louise Sang-ayon ako.

Roy Kung gayon bibili ako ng barong Tagalog na pang-okasyon ko.

Bill Ako rin!

Louise   Kayo lang ba? **Bi**bili a**ko** ng **ter**nong **sa**ya na **ya**ri sa jusi.
Wala ak**ong** ganit**ong** u**ri** ng **ter**no.

Bill   **Si**ge, wa**lang** pro**ble**ma. Da**lia**n lang **na**tin ang pamimi**li**
ka**si** mag-iim**pa**ke pa **ta**yo.

Roy   Oo *nga* pa**la**!

Talasalitaan	*Vocabulary*
tumutunog	*making a musical sound*
nakabili	*was able to buy*
noon	*then/before*
may nakalimutan	*forgot something*
naiintindihan	*understand*
pamimilihin	*things to buy*
kaya	*that's why*
pamigay	*to give around*
sa halip na	*instead of*
bibilhin	*will buy*
napakarami	*so many*
mapagpipilian	*to choose from*
pang-okasyon	*for certain occasions*
humanap	*to find*
ibibigay	*will be given*
yari sa	*made of*
daliin	*be quick*
terno	*evening gown*
nilala(ng)	*woven*
pangshopping	*for shopping*
ipambayad	*to pay with*
sang-ayon	*agree*
kung gayon	*if that is so*
oo nga pala	*oh that reminds me*
mag-iimpake	*will get packing*
ternong saya	*a lady's terno*
pamimili	*shopping*
ganito(ng) uri	*this kind*
jusi	*pineapple fibre cloth*

Translation

Louise   I need to buy some more gifts to give away. I know that I've already bought (some), but I think I've forgotten a few things.

Bill   I understand. Look, here's Priscilla's Gift Shop. If we want to buy a few things to hand out, (then) there's an enormous choice here.

Roy   All right. I also want to look for a toy Jeepney. I'm giving it to my friend Stewart.

Louise   This is nice – a bamboo wind chime for Viv and Tim. These woven handbags are for Consuelo and Clarita.

Bill   I think we'll be buying a lot of things so why don't we pay by credit card instead of cash.

Louise   That's a good idea.

Roy   In that case, then I'm going to buy myself a barong Tagalog to wear on special occasions.

Bill   I will too.

Louise   And you think it's only for you (two). I think I'll buy a long evening gown made of jusi for myself. I haven't got anything like this yet.

Bill   OK. That's not a problem, but we'll have to hurry up with our shopping because we still have the rest of the packing to do.

Roy   Oh, that reminds me… (good that you reminded me)

Exercise 3

Mga tanong: Sagutin sa Tagalog na pangungusap. Answer in Tagalog sentences. Use the glossary to help you.

1. Ano ang kailangang gawin ni Louise?
2. Saan sila pumunta upang mamili ng pampasalubong?
3. Para kanino ang tumutunog na hangin?
4. Ano ang maaaring ibigay ni Louise kina Consuelo?
5. Sabihin kung paano sila magbabayad ng kanilang pinamili.
6. Bakit kailangan nilang magmadali?

Language skills

2. *Making nouns* pang

By now you will have begun to grasp something of the versatility of the Tagalog language. One further 'trick' Tagalog has up its sleeve is the ability to form nouns from verbs, simply by adding the prefix **pang** to the verb root. For example **ligo, lakad, tulog, pasok, pasyal** etc. can be made into nouns meaning 'used for' simply by adding the prefix **pang**: pang + ligo = panligo, 'used for bathing', pang + lakad = panlakad, 'used for going out'. You will notice that words that begin with l, d and t turn the **pang** into **pan**, for example pang + tulog = pantulog; while words beginning with p makes **pang** into **pam**. Example: pang + pasok = pampasok + tulog = pantulog 'used for going to sleep', pang + pasok = pampasok, 'used for going to work or school', pang + pasyal = pamasyal, 'used to go out in'. Look at these example sentences: **Pantulog ba ang damit na iyan?**, *Is that clothing used for sleeping in?*. **Pamputol ng kahoy ito**, *This is for cutting firewood with*. **May pandagdag ka ba sa pera ko?**, *Do you have anything to add to my money?*

By adding the letter **i** to the **pang** prefix, the resulting word is transformed back into a verb, but it is different in meaning from the original verb. The new verb then carries the meaning 'to use for' and is consequently known as an instrumental verb. Here are some examples: I + pang + laba, 'wash clothes' = ipanlaba, 'to use for washing clothes'. **Ipanlaba natin ang sabong ito sa blusa mo,**

Let's use this soap to wash your blouse with. I + pang + tali 'string'
= ipantali. **Ipinantali ni Divin ang lubid sa malaking kahon,**
Divin used the string/ rope to tie around the big box.

Changing the tense of an **ipang** verb:

ipang + linis *clean* =	ipanlinis	*to clean with*	infinitive
ipan+li+linis =	ipanlilinis	*will clean with*	future
ip+inan+li+linis =	ipinanlilinis	*cleaning with*	present
ip+inan+linis =	ipinanlinis	*used to clean with*	past

Some commonly used nominalised words:

1. pantulak = *to push with*
2. pangkain = *to eat with*
3. pantulog = *to sleep with*
4. panlakad = *to walk with*
5. panlaro = *to play with*
6. pananggalang = *for protection*
7. panlaban = *to fight against with*
8. panulat = *a writing instrument*
9. panigarilyo = *money to buy cigarettes with*
10. panlasa = *taste*

✔ Exercise 4

Here are some everyday things we might see around the house.
What are they used for? Use the glossary to help you to find the
correct **pang** noun for each:

Exercise 5

Give the Tagalog 'pang' nouns for the following (the italicised word will give you a clue).

Example: a hammer to *break* with
                Answer: ***pandurog***

1. a *scratch*er
2. something you *cut* with
3. to *wash clothes* with
4. to *write* with
5. to use *to go strolling* in

Exercise 6

Having found the correct **pang** words for Exercise 5, can you make a sentence out of them?

Example: **Pambiyak ng niyog ang malaking kutsilyo**, *The big knife is for cutting the coconut with*

1. _____
2. _____
3. _____
4. _____
5. _____

Saying last goodbyes

Dialogue 3

The Cook family are saying goodbye to the Abiva family at the airport.

Bill	Maraming, maraming salamat sa pagtanggap ninyo sa amin. Pasensiya na kayo sa *nagawa* naming pang-aabala sa inyong tahanan at sa inyong katahimikan lalo na kay Jobert.
Tita Abiva	Aba, huwag kayong mag-alaala. Nasisiyahan nga kami at dito kayo tumigil. Higit sana kayong magpasensiya sa aming pagkukulang. Mas lalo kaming humihingi ng pasensiya.
Louise	Lubusan kaming nasiyahan at sana ay huwag kayong madadala sa amin. Nagbigay kami sa inyo ng kaguluhan.
Tita	Kami nga ang mas nag-aalala na *baka hindi* kayo nakatulog nang mabuti. Alam kong mas tahimik sa Inglatera kaysa dito. O, tinatawag na yata ang flight ninyo.
Mr Abiva	Huwag kayong mag-aatubiling bumalik sa amin sa susunod ninyong pagbabakasyon. Sumulat lang kayo.
Bill	Gagawin namin iyon. Pasensiya na kayo sa aming munting regalong ito.
Tita	Aba, nag-abala pa kayo. Maraming salamat. Isang napakagandang kuwadro para sa larawan ng aking pamilya!
Mr Abiva	Kay ganda! O, sige maraming salamat na *muli*.
Jobert	Susulat kayong lagi at kung maaari tumawag kayo sa akin.
Roy	Maraming salamat po sa inyo Ginoo at Ginang Abiva, nag-enjoy ako dito at maraming salamat Jobert, okey ka talaga.
Jobert	Huwag kang mag-alala, Roy. Katulad mo, nag-enjoy ako.
Louise and Bill	Maraming salamat. Aalis na kami.
Tita	Walang anuman. O sige. Paalam. *(The Cooks and the Abivas kiss)*

Talasalitaan	*Vocabulary*
pagtanggap	*receiving*
pasensiya na	*accept our apologies*
nagawa	*what's been done*
pang-aabala	*disturbance*
tahanan	*home*
katahimikan	*peace*
lalo na kay	*especially*
sa susunod	*next time*
pagbabakasyon	*vacationing*
nasisiyahan	*pleased*
tumigil	*stopped*
higit	*more*
magpasensiya	*to accept our*
pagkukulang	*shortcomings*
mas lalo	*more*
humihingi	*asking*
lubusan	*earnestly*
kay ganda	*how pretty*
huwag	*don't*
madadala	*be turned off*
nagbigay	*gave*
kaguluhan	*chaos*
mas nag-aalala	*more bothered*
baka hindi	*might not*
nakatulog	*managed to sleep*
mag-aalaala	*be worried*
paalam	*goodbye*
tahimik	*quiet*
kaysa	*than*
tinatawag	*calling*
mag-aatubili(ng)	*hestitate*
bumalik	*return*
munti(ng) regalo	*small gift*
nag-abala	*bothered*
napakaganda(ng)	*very pretty*
kuwadro	*frame*
larawan ng	*picture of*
muli	*again*
susulat	*will write*
lagi	*always*
kung maaari	*if possible*
tumawag	*call*
nag-enjoy	*enjoyed*
nang mabuti	*soundly*
alam mo ba	*do you know*

Translation

Bill	Thank you so much for letting us stay. We apologise if we have been an intrusion in your home and to your peace, especially Jobert's.
Tita Abiva	Please don't worry. In fact we were very pleased that you stayed with us. We hope you have been able to bear with our shortcomings. We're the ones who have to apologise.
Louise	We are really happy and hope that we didn't put you off coming again. We must have caused you a lot of inconvenience.
Tita Abiva	In fact, we're more worried that you might not have been able to sleep properly. I know that it's much quieter in England than it is here. Listen, I think they are calling your flight number.
Mr Abiva	Please don't hesitate to come back to our home the next time you come for your holidays. Please write.
Bill	We most certainly will. Please accept our small (parting) gift.
Tita	You should not have bothered. Thank you so much. What a lovely frame for my family's picture.
Mr Abiva	How beautiful! OK, thank you so much again.
Jobert	Please write regularly and if possible, give me a call.
Roy	Thank you so much, Mr. & Mrs Abiva. I enjoyed myself here and thank you very much Jobert, you're really ok!
Jobert	Don't worry Roy. I enjoyed it as much as you did.
Louise and Bill	Thank you so much. We've got to go now.
Tita	Don't mention it. OK. Goodbye.
	(*The Cooks and the Abivas kiss*)

Exercise 7

Bigyan ng tamang sagot:

1. Nang humingi ng paumanhin si Bill, ano ang sagot ni Tita Abiva?
2. Bakit nag-aalala si Tita Abiva na hindi nakatulog ang mag-anak?
3. Anong regalo ang tinanggap ni Tita Abiva buhat sa mag-anak?
4. Ano ang hiniling ni Jobert kay Roy?

Exercise 8

The Cook family don't want to miss their flight back to London and so are carefully monitoring the flight announcements. Listen carefully to the announcements on the tape and write down the correct flight numbers and departure times. What are the correct gate numbers for each flight? Are there any delays?

Ninoy Aquino International Airport Manila				Departures board	
Destination	Flight No.	Arrivals	Departures	Delays	Gate No.
Hong Kong					
Singapore					
Los Angeles					
Sydney					
Tokyo					
London					
Dubai					
Kualar Lumpur					

Language skills

3. Mas, lalong, kaysa sa

Richard is tall, Justin is taller, but Chris is the tallest. You will notice from this example that there are three levels or degrees of comparison in English adjectives: tall, taller, tallest. These different levels are known as the positive, comparative and superlative degrees. Take for example the adjective good. The word good is in its positive degree. When comparing two adjectives, the adjective 'good' (positive degree) becomes the word 'better' in the comparative degree, and finally ' best' in the superlative degree. In Tagalog, **mas**, **lalong** or **kaysa** + the **sa** form are used in the comparative degree, while in the superlative degree, the prefix **pinaka** is used. Look at the examples that follow:

malaki	*big* =	positive degree
mas/lalong malaki kaysa sa	*bigger* =	comparative degree
pinakamalaki	*biggest* =	superlative degree

Mas malaki ang problema ni John kaysa kay Tony
John's problem is bigger than Tony's

maliit	*small* =	positive degree
higit na maliit	*smaller* =	comparative degree
pinakamaliit	*smallest* =	superlative degree

Pinakamaliit si Louella sa magkakapatid
Louella is the smallest among the siblings

Further examples:

1. Higit na malaki ang sombrero ko kaysa sa sombrero mo
   My hat is bigger than your hat
2. Mas mahaba ang nilakad namin kaysa sa nilakad ninyo
   Our walk was longer that your walk
3. Maganda ang hardin mo pero mas maganda ang hardin ni Patricia
   Your garden is pretty but Patricia's garden is prettier
4. Higit na malayo ang Pilipinas kaysa sa India buhat sa Inglaterra
   The Philippines is farther than India from England
5. Masarap ang luto mo pero mas masarap ang luto ko kaysa sa luto mo
   Your cooking is good but my cooking is better than yours

Exercise 9

Look at the pictures and use the adjectives provided to produce a statement about each picture using the comparative degree:

Tom is taller than Benny _____

matangkad   masipag

mataba   masaya

Exercise 10

Pretend that you are Bill or Louise Cook and have just returned from your wonderful holiday in the Philippines. Write to your friends the Abivas to thank the family for their kindness. This is your chance to impress by them writing your thank you letter in Tagalog. Don't forget to use polite words and as many different types of Tagalog verbs as you can remember. Close your letter by inviting them to England to stay with you!

One-minute phrases

Alis d'yan (*ah-lees jahn*) Literally, alis means *leave* and **d'yan/ diyan**, *there*, hence: *go away from there* or, more colloquially, *get lost!!!*, *beat it!!!*

Buwena mano (*bwehnah mah-naw*) Literally, **buwena** means *good* from the Spanish word *buena* and *mano*, *hand*. It is believed that the first shopper cannot be turned down by the storekeeper as he/she will bring luck for the rest of the day.

Labas-masok (*lah-bahs mah-sawk*) Literally, **labas** means *out/outside* and **masok** or **pasok** means enter. A person who comes and goes. **Labas-masok ang mga tao sa opisina ng meyor**, *The people come and go into the mayor's office.*

Walang tawad (*wah-lahng tah-wahd*) Literally, *no discount, no bargain/last price*. This is usually what vendors say to you when you start to haggle in the markets. You can still try to ask for a discount but they usually get annoyed if you insist. If the price can be haggled they usually encourage you otherwise.

Hindi kasya (*heen-dee kahs-yah*) Meaning it doesn't fit. An expression commonly used when you are trying something on. **Hindi kasya sa akin ang sombrero mo kasi maliit ito sa akin**, *Your hat doesn't fit me because it's too small for me.*

Cultural tip

The high value Filipinos place on harmonious relationships may at first seem rather quaint to the visiting westerner. This is hardly surprising when on closer inspection, the westerner tends to value having 'a mind of his/her own' and a strong sense of autonomy. Filipino social behaviour on the other hand is expected to promote the sense of community and togetherness (**pakikisama**). One of the principal means of ensuring socially acceptable behaviour is through **hiya** or 'shame'. Filipinos report the experience of feeling 'ashamed' (**mahiya**) when they receive negative feedback from others through their body language, voice tone or verbal messages. **Hiya** is therefore a key form of social control, determining how people feel about themselves (self-esteem) as well as their social standing. A person with a strong sense of his or her own **hiya** learns how to negotiate a way through potentially sensitive or embarrassing situations. Compromise is always a key factor, ensuring that others involved do not lose face and feel **mahiya**. The Filipino will avoid at all costs making another person feel **mahiya**. To do so not only damages that person's social standing but also gains them a potential enemy. It is extremely important for the foreigner to understand this. The golden rule is very simple: Never put anyone to shame in public, even in a joking way. Others may laugh, but only out of politeness. Filipinos often laugh and smile in order to cover their sense of discomfort or embarrassment. If you have a problem with someone, look for an appropriate time and place to speak to the person alone and in private. Even if you are upset, always make sure you speak in a low voice. Be prepared to compromise in order to help the other person save face and minimise their sense of **hiya**, even if they are clearly in the wrong. This will always act in your favour, indicating to others a sensitivity on your part to the intricacies of the Filipino social relationship system. If you are ever in doubt, smile, keep your mouth shut and ask your Filipino friends for advice.

KEY TO THE EXERCISES

Unit 1
Exercise 2 1. siya 2. kami 3. ako 4. ka 5. sila 6. kayo 7. tayo 8. kayo 9. sila 10. siya. **Exercise 3** 1. hapon 2. umaga 3. tanghali 4. gabi **Exercise 4** 1. umaga 2. gabi 3. tanghali 4. hapon **Exercise 5** a3, b6, c4, d1, e5, f4 **Exercise 6** a. kayo b. ka c. ka d. ka

Unit 2
Exercise 1 May tuwalya ba kayo? May sabon ba kayo? May telepono ba kayo? May menu ba kayo? May telebisyon ba kayo? **Exercise 3** 1. Doktor sila 2. Turista ako 3. Matatangkad/ matangkad sila 4. Maganda siya 5. Amerikano ka/kayo **Exercise 5** 1. May payong ba kayo? May payong ka ba? Oo. Mayroon 2. May sasakyan ba? Oo. Mayroon 3. May pinggan ba sa mesa? Oo. Mayroon 4. May kutsilyo ba? Oo. Mayroon 5. May baso ba kayo? Oo. Mayroon **Exercise 6** 1. May libro 2. May barko 3. May mesa 4. Walang pera 5. May basura 6. May sombrero 7. Wala (ng) pasahero 8. May sanggol **Exercise 7** 1. Sino ang pagod? 2. Sino ang Reyna? 3. Anong oras na? 4. Anong kulay ng bandila?

Unit 3
Exercise 1 a. Magandang hapon sa inyong lahat b. Ito ang lola ko c. Ito ang tatay ko, _____ d. At si _____, ang kapatid ko e. Ito ang lolo ko f. Ito si _____, ang kapatid ko g. at katapusan, ang nanay ko **Exercise 2** a. Tatay b. Hipag c. Lola at Lolo d. pamangkin e. Nanay f. Bayaw g. Kuya at Ate **Exercise 3** 1. mapa 2. payong 3. posporo 4. shampoo **Exercise 4** 1. Kailangan ko ng tee-shirt 2. Gusto kong bumili ng tiket 3. May 'street guide' ba kayo? 4. Nagtitinda ba kayo ng tinapay? **Exercise 5** 1. Mainit ang panahon 2. Marumi ang kalye 3. Malinis ang kotse 4. Maganda ang bahay 5. Doktor ang lalaki

Exercise 6 a. Maraming salamat b. Maraming salamat po or
Maraming salamat sa inyo c. Maraming Salamat or Salamat d. Maraming
salamat po or Maraming salamat sa inyo e. Maraming salamat
Exercise 7 1. Hindi ito barko 2. Hindi malinis ang mesa 3. Hindi
estudyante si Amy 4. Hindi tumatakbo ang Jeepney. **Exercise 8** 1.
Wala. Walang sasakyan sa bus stop 2. Wala. Wala kaming yelo. 3 Wala.
Walang katulong si Ginoong Reyes.

Unit 4

Exercise 1 1. kumaliwa 2. kumanan 3. diretso 4. kanan 5. tumawid
kayo 6. kaliwa **Exercise 3** 1. Nasaan ang simbahan? Reply: Nasa Sto.
Domingo ang simbahan 2. Nasaan ang Jeepney stop? Reply: Nasa
Guzman Street ang paradahan ng Jeepney. 3. Nasaan ang palengke?
Reply: Nasa Cubao ang palengke 4. Nasaan ang bangko? Reply: Nasa
Makati ang bangko **Exercise 4** 1. Gusto kong bumili ng selyo para sa
pakete ko 2. Gusto kong bumili ng selyo papunta sa Amerika 3.
Magkakano ang Air Letter? 4. Nasaan ang timbangan? 5. Pakitimbang
mo nga ang pakete ko or Maaari bang timbangin mo ang pakete ko?
Exercise 6 Listening: kahon, bolpen, sulat, selyo, pakete, timbangan
Exercise 7 1. bata, payat, puti ang blusa, mahabang itim na buhok,
nakasalamin, nakapantalon 2. babaeng hindi masyadong matanda, itim
ang palda at jacket, itim ang sapatos at handbag 3. matabang babae,
pandak, hindi itim ang blusa, itim ang palda, nakarelos at singsing
4. Matandang babae, putting buhok, mahabang itim na bestida,
nakakuwintas **Exercise 8** 1. Malaking masipag na hayop 2. magandang
matalinong dalagita 3. malaking puting simbahan 4. makulay na mabilis
na Jeepney.

Unit 5

Exercise 1 1. Disinuwebe 2. Animnapu't apat 3. Nubenta y nuwebe
4. Dalawampu't pito 5. siyento kinse 6. apat na raan at walumpu
Exercise 3 1. Labinlimang piso 2. Sampung piso 3. Pitumpung piso
4. Isandaang piso 5. Isanlibong piso; total = 1195 (isanlibo isandaa't
siyamnapu't lima) **Exercise 4** 1. Alas dose beinte 2. Menos kinse para
alas tres 3. Alas siyete 4 Ala-una diyes 5. alas kuwatro medya 6. Alas sais
Exercise 5 Examples: Magkakano ang mangga, magkano ang
lanzones? Magkano ang bayabas? **Exercise 6** 1. True 2. True 3. True

4. False 5. True **Exercise 7** Gusto kong magpapalit ng dolyar
2. Magkano ang palit? 3. Ang palit ay 40 pesos 4. Nagpapalit din ba kayo
ng Australian dollars? **Exercise 8** 1. Limandaan 2. mil singko sientos

Unit 6

Exercise 2 1. Saan sila nakatira 2. Saan kayo matutulog 3. Saan nag-
aaral sina Lucy? 4. Saan po kayo bumibili ng sorbetes? 5. Saan kakain ng
almusal si Adam? **Exercise 3** 1. ka 2. bahay 3. mapa 4. Nakikita
5. kasama **Exercise 4** 1. Hindi. Masyadong malapit ito 2. Sa Sikatuna
Village 3. Sa Kalye Roxas 4. Walang kasama si Roy 5. Nasa Kalye Vito
ito. **Exercise 5** Magbabakasyon, masyadong mainit, masyadong
malayo, buhat sa, masyadong mataas. Kapitan ng eroplano, ang dating
Exercise 6 1. Dadaan ba ito sa Sikatuna Village? 2. sa Kalye
Maningning 3. Magkano + Sikatuna? Heto ang bayad. May sukli ka ba?

Unit 7

Exercise 1 1. Nasa likuran 2. Nasa harapan 3. Nasa harapan katabi ni
Toto 4. Nasa likuran 5. Nasa harapan 6)Nasa harapan katabi ni Tita
Exercise 2 Kaibigan ko si Margaret 2. Kapatid niya siya John
3. Bisita nila si Ann 4. Kaklase ko sila. **Exercise 4** 1. ng 2. namin
3. ni 4. ng 5. ko 6. ng 7. niya. **Exercise 5** 1. Bahay ni Pedro ito
2. Pagkain ng aso ito. 3. Kampana ng simbahan ito. **Exercise 6** 1.
kaibigan 2. Matangkad 3. magkakapatid 4. pinakamatanda
5. pinakabunso 6. anak ninyo 7. anak ko. 8. ilan 9. ang may-asawa. Ang
anak niya. 10. apo **Exercise 7** 1.d 2.e 3.b 4.a 5.c **Exercise 8** 1. ang
piknik natin 2. mas matanda sa dalawa 3. tatlong taon 4. mas bata
5. hindi mo ba alam 6. kapatid siya ng aking nanay 7. ng malamig na
inumin 8. ang piknik na ito **Exercise 9** 1. Siya ay anak mo 2. Ako ay
may tiket 3. Ang tubig ay malamig 4. Ngayon ay mainit 5. Ang handa mo
ay masarap.

Unit 8

Exercise 1 1. Apat kami. 2. May mesa ba kayo para sa apat (na tao)?
3. Gusto ko ng malamig na tubig. 4. Gusto ko ng San Miguel beer.
5. May malaking mesa ba kayo? **Exercise 2** 1. False 2. True 3. True
4. False 5. False 6. True **Exercise 3** 1. mga aklat 2. mga babae 3. mga
bahay **Exercise 4** 1. May mga bisita na sa bahay 2. Mga estudyante ba

kayo? 3. Hindi sila mga Pilipino
4. Kailangan ko ang mga silya at mesa. 5. Mga sariwang prutas ang mga
ito **Exercise 5** 1. Oo. Suka nga para sa bangus 2. Oo. Maaari bang
bigyan mo ako ng asin? 3. Gusto ko ng sarsa 4. May toyo ba kayo?
Exercise 6 1. mga dalawang kilong 2. mga tatlong yarda. 3. Mga alas-
dos 4. Mga siyam 5. mga walong tao **Exercise 7** Customer
1. adobong manok sa gata, kanin at malamig na guyabano 2. pansit,
guinataan, malamig na buko juice 3. lechon, kanin, pansit at malamig
na Coke.

Unit 9

Exercise 1 1.f 2.d 3.e 4.a 5.c 6.b **Exercise 2** 1. Para sa kape ang
gatas 2. Para sa bintana ang kurtina 3. Para sa sulat 4. Para sa ulan
5. Para sa pagtulog ang kama 6. Para sa biyahe ang maleta 7. Para sa
tubig. **Exercise 3** 1. Magandang umaga 2. ngipin ko 3. gamot 4 Okey
lang. Maraming salamat 5. Magkano iyan 6. ang bayad 7. Walang
anuman **Exercise 4** 1. buhok 2. ulo 3. mata 4. panga 5. tiyan 6. kamay
7. daliri 8. binti 9. paa 10. talampakan **Exercise 5** Tama. 2. Mali.
Nasa harapan ang dibdib. 3. Tama. 4. Mali. Nasa paa ang talampakan.
5. Mali. Nasa bibig ang labi. 6. Tama **Exercise 6** 1. Ang sakit ng ulo
ko. 2. Hatsing! May sipon ako. 3. Masakit ang paa ko.

Unit 10

Exercise 1 1.b 2.c 3.c 4.b **Exercise 2** 1. Sa akin ang maletang ito
2. sa bata ba ang bisikleta/ 3. Sa kanila ang bagong Jeepney 4. Hindi sa
iyo iyan 5. Kay Beth ang tsinelas. 6. Kina Philip ba ito? **Exercise 3**
1. dilaw 2. puti 3. pula 4. asul 5. kulay pilak 6. biyoleta 7. itim 8. berde
9. ginto **Exercise 4** 1. Hindi. Kay Amy ang itim na tote bag 2. Hindi.
Kay Paul ang itim na tote bag 3. Hindi. Kay Stephen ang duffel bag
4. Kay Dad ang denim tote bag 5. Oo. Kay Lucy ang dilaw na plastic bag.
Exercise 5 1. Kanino ang mga iyon? 2. Kaninong bahay ito? 3.
Kaninong guro si Cora? 4. Kanino iyan? 5. Kanino ang mga gulay na ito?
6. Kanino ang mga berdeng mangga? 7. Kanino ang maleta?
8. Kaninong anak si Joanna? 9. Kaninong maleta ito? 10. Kaninong
kamera iyan? **Exercise 6** 1. bata, 2. beach, 3. turista, 4. bata, 5. turista,
6. beach, 7. bata, 8. turista, 9. beach, 10. bata, 11. beach, 12. turista,
13. bata, 14. beach, 15. bata, 16. turista, 17. beach, 18. turista
Exercise 7 1. sa tindahan 2. sa paliparan 3. sa dagat 4. sa tindahan ng
laruan 5. sa palengke 6. sa palaruan 7. sa kalye **Exercise 8** 1. sa hapon

2. Sa Linggo 3. sa gabi 4. sa tanghali 5. sa hapon 6. sa umaga
7. sa isang lingo

Unit 11

Exercise 2 1. gusto 2. kailangan 3. ayaw 4. dapat 5. ibig
Exercise 3 1. Hindi masyadong mahaba 2. Hindi 3. Sa tabi
4. Huhugasan muna ng barbero ang buhok ni Bill 5. Gusto rin ni Bill ng
masahe **Exercise 4** 1. ang bagong kotse 2. ng katulong 3. ng aking
tulong 4. magpagupit 5. ng malamig na kape **Exercise 5** 1. Kailangan
(Do you want a pencil?) 2. Ibig (Baby wants to buy some bananas from
the market) 3. kailangan (Why do you need a blackboard?) 4. gusto Who
do you want to go with you to the cinema? 5. Ibig (Do you like a cold
Pepsi?) **Exercise 6** 1. Mahaba ang inyong buhok 2. Bagay sa inyo ang
mahabang buhok 3. Kailangan kong hugasan ang inyong buhok.
Exercise 7 1. Maikli sa harapan, medyo mahaba sa likuran 2. putulin
nang kaunti ang tagiliran, medyo kulot, medyo kingki 3. pakiputulan ang
hulihan, huwag masyadong maikli, hanggang batok lang.
Exercise 8 1. Magandang umaga naman 2. gusto kong magpagupit 3.
Maaari bang ngayon na ako magpagupit? 4. Hindi na salamat. Gupit lang
5. Gusto ko maikli ang gupit 6. Gupit na lang muna 7. Maraming salamat
Exercise 9 1. sa matatanda 2. sa iyo 3. sa kaniya 4. sa akin 5. sa atin
6. sa kaniya

Unit 12

Exercise 1 1. kailangan 2. pantalon at kamisadentro 3. maluwag
4. sarisaring kulay 5. maganda 6. pumili 7. sombrero **Exercise 2** 1.
bibili ako ng laruan bukas 2. Kumakain kami ng gulay araw-araw
3. Gumawa tayo ng laruan 4.) Humihiram si Ely ng libro sa akin 5. Iinom
kami ng malamig na beer sa kantina ngayon. **Exercise 4** 1. gusto ko
ng berdeng palda 2. Ayaw ko ng mahabang palda 3. Kailangan ko ito sa
Lunes 4. Nasa bahay ang palda ko. **Exercise 5** 1. lumalaki
2. gumaganda 3. luminis 4. lumayo **Exercise 6** lumalaki, lumiwanag,
luminaw, sumarap **Exercise 7** 1. Kanina sumikat ang araw 2. sa amin
noong isang linggo 3. tag-init 4. umuulan 5. Madilim ang langit.
Exercise 8 1. Bumabaha sa Maynila. 2. Hindi. Sa Kanluran ito
lumulubog 3. Sumisikat ang araw sa Pilipinas mga alas 6:00 nang umaga
4. May ingay kung kumukulog at kumikidlat 5. Hindi. Sumisikat ang
buwan sa gabi. **Exercise 9** Kumikidlat 2. umulan 3. bumaha

Exercise 10 1. maulap, maaaring umulan sa Hilagang Luzon
2. Mainit 3. Mainit ang araw

Unit 13

Exercise 1 1. False 2.True 3. False 4. True 5. True 6. False 7. False
8. True 9. True 10. False **Exercise 2** 1. Hindi ko gustong bumili ng
tiket 2. Hindi puwede bukas nang umaga. 3. Hindi humihinto ang bus
nang mga alas 7:30 4. Malayo ang Banaue buhat sa Maynila 5. Hindi
mabuti ang alas 4.30 nang umaga. **Exercise 3** 1. Huwebes
2. Septyembre 3. Nobyembre 4. Linggo 6. Miyerkoles 6. Hunyo
7. Sabado **Exercise 4** 1. Sa ika-30 ng Agosto ang kaarawan niya 2. Sa
Lunes ang simula ng pasukan 3. Dadalaw kami sa iyo sa Sabado, ika-
sampu ng Mayo. 4. Noong Martes, ika-14 ng Hunyo ang komperensiya
5. Pupunta kami sa zoo sa Linggo, ika-3 ng Septyembre 6. Sa Sabado ka
ba aalis? 7. Sino ang darating sa Huwebes, ika 5 ng Enero? **Exercise 5**
1. magluto 2. maglaba 3. maglaro **Exercise 6** 1. Maglaro tayo 2.
Naglinis na ako ng kotse 3. Naghuhugas ng pinggan si Maria 4.
Magdasal tayo 5. Magluluto sina Lina. **Exercise 7** 1. Mga sampung
oras 2. Hindi 3. Tarlac 4. Lima **Exercise 8** 1. Alas 7.45 ang dating ng
bus galing sa Baguio. 2. Umalis ito sa Baguio kaninang alas 9.00 ng
umaga. 3. Hihinto ito sa Ilocos, Pangasinan, Tarlac, Pampanga at
Bulacan **Exercise 9** 1. 81 pesos
2. Mali. Ang numero ng tiket ay: anim, dalawa, dalawa, tatlo, talo, anim
3. wala. 4. 10–60 5. Hindi. 6. Hindi **Exercise 10** 1. maligo
2. nakikinig 3. naupo 4. mahiga 5. natulog **Exercise 11** 1. Anong oras
hihinto ang bus sa Pampanga? 2. Saan pa kayo hihinto? 3. Mayroon bang
kubeta doon? 4. Gusto kong pumunta sa kubeta **Exercise 12**
1. Magandang umaga 2. Oo. Pero hindi ko sigurado kung anong oras ito
babalik sa Maynila 3. Bukas nang hapon ang balik naming 4. Alas tres.
Okay lang 5. Isang biyahe lang. Para sa tatlong adults 6. Heto ang bayad
namin 7. Maraming salamat din. **Exercise 13** 1. nakapaglalaro
2. makakaalis 3. makakabili 4. makakapagluto 5. nakatulog

Unit 14

Exercise 1 1. Kasi maganda ang panahon 2. Mamamasyal muna
3. Mga mangingisda 4. Oo. Sa palagay ko, mura ang pag-arkila ng
bangka 5. Hindi. Pagbalik na nila. **Exercise 2** 1. Mamimitas ako ng

prutas bukas 2. Mangingisda sila sa Miyerkoles 3. Maraming
mandurukot sa palengke 4. Mamamasyal ako mamayang gabi 5. Mamili
tayo! **Exercise 3** 1. mamimitas 2. mangisda 3. namimili
4. nandurukot 5. nanahi **Exercise 4** 1.a 2.a 3.a **Exercise 5** 1.
Malapit na ang pasko 2. Hindi pa ako nakakakain 3. Sa Sabado na ba ang
binyag ng anak mo? 4. alam mo ba ang sagot sa tanong? 5. Kumakain pa
ba sila? **Exercise 6** 1. Si Bill 2. Malalaking isda 3. Nakakapangisda
sila 4. Oo. Nasiyahan sila 5. Lumangoy sila. **Exercise 7** 1.
Namamangka ang pamilya Cook. 2. Lumalangoy ang pamilya Cook.
Exercise 8 1. Nakabili 2. nakakapaglaro 3. nakahiram 4. nakakaalis
5. makabalik. **Exercise 9** 1. Makakapangisda 2. Makakabili 3.
nakakain 4. nakabisita 5. Nakakain **Exercise 10** 1. Salamat.
Nakapamahinga kami. Nakapangisda rin kami 2. Oo. Nakapangisda kami
ng tulingan at dalawang Lapulapu 3. Oo! Sana makabalik kami sa
susunod na taon at makahuli nang maraming isda 4. Heto ang bayad
namin sa bangka 5. Maraming salamat din.

Unit 15

Exercise 1 1. Tinanong nila si Roy kung ibig niyang maging ninong.
2. Apat 3. Sa kapilya sa bukid 4. Oo 5. si Jobert. **Exercise 2** 1. Bukas
ba ninyo bibilhin ang bagong stereo? 2. Ginagawa niya ang bulaklak na
papel 3. Tinatahi mo ba ito? 4. Tinutugtog niya ang kundiman sa piyano
5. Nililinis ko pa ang kuwarto ko 6. Piliin mo ang sariwang gulay.
Exercise 3 1. Maaari bang kunan kita ng retrato? 2. Maaari bang
kunan mo ako ng retrato? 3. Gusto ko ang damit mo, maganda ito/ Ang
ganda ng damit mo! 4. sumama ka sa amin. **Exercise 4** 1. iibigin,
iniibig, inibig 2. kakainin, kinakain, kinain 3. lilinisin, nililinis, nilinis
4. susulatin, sinusulat, sinulat 5. tatapusin, tinatapos, tinapos
Exercise 5 1. hinuhuli 2. kinain 3. tatahiin 4. sasabihin 5. nilinis
Exercise 6 1. kinukuha, binili 2. nililinis, kinukuskos 3. niluluto,
sinasaing **Exercise 7** 1. Ninong ka rin ba? 2. Ilan kayong ninong?
3. Narito ba ang mga magulang mo? 4. Pupunta ka ba sa salu-salo?
Exercise 8 1.4 2.2 3.1 4.3 **Exercise 9** 1. pala 2. nga 3. kaya
4. yata 5. ba

Unit 16

Exercise 1 1. Maaari bang ipakihulog mo ang mga sulat ko?
2. Labindalawa 3. Sapagka't walang selyo si Louise 4. sa Post Office.

Exercise 2 1. ibinibigay 2. itinatapon 3. isinusukat **Exercise 3**
1. ibibigay 2. isasama 3. ipinirito 4. isinulat 5. iniluluto 6. inihulog 7.
itatapon 8. inilagay **Exercise 4** 1. Kasi maraming naitulong si Jobert
sa pamilya Cook 2. Dahil sa malaki ang itinulong ng pamilya kay Jobert
sa London 3. Dinala nila si Jobert sa iba't ibang lugar, ibinili nila sa
Jobert ng kailangan niya 4. Aba, oo. **Exercise 5** 1. Maraming bumibili
ng libro dito araw-araw 2. May kumakatok yata sa pinto 3. May kinuha
ako kahapon sa kaniya 4. Walang sumama sa akin sa ospital noong
Linggo 5. May naglalaro na naman ng tennis sa kabila. **Exercise 6**
1. Tumayo ka! 2. Maupo po kayo. 3. Matulog na tayo. 4. Maari po bang
huwag kayong manigarilyo? 5. Mamasiyal tayo. **Exercise 7**
1. Magandang umaga 2. May semento ba kayo 3. Puwede bang
ipagreserba mo ako ng sampung sako? 4. May Marine plywood ba kayo?
5. Aluminum roofing sheets, mayroon ba kayo? 6. Mabuti. Puwede bang
ipagreserba mo ako ng labindalawang sheets? 7. Oo. Dalawang kilo nga
8. Wala na. Iyan lang. Pupunta ako riyan nang mga tanghali 9. Paalam.

Unit 17
Exercise 1 1. Mali 2. Tama 3. Mali 4. Tama. **Exercise 2** ninong,
simbahan, pulot-gata, ninang, retratista, singsing, pagkain **Exercise 3**
1. Kakainan ko ng pansit ang plato 2. Tinutulungan ko siya
3. Lalagyan namin ng rosas ang halaman dito 4. Gusto kong bigyan si
Larry nito 5. Lalagyan ba natin nito doon? 6. Huwag mong aalisan ng
libro ang mesa **Exercise 4** 1. tutulungan 2. nilakihan 3. sinuklian
4. sasamahan 5. binigyan 6. hinalikan 7. sarapan 8. palitan **Exercise 5**
1. Paglabas… 2. Maraming kumuha…. 3. Maraming sasakyan…
4. Dumating ang bagong…. 5. Inihanda ng mga tagapagluto….
6. Maraming pagkain 7. Ang mga nagluluto 8. Tumulong sa paghahain
9. Habang kumakain 10. May tugtugin… 11. Isa sa mga tugtugin
12. Inanyayahan ng mga panauhin 13. Tuwang-tuwa 14. Napagod sa
pagsayaw 15)Sa dulang, nagbigay ng… 16. Nagbigay din 17. Isa-isang
nagpaalam **Exercise 7** 1. Nasusulatan mo na ba si Sophie?
2. Maitatapon ni Harry ang basura lagi 3. May binubuksan siyang kabinet
ngayon 4. Hindi masasamahan ni Caroline si Phil sa bayan mamayang
gabi 5. Sino ang naisakay mo sa kotse kagabi? **Exercise 8** 1. Ang
paghalik sa kamay ng mga lolo at lola. 2. Ang lola 3. Upang maging
puhunan 4. Ang unang makarating sa bahay ang boss **Exercise 9**
1. siya mismo 2. Mismong kami 3. nila mismo 4. ikaw, mismo 5.

Mismong sina Fred **Exercise 10** 1. natutulog 2. nakikipag-usap sa kaibigan 3. naliligo 4. naglalaba 5. namamasiyal 6. umiinom

Unit 18

Exercise 1 1. pista 2.mamayang gabi 3. mga damit at mga laruan 4. dapat mayaman siya 5. pag-akyat sa kawayan, pagsungkit ng laso, pagsakay sa kalabaw 6. upang ilibot sa bayan 7. ang tenyente
Exercise 2 1. kapalaran 2. katamaran 3. kawalan 4. kayamanan 5. kabahayan 6. kamalian **Exercise 3** karunungan 2. kasinungalingan 3. kalalakihan, kababaihan 4. karapatan 5. kakayahan **Exercise 5** 1. False (gusto) 2. False (upang maghanda 3. False. (ginagastos kaagad) 4. False. (Hindi mabuti) 5. False. (Hindi mabuti para sa lahat.
Exercise 6 1. Oo, pupunta kami sa pista 2. Mahilig akong sumayaw 3. Saan makakabili ng pagkain at inumin? 4. Salamat, sumama ka sa amin. 5. O sige, hahanapin ka namin mamaya 6. Paalam.
Exercise 7 1. Makikikain si Auntie Marge sa kanila mamaya. 2. Kanino ka nakiupo? 3. Makikipamili ka ba kina auntie dot? 4. Nakikipag-away na naman si Jose 5. Nakikipag-usap pa ako kay Janet.
Exercise 8 1. Maaari bang makipag-usap kami kay Ginoong Reyes? 2. Puwede bang makitulog ako sa kanila? 3. Huwag sana kayong makipag-away sa mga bata 4. Maaari bang makisakay kami kina Baby? 5. Puwede bang makipagluto ang mga bisita dito? **Exercise 9** 1. Nag-aaral siyang humawak ng kalabaw 2. Medyo kausapin ang kalabaw 3. Oo. Maaari siyang sumakay sa kalabaw 4. Nagtrabaho siya sa isang sabsaban ng kabayo sa Inglaterra. **Exercise 10** 1. Ganoon kabait si ginoong Cruz sa amin 2. Ganito ba ang paggawa ng silyang rattan? 3. Paano ang pagsara ng kahong ito? 4. Hindi ba ganito ang pagluto ng adobo? 5. Sabihin mo sa akin ang pagtugtog ng himig na ito. **Exercise 11** 1. ganito 2. ganiyan 3. ganiyan 4. ganito 5. ganoon 6. ganito 7. ganiyan 8. ganoon 9. ganito 10. ganiyan 11. ganoon 12. ganito

Unit 19

Exercise 1 1. mga punong-kahoy 2. rosal, sampaguita, rosas, camia 3. Gumawa siya ng palaisdaan 4. Nagpaluto ng kakanin si Kiko 5. Maganda ang buhay sa bukid: may mga punong-kahoy, masarap ang pagkain, may mga bulaklak etc. **Exercise 2** 1. Nagpapakuha ako ng libro sa kanila 2. Magpapalabas ba tayo ng silya? 3. Nagpapasok ba si Henry ng mga maleta kanina? 4. Saan ka nagpapabibili ng gulay at

prutas? 5. Nagpabasa siya ng aklat sa klase. **Exercise 3** 1) Seven
2) a) Medyo huli na ako OR Alas_____ ako nakarating. b) Oo, natrapik
ako. c) Nasa kusina ang Nanay ko. d) Hindi lahat. Nagpaluto ako ng
ibang putahe. w) Oo. d) May kilala akong masarap magluto. Chef siya.
Exercise 4 1. Gusto niyang magpakain ng mga baboy 2. Si Kiko
3. Mga manok 4. Kasi pinagluto na ni Kiko ang Misis niya ng almusal.
Exercise 5 1. pasusulatin 2. pinaglinis ng kotse 3. pagtatahiin ng
bestida 4. nagpapagupit 5. nagpapaganda **Exercise 6** 1. Nagpapaligo
si Mang Kiko ng kalabaw sa ilog 2. Nagpapakain ng manok si Roy
3. Nagsasampay ng damit ang asawa ni Mang Kiko 4. Pinaaalis ng
batang babae ang mga ibon 5. Nagpapalipad ng saringgola ang batang
lalaki. **Exercise 7** 3. Pinagbuti ni Elvie ang kaniyang trabaho kagabi
1. Pasasamahin ko si Michael kay Jim sa bayan sa isang linggo
2. Pinamili namin si Lisa kahapon 1. Pinapag-aral ni Lina si Georgina
kanina. 2. Pinasulat daw ni Patricia si Larry noong isang buwan.
Exercise 8 1. damo 2. si roy 3. hinog na ang guyabano 4. para inumin
ng mga hayop 5. sa loob ng murang niyog. **Exercise 9** 1. pinatutulog
2. pinatatakbo 3. pinaglilinis **Exercise 10** 1. ipalalagay 2. ipasok
3. ipamimigay 4. ipinaaayos 5. papintahan

Unit 20

Exercise 1 1. Isang kalabaw na inukit sa kahoy 2. magdaramdam si
Kiko 3. mga pagkain lang 4. Malaking abala ang ibinigay nila kay Kiko
Exercise 2 1. Kasimbait ni Remy si Bing. (Remy is as kind as Bing)
2. Kasimputi ng camia ang rosal. (Camia is as white as rosal)
3. Kasintaas ng St. Paul's Cathedral ang BT Tower (The BT Tower is as
tall as St. Paul's Cathedral) 4. Kasinluwang ng pantalon ko ang pantalon
mo (My trousers are as wide as your trousers) 5. Kasingkipot nito iyan.
(This is as tight as that) 6. Hindi kasingganda ang hardin ko ng hardin mo
(My garden is not as pretty as yours) 7. Magkasimbuti ang gulay at
prutas (Vegetables and fruits are equally good) **Exercise 3** 1.
Kailangan niyang bumili ng pampasalubong 2. sa Priscilla's Gift Shop 3.
para kay Viv at Tim 4. nilalang handbag 5. sa pamamagitan ng credit
card
6. mag-iimpake pa sila. **Exercise 4** 1. panlakad 2. pambayad
3. pangkain **Exercise 5** 1. pangkamot 2. pamputol 3. panlaba
4. panulat 5. pamasyal **Exercise 6** 1. Pangkamot ng likod ang patpat
2. Pamputol ng kahoy ang itak 3. Panlaba ang sabon 4. Panulat ang lapis

5. Pamasiyal ang gomang sapatos. **Exercise 7** 1. Aba, huwag kayong mag-alaala 2. Mas tahimik sa Inglaterra 3. Magandang kuwadro para sa kaniyang pamilya 4. sumulat lagi si roy o kaya'y tumawag.

Exercise 9 1. Mas matangkad si Tom kaysa kay Benny 2. Higit na masipag si Benny kaysa kay Tom. 3. Mas mataba si Benny kaysa kay Tom. 4. Mas masaya si Benny kaysa kay Tom

Exercise 10 Self-assessment (Ask your Filipino friends to help)

VERB LIST

Stem	Meaning	-um-	mag+	mang+	+in	i+	+an
abang	*to wait for*	x	x	mang-abang	x	x	abangan
abay	*to accompany*	umabay	x	x	x	x	abayan
abot	*to arrive, reach*	umabot	x	x	abutin	x	abutan
ako	*to claim*	umako	x	mang-ako	akuin	x	x
aksaya	*to waste (time)*	umaksaya	mag-aksaya	x	aksayahin	x	x
akyat	*to climb*	umakyat	x	x	akyatin	x	akyatan
alaala	*to remember*	umalaala	x	x	alalahanin	x	x
alam	*to know*	x	x	x	alamin	x	x
alay	*to offer/dedicate*	x	mag-alay	mang-alay	x	ialay	alayan
alibadbad	*to be nauseous*	x	x	x	alibadbarin	x	alibadbaran
alis	*to leave*	umalis	mag-alis	x	alisin	x	x
alis	*to remove*	x	x	x	alisin	x	alisan
alsa	*to raise/rise/strike*	umalsa	mag-alsa	x	x	x	x
ambag	*to contribute*	umambag	mag-ambag	x	x	iambag	ambagan
anak	*to treat as one's own child*	x	mag-anak	x	anakin	x	x
anak	*to have a baby*	x	x	manganak	x	x	x
aral	*to study*	x	mag-aral	x	x	x	x
araw-araw	*to do something daily*	x	x	x	araw-arawin	x	x
awit	*to sing*	umawit	x	x	awitin	x	awitan
ayos	*to tidy up*	umayos	mag-ayos	x	ayusin	x	ayusan
baba	*to descend/go down*	bumaba	x	x	babain	x	babaan
bago	*to change*	bumago	x	x	baguhin	x	x
bagsak	*to drop/fall*	bumagsak	magbagsak	x	x	ibagsak	bagsakan
bagyo	*to be hit by typhoon*	bumagyo	x	x	bagyuhin	x	x
bahin	*to sneeze*	bumahin	x	x	x	x	bahinan
balik	*to come back*	bumalik	x	x	x	x	x

balik	*to return something*	x	magbalik	x	x	ibalik	x
bangon	*to get up (from lying down)*	bumangon	magbangon	x	x	ibangon	x
bantay	*to guard*	x	magbantay	x	x	x	bantayan
baon	*to bring provision*	x	magbaon	x	baunin	x	x
baon	*to bury*	bumaon	magbaon	x	x	ibaon	x
basa	*to read*	bumasa	magbasa	x	basahin	x	basahan
basa	*to wet*	x	magbasa	mambasa	basain	x	x
basag	*to break (as in glass)*	bumasag	magbasag	mambasag	basagin	x	x
bastos	*to be bad mannered/ rude*	bumastos	x	mambastos	bastusin	x	x
bata	*to become young*	bumata	x	x	x	x	x
bata	*to suffer*	x	magbata	x	batahin	x	x
batid	*to know*	x	x	x	batirin	x	x
bili	*to buy*	bumili	magbili	mamili	bilhin	ibili	bilhan
bili	*to sell*	x	x	x	x	x	x
bola	*to fool someone*	x	x	mambola	bolahin	x	x
bubo	*to spill*	x	magbubo	x	x	ibubo	bubuan
bukas	*to open*	bumukas	by itself	x	x	x	x
bukas	*to open something*	x	magbukas	x	x	ibukas	buksan
bukid	*to farm*	x	magbukid	mambukid	bukirin	x	x
buhay	*to give life*	x	magbuhay	x	buhayin	x	x
buhay	*to live*	bumuhay	x	mamuhay	x	x	x
bunga	*to bear fruit*	bumunga	magbunga	x	x	ibunga	x
busog	*to make full (appetite)*	bumusog	x	x	busugin	x	x
buwis	*to pay tax*	x	magbuwis	x	x	x	buwisan
kaibigan	*to befriend*	kumaibigan	x	x	kaibiganin	x	x
kailangan	*to need*	kumailangan	x	mangailangan	kailanganin	x	x
kain	*to eat*	kumain	magkain	mangain	kainin	ikain	kainan
kagat	*to bite*	kumagat	x	mangagat	kagatin	ikagat	kagatan

Root	English						
kaliwa	to turn left	kumaliwa	x	mangaliwa	kaliwain	x	x
kamay	to use the hand	x	magkamay	x	kamayin	x	x
kanta	to sing	kumanta	x	x	kantahin	x	kantahan
kapit-bahay	to visit neighbours	x	x	mangapit-bahay	x	x	x
kilala	to know	kumilala	x	mangilala	kilalanin	x	x
kilos	to move	kumilos	x	x	x	ikilos	x
kita	to earn	kumita	x	x	kitain	x	x
kita	to meet up	x	magkita	x	kitain	x	x
kuha	to get/take	kumuha	x	manguha	kunin	ikuha	kunan
kulang	to lack	x	magkulang	x	kulangin	x	x
kulay	to colour	x	magkulay	x	x	ikulay	kulayan
dala	to carry	x	magdala	x	dalhin	x	x
dala	to bring to someone	x	x	x	x	x	dalhan
dala	to catch fish with a net	x	magdala	mandala	dalahin	x	x
dalangin	to pray	dumalangin	x	manalangin	dalanginin	idalangan	dalanginan
dalaw	to visit	dumalaw	x	x	dalawin	idalaw	x
dali	to make quick	x	x	x	daliin	x	dalian
dama	to feel	dumama	magdama	x	damahin	x	x
damihan	to make many	x	x	x	x	x	x
damit	to wear clothes	x	magdamit	manamit	damitin	idamit	damitan
dapat	to be a must/ought to	x	x	x	x	x	x
dumi	to dirty	dumumi	magdumi	x	x	x	dumihan
dusa	to suffer	x	magdusa	x	x	x	x
eskandalo	to create a scandal	x	mageskandalo	x	eskandaluhin	x	x
eskoba	to brush clothes	x	mageskoba	x	eskubahin	x	eskubahan
gabi	to be overtaken by night	gumabi	x	x	gabihin	x	x

Root	Meaning						
galing	to come from	x	x	manggaling	x	x	x
galing	to become well	gumaling	x	x	x	x	x
galit	to be angry	x	x	manggalit	galitin	x	x
gamit	to use	gumamit	x	x	gamitin	x	gamitan
gamot	to treat/ cure	gumamot	x	manggamot	gamutin	x	x
gana	to have appetite	x	x	x		x	ganahan
ganda	to make beautiful	gumanda	x	x		x	gandahan
gata	to cook in coconut milk	x	maggata	x		igata	gataan
gawi	to turn towards	gumawi	x	x	x	igawi	gawian
gibik	to shout for help	gumibik	x	x	x	x	gibikan
giling	to grind	gumiling	x	x	gilingin	x	x
gising	to wake up	gumising	x	manggising	gisingin	x	x
gusto	to like	gumusto	x	x	gustuhin	x	x
gutom	to feel hungry	gumutom	x	manggutom	gutumin	x	x
hakot	to load baggage	humakot	maghakot	x	hakutin	x	hakutan
hagilap	to search for/ look for	humagilap	maghagilap	manghagilap	hagilapin	ihagilap	x
hagis	to throw	humagis	maghagis	manghagis	x	ihagis	hagisan
hangin	to blow (as in wind)	humangin	x	x	x	x	hanginan
hapo	to suffer from tiredness	x	x	x	hapuin	x	x
hasik	to plant seed	x	maghasik	x	x	ihasik	hasikan
hayag	to reveal	x	maghayag	x	x	ihayag	x
higa	to lie down (a **ma** verb)	mahiga	x	x	x	ihiga	higaan
hila	to pull	humila	maghila	manghila	hilahin	x	x
hindi	to say no/ turn down	humindi	x	x	x	x	hindian
hintay	to wait	x	maghintay	x	hintayin	x	x

hinto	*to stop*	huminto	x	x	x	ihinto	hintuan
hipo	*to touch*	humipo	x	manghipo	hipuin	x	hipuan
hiram	*to borrow*	humiram	x	manghiram	hiramin	ihiram	hiraman
hithit	*to smoke* (ie cigarette etc.)	humithit	x	x	hithitin	x	x
hiyaw	*to shout*	humiyaw	x	x	x	ihiyaw	hiyawan
hubad	*to undress*	x	maghubad	x	hubarin	x	hubaran
hugas	*to wash*	x	maghugas	x	x	x	hugasan
hulog	*to drop*	x	maghulog	x	x	ihulog	hulugan
iba	*to change*	x	mag-iba	x	ibahin	x	x
ibig	*to love/ like*	umibig	x	mangibig	ibigin	x	x
idlip	*to have a short nap*	umidlip	x	x	x	x	x
igib	*to fetch water*	umigib	x	x	x	x	x
imik	*to talk/ speak*	umimik	x	x	x	x	imikan
isip	*to think*	umisip	mag-isip	x	isipin	x	x
init	*to become hot*	uminit	mag-init	x	initin	x	x
inom	*to drink*	uminom	x	x	inumin	x	inuman
isda	*to go fishing*	x	x	mangisda	x	x	x
itim	*to become dark*	umitim	x	mangitim	x	x	x
laba	*to wash clothes*	x	maglaba	x	x	x	labhan
labas	*to go outside*	lumabas	x	x	labasin	x	labasan
lakad	*to walk*	lumakad	maglakad	x	lakarin	ilakad	lakaran
lagay	*to place/ put*	lumagay	maglagay	x	x	ilagay	lagyan
laglag	*to fail/ fall*	lumaglag	maglaglag	x	x	ilaglag	laglagan
lala	*to become seriously ill*	lumala	x	x	x	x	x
lamok	*to be infested with mosquitoes*	x	x	x	lamukin	x	x
lapit	*to come close/ near*	lumapit	x	x	x	ilapit	lapitan
laro	*to play*	x	maglaro	x	laruin	x	x
lasap	*to taste/ experience*	lumasap	x	x	lasapin	x	x
lasing	*to get drunk*	lumasing	maglasing	x	lasingin	x	x

Root	Meaning						
lawig	*to take a long time*	lumawig	maglawig	x	x	ilawig	lawigan
layag	*to sail*	lumayag	maglayag	x	x	x	x
layo	*to distance oneself*	lumayo	x	x	x	ilayo	layuan
libak	*to mock, humiliate*	lumibak	x	manglibak	libakin	x	x
libing	*to bury*	x	maglibing	x	x	ilibing	x
ligo	*to take a bath (a **ma** verb)*	maligo	x	x	x	x	liguan
ligpit	*to keep / tidy up*	x	x	x	x	x	x
limos	*to give alms*	x	maglimos	x	x	ilimos	limusan
limot	*to forget*	lumimot	x	x	limutin	x	x
lindol	*to have an earthquake*	lumindol	x	x	x	x	x
linis	*to clean*	x	maglinis	x	linisin	x	linisan
lingkod	*to serve*	x	maglingkod	x	x	x	x
lipad	*to fly*	lumipad	x	x	liparin	ilipad	x
litaw	*to appear*	lumitaw	x	x	x	ilitaw	litawan
liwanag	*to become brighter*	lumiwanag	magliwanag	x	liwanagin	x	liwanagan
loko	*to fool*	lumuko	magloko	manloko	lokohin	x	x
lukso	*to jump*	lumukso	x	x	luksuhin	x	luksuhan
lugas	*to fall off*	lumugas	x	x	lugasin	x	x
lulon	*to swallow*	lumulon	x	x	lulunin	x	x
may-ari	*to own/ claim*	x	magmay-ari	x	x	x	x
meryenda	*to have a snack*	x	magmeryenda	x	meryendahin	x	x
mahal	*to make dear/ expensive*	x	magmahal	x	x	x	mahalan
mahal	*to love*	x	x	x	mahalin	x	x
minindal	*to have a snack*	x	magminindal	x	minindalin	x	x
miting	*to have a meeting*	x	magmiting	x	x	x	x
mukha	*to be similar to/ look like*	x	magmukha	x	x	x	x
mungkahi	*to suggest*	x	magmungkahi	x	x	imungkahi	x
mura	*to become cheaper*	x	magmura	x	x	x	murahan
nakaw	*to steal*	x	magnakaw	x	nakawin	x	nakawan
nais	*to desire/ wish*	x	magnais	x	naisin	x	x

ningas	to have flame	x	magningas	x	x	x	x
ngiti	to smile	ngumiti	x	x	x	x	ngitian
nguya	to chew	ngumuya	magnguya	x	nguyain	inguya	x
obserba	to observe	x	mag-obserba	x	obserbahin	x	obserbahan
opera	to operate	umopera	mag-opera	x	uperahin	x	uperahan
oo	to say yes	umoo	x	x	x	x	uuhan
oras	to measure the time of	x	mag-oras	x	orasin	x	orasan
paa	to be barefooted	x	magpaa	x	paahin	x	x
paalam	to bid goodbye	x	magpaalam	x	x	x	x
pakli	to reply answer	pumakli	x	x	x	ipakli	x
paksiw	to cook this native dish	x	magpaksiw	x	paksiwin	ipaksiw	x
pakumbaba	to be humble	x	magpakumbaba	x	x	x	pakumbabaan
pakundangan	to have respect	x	magpakundangan	x	x	x	x
pagitan	to be a go-between	pumagitan	x	mamagitan	x	ipagitan	pagitanan
pahimakas	to say farewell	x	magpahimakas	x	x	ipahimakas	pahimakasan
pahintulot	to give permission	x	magpahintulot	x	x	ipahintulot	pahintulutan
pahinga	to take a rest	x	magpahinga	mamahinga	x	x	pahingahan
pait	to become bitter	pumait	x	x	x	x	x
palamuti	to decorate	x	magpalamuti	x	x	ipalamuti	palamutihan
palayaw	to nickname	x	magpalayaw	x	x	ipalayaw	palayawan
palengke	to go to the market	x	x	mamalengke	x	x	x
panaginip	to dream	x	x	managinip	panaginipin	x	panaginipan
panalangin	to pray	x	x	manalangin	x	ipanalangin	panalanginan
pangako	to promise	x	magpangako	mangako	x	ipangako	pangakuan
paniwala	to believe	x	x	maniwala	x	x	paniwalaan
pangamba	to worry	x	x	mangamba	x	x	pangambahan
pasok	to enter	pumasok	x	x	pasukin	x	pasukan
para	to stop a bus/ Jeepney	pumara	magpara	x	parahin	ipara	parahan
pasko	to spend Christmas	x	magpasko	x	x	x	x

Root	Meaning						
pasiya	to decide	x	magpasiya	x	x	ipasiya	pasayahan
pasyal	to take a stroll	x	magpasyal	mamasyal	x	x	x
patay	to die	x	x	mamatay	x	x	x
patay	to kill	pumatay	magpatay	x	patayin	x	x
patnubay	to guide	pumatnubay	magpatnubay	mamatnubay	x	ipatnubay	patnubayan
patnugot	to direct	pumatnugot	x	mamatnugot	x	x	patnugutan
patubig	to irrigate	x	magpatubig	x	x	x	patubigan
patuloy	to continue	x	magpatuloy	x	x	x	x
pawis	to sweat	x	magpawis	mamawis	pawisin	x	pawisan
pikit	to close eyes	pumikit	magpikit	x	x	ipikit	pikiran
pihit	to turn	pumihit	magpihit	x	pihitin	x	x
pila	to queue up	pumila	x	x	x	ipila	pilahan
pili	to select/ choose	pumila	magpili	mamili	pilin	ipili	pilian
pilipit	to twist	pumilipit	magpilipit	mamilipit	pilipitin	ipilipit	x
pilit	to insist	x	magpilit	mamilit	x	x	x
pirma	to sign	pumirma	x	x	x	ipirma	pirmahan
pisan	to put together/ to join	pumisan	magpisan	x	x	ipisan	x
pista	to attend fiesta	x	magpista	mamista	x	x	x
pito	to whistle	pumito	x	x	x	x	pituhan
radyo	to have the radio on	x	mag-radyo	x	x	x	x
rikisa	to search	x	magrikisa	mangrikisa	rikisahin	x	rikisahan
regalo	to offer a gift	x	magregalo	x	x	iregalo	regalahan
relos	to wear a watch	x	magrelos	x	x	x	relosan
repeke	to peal (as in bells)	rumepeke	magrepeke	x	repekehin	irepeke	x
rosaryo	to recite the rosary	x	magrosaryo	x	x	x	x
reseta	to prescribe	x	magreseta	x	x	ireseta	resetahan
resibo	to issue/ give a receipt	x	magresibo	x	x	iresibo	resibuhan
sabi	to say	x	magsabi	x	sabihin	x	sabihin
sakal	to choke	magsakal	manakal	sakalin	x	x	x
sakay	to ride	sumakay	magsakay	x	x	isakay	sakyan

sakdal	*to charge or accuse in court*	x	magpasakdal	x	isakdal	x	x
sakmal	*to snatch*	sumakmal	x	manakmal	x	x	x
sakit	*to hurt*	sumakit	x	manakit	x	x	x
sagana	*to be abundant*	x	magsagana	managana	x	x	x
saglit	*to visit someone for a short time*	sumaglit	magsaglit	managlit	saglitin	isaglit	saglitan
sagot	*to answer*	sumagot	x	x	sagutin	isagot	sagutan
sagot	*to be answerable to one's actions*	x	x	managot	x	x	x
salat	*to feel*	x	x	manalat	salatin	x	x
salita	*to speak/ talk/ say*	x	magsalita	manalita	salitain	x	x
saliw	*to accompany (instrument)*	sumaliw	magsaliw	x	x	isaliw	saliwan
sanay	*to practice*	x	magsanay	x	sanayin	x	x
sangguni	*to consult*	sumangguni	magsangguni	manangguni	x	isangguni	sanggunian
saplot	*to wear clothes*	x	magsaplot	x	saplutin	isaplot	saplutan
sarap	*to make delicious*	x	x	x	x	x	sarapan
sarili	*to live on one's own*	x	magsarili	manarili	x	x	x
sayaw	*to dance*	sumayaw	magsayaw	x	sayawin	isayaw	x
saysay	*to narrate*	x	magsaysay	x	x	isaysay	saysayan
sigaw	*to shout*	sumigaw	x	manigaw	x	isigaw	sigawan
sulat	*to write*	sumulat	magsulat	x	sulatin	isulat	sulatan
simula	*to start/ begin*	x	magsimula	x	x	x	simulan
subo	*to put some food into mouth*	x	magsubo	x	x	isubo	subuan
suka	*to vomit*	sumuka	magsuka	x	x	isuka	sukahan
sulak	*to boil*	sumulak	magsulak	x	x	x	x
sumpa	*to swear an oath*	sumumpa	x	manumpa	sumpain	isumpa	x
sunod	*to follow*	sumunod	x	x	sunurin	isunod	sundan
sunog	*to burn*	sumunog	magsunog	manunog	sunugin	x	x
suot	*to wear*	x	magsuot	x	suutin	isuot	x
suweldo	*to receive salary*	sumuweldo	x	x	x	x	x
taas	*to grow/ to rise*	tumaas	x	x	x	x	x

taas	*to raise*	x	magtaas	x	x	itaas	taasan
taba	*to become fatter*	tumaba	x	manaba	x	x	x
tabi	*to be at one side*	tumabi	x	x	x	x	tabihan
takbo	*to run*	tumakbo	x	x	takbuhin	x	takbuhan
takal	*to measure*	tumakal	magtakal	x	takalin	itakal	takalan
taklob	*to cover*	x	magtaklob	x	x	itaklob	takluban
tadtad	*to chop into pieces*	tumadtad	magtadtad	x	tadtarin	itadtad	x
tadyak	*to kick*	tumadyak	x	manadyak	x	x	tadyakan
tago	*to hide*	x	magtago	x	x	itago	x
tagumpay	*to succeed*	x	magtagumpay	managumpay	x	x	x
tahi	*to sew*	tumahi	magtahi	manahi	tahiin	itahi	x
talon	*to jump*	tumalon	x	x	talunin	x	x
talumpati	*to make a speech*	x	magtalumpati	manalumpati	x	italumpati	talumpatian
tama	*to tally/ to agree*	x	magtama	x	x	itama	x
tanim	*to plant*	x	magtanim	x	x	itanim	tamnan
tanod	*to keep guard*	x	magtanod	x	x	x	tanuran
tanong	*to ask*	x	magtanong	x	tanungin	itanong	x
tanggap	*to accept/ receive*	tumanggap	magtanggap	x	tanggapin	x	x
tapon	*to throw*	x	magtapon	x	x	itapon	tapunan
tapos	*to finish*	tumapos	magtapos	x	tapusin	x	x
tawa	*to laugh*	tumawa	magtawa	x	x	x	tawanan
tawag	*to call*	x	magtawag	x	tawagin	x	tawagan
tawag	*to call on the telephone*	tumawag	x	x	x	x	x
tayo	*to stand up*	tumayo	magtayo	x	x	itayo	tayuan
tayo	*to erect (a building etc.)*	x	x	x	x	x	x
tikim	*to taste*	tumikim	x	x	x	x	tikman
tamasa	*to enjoy*	x	magtamasa	x	tamasahin	x	x
tinda	*to sell*	x	magtinda	x	x	itinda	x
tira	*to live (in a place)*	tumira	x	manira	x	x	tirahan
tiyaga	*to be patient*	x	magtiyaga	x	x	x	x
tubo	*to grow*	tumubo	x	x	x	x	x
tugon	*to reply/ answer*	tumugon	x	x	x	x	x
tugtog	*to play an instrument*	tumugtog	magtugtog	x	tugtugin	itugtog	tugtugan

tulala	to ignore	x	magtulala	x	x	x	tulalaan
tulay	to cross a bridge	tumulay	x	manulay	tulayin	x	tulayan
tulog	to sleep (**ma** verb)	matulog	x	x	x	itulog	tulugan
tuloy	to enter	tumuloy	magtuloy	x	x	x	x
tuloy	to continue	x	x	x	x	ituloy	x
tumba	to tumble down	tumumba	x	x	tumbahin	itumba	x
tunaw	to melt	tumunaw	magtunaw	x	tunawin	x	x
tupad	to fulfil	tumupad	x	x	tuparin	x	x
tupok	to be burned	x	x	x	tupukin	x	x
turo	to teach	tumuro	magturo	x	x	ituro	turuan
turo	to point	x	x	x	x	ituro	x
tuwang	to help	tumuwang	magtuwang	x	x	x	x
ubo	to cough	umubo	x	x	ubuhin	x	x
ubos	to consume/ exhaust	umubos	x	x	ubusin	x	ubusan
ulinig	to listen to	x	x	x	ulinigin	x	ulinigan
ulit	to repeat	umulit	x	x	ulitin	x	x
umaga	to be caught by the dawn	x	mag-umaga	x	umagahin	x	x
ulan	to rain	umulan	x	x	ulanin	x	ulanan
untag	to remind	umuntag	x	x	untagin	x	x
uwi	to go home	umuwi	x	x	x	x	uwian
una	to go ahead first	umuna	mag-una	manguna	unahin	x	x
unawa	to understand	umunawa	x	x	unawain	x	x
upo	to sit down (**ma** verb)	maupo	x	x	x	x	upuan
usap	to converse	x	mag-usap	x	x	x	x
wakas	to end	x	magwakas	x	x	x	wakasan
wala	to lose	x	x	x	x	iwala	x
walang-hiya	to be shameless	x	magwalanghiya	x	x	x	x
yabong	to grow	yumabong	magyabong	x	x	x	x
yamot	to annoy	x	x	x	yamutin	x	x

TAGALOG–ENGLISH GLOSSARY

Trying to get your tongue around unfamiliar words in a new language is often something of an uphill struggle. It can be frustrating to discover that words are not always pronounced as they appear on the page. With this in mind, we have provided three small symbols or 'accents' to help you find the correct stress or sound for each word in the Tagalog–English Glossary. The accents are as follows:

´ This accent serves to lengthen the sound of the vowel. For example, the Tagalog word **lata** (or 'tin' in English) would be pronounced *'lah-tah'*, with the stress on the first syllable. The first 'a' sound is long, something akin to the long 'a' in the English words 'bar' or 'car'. (In the unit dialogues this stress is shown by making the stressed syllable **bold**.)

` This accent is only ever found on the last vowel of a word. It informs you that the vowel sound is shorter than the vowel with the ´ accent. For example, the Tagalog word **kasápì** (*to be a member of*) would be pronounced *'ka-sah-pee'*, with a long 'ah' sound and a short 'ee' sound.

^ This accent is found on a number of words ending with a vowel. It indicates a glottal stop – a short, abrupt sound, almost as though the pronunciation of the vowel has been interrupted, like a tape recorder being switched off. For example, the Tagalog words **basâ** (*wet*) and **bása** (*to read*) are distinguished from one another by their very different accents. (Glottal stops are shown in the unit dialogues by *italics*.)

áalis *will leave*
áalmusalin *what someone's having for breakfast*
abá *oh! / hey! / well!*
abála *disturbance*
abá oó / aba oo naman *of course*
ábay *consort*
abá ópò *certainly, sir*
(mga) ábay sa kasál *wedding assistant(s)*

adóbong pusít *squid adobo*
áking ináanak *my godchild*
aklát (libro) *book*
akó rin *me too*
alám *know*
alam mo bá *do you know*
alas dós nang hápon *2.00 p.m.*
alas dóse *12.00*
alas nuwébe y médya *9.30*

alas saís y médya *6.30*
alín *which one*
alís *departure*
almusál *breakfast*
Amérika *America*
áming *our*
áming anák / anak namin *our child*
ámpalaya *bitter melon*
anák *son / daughter / child*
ang *the*
ang bahálà *will look after*
ang datíng *the arrival*
ang gágawâ *will do*
ang mga itó *these*
ang mga iyán *those*
ang bill ngà námin *our bill, please*
ang kailángan ninyó *what you need*
ang kaínin mo *what you have to eat*
ang kináin mo *what you ate*
ang gusto ninyó(ng) *what you like*
ang íbig ninyo *what you want*
ang maiklíng gupít *short cut*
ang nakáin mo *what you have eaten*
ang paboríto ko(ng) *my favourite*
ang pangálan ko *my name*
ang púnta *the destination / going to*
ang súkat *the size*
ang súkat ko *my measurement*
anó(ng) *what*
anó ang mga óras ng *what are the times of*
anó namán itó? *and what is this?*
ano pá *what else*
ano pò ang maipaglílingkod ko *what (service) can I do*
ano pong gupít *what (kind of) haircut*
anóng edád *how old*
anóng óras *what time*
anóng pangálan ninyó *what's your name? (formal)*
anu-anó *what (plural)*
apó *grandchild*
apritáda *a kind of dish*
áraw *day / sun*
araw-áraw *every day*
asáwa *husband / wife*
asáwa niyáng *his/her spouse*
asín *salt*
at *and*
ate *older sister*
at sakâ *and also*
áyaw ko / ayoko *I don't like*

bábahâ *will flood*
babáe *female/ woman*
babágay pò sa inyó *it will suit you*
babágyo *there will be a typhoon*
bakâ *might/ cow*
baká hindî *might not*
bakánte *vacancy*
bakasyón ka bá *are you on vacation?*
bákit *why*
bákit hindî *why not*
bágay *thing*
bágay ba sa ákin *does it suit me*
bágo *new*
bágo(ng) binyag *newly baptised*
bágo(ng) kasal *newly wed*
bahálà na *come what may*
báhay *house*
baldé *bucket*
bále wala *means nothing*
bandá *band*
bangkâ *boat (canoe)*
bandéra / bandila *flag*
bangâ *earthen pot*
bangús *milkfish*
barkó *ship*
báryo *barrio/ village*
báso *drinking glass*
bátà *child*
bátok *nape*
basúra *rubbish*
báwa't óras *each hour*
bayábas *guavas*
báyad ko *my payment*
bayáw *brother-in-law*
bíbigyan kitá *I'll give you*
bíbili *will buy*
bíbili akó ng *I'll buy/ I'm going to buy*
biglá(ng) *suddenly*
bigyán mo akó *give me*
bibíg mo *your mouth*
bíbilhin *will buy*
bíbili akó *I will buy*
bibingká *a local delicacy*
bili ná *come and buy*
bilobiló *a local delicacy in coconut milk*
binátà *bachelor*
binigyán *was given*
binyág *baptism*
binyágan(g) ito *this baptism*
bintánà *window*
bisíta *guest/ visitor*

biyáhe *travel*
blusá *blouse*
bólpen *pen*
bubúti *will become better*
búkas *tomorrow*
búkas nang gabí *tomorrow night*
búkas nang hápon *tomorrow afternoon*
búkas nang tangháli̇̀ *tomorrow midday*
búkas nang umága *tomorrow morning*
búhat sa *from*
búhay *life*
buhók ninyo (*also* inyong buhok)*your hair*
bulaklák *flower*
bumabâ ka *you alight / you get off*
bumalík *return*
bumílang *counted*
bumilí *to buy*
bumíbilí *buying/ buy*
bumúbulong *whispering*
buntál *a kind of Philippine fibre*
buóng lugár *whole place*
burdádo(ng) *embroidered*
ka *you* (singular)
kaagád *immediately*
kaakit-ákit *attractive*
kabayánan *town*
kabáyo *horse*
kadálasan *often*
kailán *when*
kakáin *will eat*
kakánin *rice cakes*
kakláse *classmate*
kagabí *last night*
kagulúhan *chaos*
kahápon *yesterday*
kahápon nang hápon *yesterday afternoon*
káhit *even though*
káhit saán *anywhere*
kahón *box*
káhoy *wooden*
kaibígan *friend*
kailán *when*
kailángan ko (ng) *I need*
kailángan po námin *we need (**formal**)*
kalabása *squash / pumpkin*
kalabáw *water buffalo*
kalimútan *forget*
kaliwâ *left*
kalsáda / kalye *street*
kálye *road / street*
káma *bed*

kamáy *arm*
kamátis *tomatoes*
kámera / kodak *camera*
kamí *we*
kánin *boiled rice*
kanína *a while ago*
kaníno *whose*
kaníno pa *whose else*
kaniyá(ng) *her*
kánto *corner*
kaopisína ko *my officemates*
kapág *if/ when*
kapaligirán *environment*
kapatíd *sister/ brother*
karamíhan *many of*
kapitán *captain*
karósa *cart*
kasabáy *at the same time*
kasabihán *saying/adage*
kasál / kasálan *wedding*
kasáma *companion/ together with / with /
    including*
kasáma ba *is it included?*
kasáma ko *I'm with*
kasáma nilá *accompanied by them*
kasí *because*
katabí kó *next to me*
katahimíkan *peace*
(ng) katawán *(of the) body*
katóliko *Catholic*
katúlad ng *like*
kaugalián *custom*
kaunting masáhe *a little massage*
kausápin *talk to*
kawáyan *bamboo*
kay [**+ name**] *for [+ name]*
kay / ke mahál ngà *in fact it's expensive*
kay gandá *how beautiful*
kayâ múna tayo *why don't we first*
kayâ *that's why*
kaya palá *no wonder*
kayó *you (**plural informal/ formal
    singular**)*
kayo namán *oh! please!*
káysa *than*
kinákabitán *being attached*
ko *my*
kótse *car*
kubéta *toilet*
kukúnan *will take (a photograph)*
kukúnin *will get / fetch*

kúlay *colour*
kumáin *eat*
kumakáin *eating*
kumánan *turn right*
kumaliwâ *turn left*
kumbidádo *invited*
kumúha *took*
kumústa kayó *how are you (formal
    singular / informal plural)*
kúnan *to take*
kundî *instead*
kung *if*
kung áyaw ninyó *if you don't like*
kung bákit *why*
kung ganoón /gayon *if that's the case*
kung gústo mo(ng) *if you want*
kung hindî *if not/ had not been*
kung maaárì *if possible*
kung mínsan *sometimes*
kung puwéde sána *if possible*
kung saán *where*
kung támà *if right*
kurtína *curtain*
kutsílyo *knife*
kutsintâ *a delicacy*
kuwárta *money*
kuwádro *frame*
kuwárto *room / quarter / one fourth*
kúya *older brother*
daán *road / way*
dágat *sea*
dáhil sa *because*
dáhil lang sa *just because of*
dalandán / dalanghítà *oranges*
dalawá *two*
dalawandaáng píso *200 pesos*
dalawampúng ányos *20 years old*
dalawáng reséta *two prescriptions*
daliín *be quick*
damít-pangkasál *wedding dress*
damó *grass*
dápat *must / should*
dárating *will arrive*
datíng *arrival*
dekorasyón(g) *decoration*
dilà-dílà *a delicacy*
díla mo *your tongue*
diláw *yellow*
direksiyón *direction*
dirétso *straight*
'di sa ákin *of course it's mine*

disiótso pésos *18 pesos*
díto/ ríto *here*
díto lang po sa ibaba *just here below*
díto múna *just here*
doón *there*
doséna *dozen*
dos singkuwénta *2.50 pesos*
dúlang *table*
dumárating *arriving*
dumídilim *becoming dark*
dumirétso *to walk straight ahead*
estudyánte *student*
éto (see heto) *here is*
éto lang *just this*
éto po *here you are madam/ sir*
gaáno kalakí *how big*
gabí *night*
gáling sa *from*
gamót *medicine*
ganito pô *like this, sir*
ganito(ng) úrì *this kind*
ganiyán *like that*
ganoón *like that*
ganoón bá *is that so / oh, my!*
ganoón láng *just like that*
ganoón ngà *really like that*
gáganapín *will be held*
gágastusin *will be spent*
ganiyán *like that*
gasolína *petrol*
gátas *milk*
gawín *be made*
gawin kó *I'd do*
ginágawâ *be made*
gínang *Mrs*
ginisáng gúlay *sauteed vegetables*
gúlay *vegetables*
gumabí *to become night*
gumandá *to become fine/beautiful*
gumawâ *to make*
gúrò *teacher*
gustó *like/ want*
gústo kó(ng) *I like / I want / I love*
gústo ninyó *you like*
gústo kong *I'd like*
gústo ko rín *I also like*
gústo pa namín ng *we want some more*
gústo po ba ninyó *do you like/ would
    you like*
guyabáno *guyabano fruit (large, soft white)*
halíkayo *come on everyone*

hábang *while*
haláman *plants*
handâ *food preparation*
handaán *reception*
hanggáng *until*
hanggáng itaás *reaching the top*
hanggáng sa *until*
hápon *afternoon*
hapúnan *supper*
harapán *front*
hátinggabi *midnight*
hawákan *hold*
háyop *animal*
héto / heto po *here you are / here, sir*
héto ang bayad *here's the payment*
héto na *here comes*
higít *more*
hípon *prawns*
híhintò *will stop*
hindî *no*
hindî ba *isn't it?*
hindi ba mahál *not expensive (I hope)*
hindí ko gustó *I don't like*
hindi na bále *never mind*
hindi namán *not quite / not so*
hindi na pô *not anymore*
hindi pa *not yet*
hindí pò *no, sir*
hindi sa ákin *not mine*
hinóg *ripe*
hintayín mo akó *you wait for me*
hípag *sister-in-law*
huhugásan ko lang *I'll just wash*
humánap *to find*
humángin *was windy*
humíhingî *asking*
humíhiram *borrowing*
huwág *don't*
ibáng kúlay rin *other colours, too*
iba't ibáng *different kinds*
íbig námin *we want / like / would like*
ibigáy *to give*
ibíbigay *will be given*
íbig n'yo ná *would you like now*
íbig po ba ninyó ng *do you want / like a*
ibilí *to buy for*
ibinigáy *handed / gave*
ibinuká *opened*
ikalimáng gusáli̇̀ *fifth building*
ikatatló *third*
ikáw ba talagá *is it really you?*

ikinagágalak ko kayóng makilála *I'm
    pleased to meet you*
ikinasál *got married*
idéya *idea*
iláng béses *how many times*
ihúlog *to post* (literally, *to drop*)
ihuhúlog *will post*
íinom *will drink*
íinumin *will be drunk*
ilabás *show/bring out*
ilán(g) *how many/ a few*
ilangílang *ilangilang (flower)*
ililígid *will be driven around*
inahín *hen*
inanyayáhan *invited*
inasikáso *dealt with/attended to*
ináyos *fixed / arranged*
iniabót *handed over*
inihandâ *prepared*
inihatíd *took to*
iníhaw *grilled*
inípon *the savings*
inyong buhók *your hair*
Inglatérra *England*
inumín *drinks*
inúkit *carved*
ipakihúlog mo *could you post*
ipalálagay *will cause to put*
ipambáyad *to pay with*
ipatápon *will cause to throw*
ipapípitas *will have something picked*
isá *one*
isa ká sa mga *you're one of the*
isáma *to include*
isáng kahón *one box*
isáng doséna(ng) *one dozen*
isáng gabí *per night*
isáng pláto(ng) *a plate of*
isáng taón *one year*
isdâ *fish*
isináma *accompanied*
isinúkat *tried it on*
isúkat ninyó *you try*
itátanong *will ask*
itím *black*
itó *this*
itong itím *this black (one)*
itutúrò *will show/ point*
iwásan lang *please avoid*
iyán *that*
iyan láng *that's all (just those)*

iyón(g) *that*
labánan *contest*
labíndalawá *twelve*
labinlimá *fifteen*
lági *always*
lahát *everybody*
lahat-lahát *all in all / altogether*
laláki *man/ male*
lakárin *to walk (it)*
lálò na *especially*
lamán *contents*
lang *only/ just*
lángit *sky*
lanzónes *lanzones (fruit similar to lychee)*
láot *sea*
lápis *pencil*
laráwan *photograph / picture*
laruán(g) *toy*
likurán *behind / at the back*
lima(ng) píso *five pesos*
limandaán(g) *500*
Linggó *Sunday*
línggo-linggó *every week*
litsón *suckling pig*
lóla *grandmother*
lólo *grandfather*
lúbusan *earnestly*
lugár *place*
lumákad *to walk / move*
lumangóy *to swim*
maaári *can*
maaári ba(ng) *is it possible/(see puwede bang)*
maaábot *be able to reach*
mabáhò *smelly*
mabaít *kind*
mabangó *fragrant*
mabilís *fast*
mabúti *good*
mabúti kung ganoón *that's good*
mabúti rin namán *I'm fine, too*
mabúti po namán *I'm fine, too (formal)*
makapág-almusál *can have breakfast*
makapágbánat *to be able to stretch*
makapághandâ *be able to prepare*
makapál *thick*
makatáwag *to be able to call*
makatutúlong *will be able to help*
makúlay *colourful*
madádalâ *be turned off*
madalî(ng) *easily*

madalí lang *just easy*
magalíng *good at/ clever*
mag-áatubili *hesitate*
mag-alalá *worry*
mag-almusál *to have breakfast*
magandá *beautiful*
magandáng umága *good morning*
magandáng gabi pô *good evening (formal)*
magandáng hápon *good afternoon*
mag-aáral *will study*
magbábakasyon *will go on vacation*
magbábasa *will read*
magbabáyad *will pay*
magbiyáhe *to travel*
magkáno *how much*
magkáno namán *how much is it?*
magkakáno *how much each*
magdádagdag *will add*
magdáramdam *will feel bad*
mag-enjoy *to enjoy*
maghandâ *to prepare*
mag-ímpake *will get packing*
mag-isíp *to worry/think deeply*
magpalamíg muna *have some refreshment first*
magpápakain *will feed*
magpápagod *to become tired*
magpápalit *to change (money)*
magpagupít *have a haircut*
magpasénsiya *to accept our shortcomings*
magsúkat pa *try some more*
magtanóng *enquire*
magúlang *parents*
magustuhán sana ninyo *I hope you'd like it*
mahábà *long*
mahírap *difficult/ poor*
mahiyâ ka namán *are you without shame*
mahúsay *fine / very good at*
maiklî *short (i.e. pencil)*
maiklíng buhók *short hair*
maínit *hot*
malaki *big*
malakí-lakí *quite big*
malamíg *cold*
malápit *near*
maláyò *far*
maléta *suitcase*
maligáya(ng) *happy*
maligáyang pagdatíng *welcome*
malínis *clean*
maliít *small*

maliít sa ákin *small for me*
malulúgi *I'll lose*
maluwáng *loose*
mámayâ *later*
mamangkâ *to go boating*
mamasyál *to take a stroll*
mámayang gabí *tonight*
manggá *mango*
mangingisdâ *fisherman*
manók *chicken*
manoód *watch*
mantikílya *margarine*
mápa *map*
mapagpípilian *to choose from*
marámi *many / plenty*
maráming salámat *thank you very much*
marumí *dirty*
marúnong *know*
masakít *hurting / painful*
masaráp *delicious/ great / nice/ good*
masayá *happy*
mas bágay *suits better*
mas lálò *more*
mas maága *earlier*
mas malakí *bigger*
mag-aalalá *more bothered/ be worried*
masúsunod *will be followed*
masyádo(ng) *very / too / quite / extremely*
mataás *high*
matabáng *bland / flat in taste*
mata mó *your eyes*
matatandâ *the old ones*
matatápos na gawáin *jobs will be finished*
matúto *will learn*
matutúlog *will sleep*
mawáwalâ *will disappear*
may *has/have, there is/ there are*
mayáman *rich*
mayáman namán kayó *anyway, you are rich*
máy binili akó(ng) *I bought*
may kilála akó *I know someone*
may mésa ba kayó *do you have a table*
may makakaínan bang *is there any place to eat*
may nakalimútan *forgot something*
may napílì *has selected/ chosen*
mayroón / meron *has/have there is/ there are*
médyo *sort of / somewhat*
médyo maliít *slightly small*

médyo masikíp *slightly small*
médyo nagúlat *somewhat surprised*
mésa *table*
mésa ninyó *your table*
mechádo *pork / beef with tomato sauce, pepper and potatoes*
minsánan *in one go*
mga pluraliser, similar to the English 's'
mga alás siyéte medya *about 7.30*
mga limá *about five*
modistá *dressmaker*
mukhá(ng) *looks / appears / seems*
mukháng malínis *looks quite clean*
mulî *again / once more*
múna *first, for the time being*
muntí(ng) regálo *small gift*
múra *cheap*
múra na pò *it's already cheap, ma'am*
múra ang halagá *the price is cheap/ right*
múrang niyóg *young coconut*
múrang-múra *very cheap*
na *now/ already*
naáyos *managed to arrange*
na namán *again*
na binilí ko dito *that I bought here*
naka-arkilá *was able to hire*
nakákahiyâ *embarrassing*
nakákapangisdâ *are able / manage to catch fish*
nakakitá *happened to see / was able to see*
nakaháwak *managed to handle*
nakaháwak *holding on to*
nakahigâ *lying down*
nakatayô *standing*
nakapamasyál *managed to take a stroll*
nakatirá *living*
nakíta ba ninyó *did you see?*
nakikíta mo *you see*
nág-abalá *bothered*
nagawâ *what's been done*
náiintindihán *understand*
naiísip *able to think about*
náis po ba ninyó *do you want*
nag-aáral *studying / study*
nagbigáy *gave*
nag-enjóy *enjoyed*
naghandâ *prepared food*
nagkoronasyón *crowned*
nag-iípon ng péra *saving money*
nag-íisa *alone*
naglulútò *cooking*

nagmamáno *kissing the hand*
nag-paálam *said goodbye*
nágpagupit *had a haircut*
nagpalútò *caused someone to cook*
nagpápa-akyát *ask someone to climb*
nagpápabango *making (something) fragrant*
nagpapakáin *give them food*
nagpápaganda *making(something) pretty*
nagpápalaki *making (something) grow*
nagpápalit din ba kayó *do you also change?*
nágpasalamat *gave thanks*
nagpuntá *went*
nagséseremonya *officiating*
nagtátaka *wondering*
nagtátae akó *I've got diarrhoea*
nagtítinda ba kayó *do you sell*
nagtrabáho *worked*
nagustuhán *I liked*
nag-úunahan *beating each other* (in a race)
nahíhiyâ *embarrassed*
namámangkâ *boating*
nakabálot *wrapped*
nakabilí *was able to buy*
nakapamangkâ *was able to go boating*
nakatúlog *managed to sleep*
namán *too / on the other hand*
námin *our*
nanálo *won*
nánay *mother*
nang gabí *at night*
nang hápon *in the afternoon*
nang ibigáy *when (it) was given*
nangingísdâ *fishing*
nang maága *early*
nang mabúti *soundly/ well/ better*
nang maluwág *loosely*
nang umága *in the morning*
nangungútang *borrow money*
nápakagandá *very pretty*
napakarámi(ng) *so many*
napágod *got tired*
nápansin *noticed*
nárito ná *here now / here comes*
nása (prefix) *at / on / in / at the / on the / in the*
násaan *where*
nása parke *at the park*
nasiyáhan *was pleased*
naúbos *finished / consumed*
naupô *sat down*
ngayón *now/ today*

ngayón láng *just now*
ngayóng linggó *this week*
ngumitî *smiled*
nilála(ng) *woven*
nínang *godmother*
nínong *godfather*
ninyó *your*
nitó *this,* (in the **ng** form) *of this*
niyá *his / her*
niyáng *of that*
ng *of/ of the*
ng bandána *a scarf*
ng ibá *other ones*
ngâ *please / indeed / it's true*
ngayón *now / today*
ngayóng alas dós *today at 2 o'clock*
ngayóng hápon *this afternoon*
ngayóng umága *this morning*
ng mga anák *of the children*
ng size ninyó *your size*
noón *then / before*
noóng *when / during*
noóng isáng linggó *last week*
número *number*
o kayá'y *or/otherwise*
okey láng *just all right*
o, síge *all right*
oo, mabúti *yes, good*
oo ngà *I agree*
oo nga palá *by the way*
ópò *yes (**formal**)*
óras *time*
pa *still*
paálam *goodbye*
paarkiláhan *a place to hire*
pakaínin *to serve / feed*
pakéte *parcel*
pakiabót sa akin *please pass to me / hand to me*
pakilagáy *please put/ place*
pakipára mo *please stop at*
pakiúlit mo ngâ *please repeat*
págbabakasyón *vacationing*
pagbalík *when you return*
pagháwak *how to hold*
pagkáin *food / eating*
pagkatápos *afterwards / then*
pagháwak *handling / holding*
paglabás ninyó *once you've come out*
pagtanggáp *reception*
págtataním *planting*

paikliín *be shortened*
palagyán *will ask to be put*
palarô *games*
palawít *bunting*
palígid *around*
pálda *skirt*
pangálan *name*
pangalawáng order *second order*
pang-shopping *for shopping*
pag-akyát *climbing*
pág-alalá *concern*
pagkatápos *afterwards*
pagkukúlang *shortcomings*
paghaháin *offering*
paglabás *upon leaving*
páglalakbáy *trip*
pagód *tired*
pagsakáy *riding*
pagsayáw *dancing*
págsisilbi *serving*
pagsungkít *hooking with a pole*
pagtakbó *running*
págtatae *diarrhoea*
pala' *so!*
pála *spade*
palaisdaán *fishpond*
palarúan *playground*
paláyan *rice field*
paléngke *market*
páliguan *bathroom*
(ang) palít *exchange*
páliparan *airport*
pamangkín *niece / nephew*
pamasáhe *fare*
pamaypáy *fan*
pambálot *wrapping paper*
pamigáy *to give around*
pamilyá *family*
pamimilí *shopping*
pamímilihin *things to buy*
pamintá *pepper*
pámpalamig *refreshment*
pampasalúbong *gifts*
panahón *weather / time*
panaúhin *guests*
pandalawáhan *double*
pangálan *name*
pang-aabála *disturbance*
pang-isáhan *single*
pang-okasyón *for certain occasions*
pansít *noodles (cooked the Filipino way)*

panyolíto *handkerchiefs*
papalitán namin iyan *we will replace it*
papáya *pawpaw*
papuntá sa *going to*
paputók *fireworks*
pára *so that / in order to*
paráda *parade*
párang *seems / like / as if*
pára kaníno *for whom*
pára sa *for*
pára sa akín *for me*
pára sa ámin/ atin *for us*
pára sa anák ko(ng) *for my son*
pára sa áraw ng kasal ko *for my wedding day*
pára sa inyó *for you*
pára sa sakít ng tiyán *for stomach ache*
párke *park*
párì *priest*
pasalúbong *gift*
pasahéro *passenger*
pasapórte *passport*
pasénsiya na *accept our apologies*
páyong *umbrella*
pechay *pak choi*
péra/ pera ko *money / my money*
péro *but*
pinakabunsó *youngest*
pinakakáin *give food / feed*
pinakamalápit *nearest*
pinagamásan *had it cleaned*
pinaglútò *asked to cook/cooked for*
pinapágod ka *tiring you*
pinggán/plato *plate*
pínya *pineapple*
pirmahán lang *(just) please sign*
pisára *blackboard*
pistá(ng) *feast day*
pistá(ng) bayan *town fiesta*
pitákà *wallet*
platíto *saucer*
pósporo *a box of matches*
probléma *problem*
prútas *fruit*
puhúnan *capital*
pulá(ng) handbag *red handbag*
pumíli pa *choose some more*
pulútan *finger food to go with drinks*
pulót-gatâ *honeymoon*
pumíli po kayó *please choose*
pumunta ká *you go/ you visit/ stop by*

púnong-káhoy *fruit trees*
púpunta *will go*
puwéde *can*
puwéde akó *I'm available*
puwéde ba(ng) *is it possible / could you*
puwéde na *will suffice/ that will do*
puwéde na pò bá *is it all right, sir / ma'am?*
puwésto *stalls*
raw/ daw *apparently*
resíbo ninyó *your receipt*
rekomendádo *recommended*
regálo *gift*
regálong ito *this gift*
rénda *reins*
repólyo *cabbage*
reséta ng doktor *doctor's prescription*
retratísta *photographer*
retráto *picture*
réyna *queen*
rin/ din *also / too / as well*
rosál *gardenia*
sa (preposition) *to / in / at/ on / at the / in the/ on the*
saán *where (direction)*
saán akó pípirma *where do I sign*
(ang) sa ákin *(what is) mine*
sa áraw *during the day*
sabáy na *do it together / at the same time*
Sábado *Saturday*
sa báryo *at the barrio*
sa báhay *at my place / at my home*
sabáw *thin soup / stock*
sabíhin *tell / say*
sábong *cockfight*
sabsában *stable*
sabungán *cockpit*
sa kaniyá *to him / her*
sáko *sack*
sa kápitbáhay natin *our neighbours'*
ságing *banana*
sa halíp na *instead of*
sa inyó *to you (singular formal / informal plural)*
sa inyóng lahát *to you all*
sa isáng *to one / against one*
sa isáng áraw *the day after tomorrow*
sa isang linggó *next week*
sa loób ng *in(side)*
sa (loób ng) isang araw *in one day*
salámat *thank you*
sa lahát nang oras *at anytime*

sa lugár na ito *here in this place*
salu-sálo *party*
sa may *near*
sampagúita *the national flower*
sána *I hope*
sandalì láng *wait a minute*
sang-áyon *agree*
sang-áyon sa *according to*
sanggól *baby*
sa palagay kó *in my opinion*
sarisári(ng) *assorted*
saríwa(ng) *fresh*
saríwang lumpiâ *fresh spring rolls*
sársa *sauce/ dressing*
sasabíhin *will tell*
sasakyán *vehicle*
sa súsunod *next time*
sa tabí *next/ beside*
sa timbángan *on the scales*
sa trabáho *at work*
sa tuktók *at the top*
sa umága *in the morning*
sa únang béses *for a first time*
sélyo *stamp*
siksíkan *crowded*
síge *all right / OK / so long*
síge lang *OK*
sigúro *perhaps*
sîli *pepper (chilli or bell pepper)*
silíd-tulugán *bedroom*
sílya *chair*
simbáhan(g) *church*
sinabúgan *sprinkled with / showered with*
sinasábi lang *just say*
sinigáng na bangús *stewed milkfish (with vinegar or tamarind and garlic)*
síno *who*
sóbra siguro *perhaps too much*
sóbre *envelope*
sombréro *hat*
sópas manók *chicken soup*
sorbétes *ice cream*
subáli't *but*
súlat *letter*
sumakáy *ride*
sumáma *to come / go with*
sumasáma (from *masama*, adj.) *becoming worse*
sumayáw *danced*
sumisíkat *shining*
sumúlat *write*

sumunód po kayó sa ákin *please follow me*
sungáyin *charge with his horn*
susúlat *will write*
street guide *street guide*
táksi *taxi*
tagá *from (place of origin)*
tagapagdalá ng singsíng *ring bearer*
tagapaglútò *cook*
tahánan *home*
tahímik *quiet*
talagá *really*
talóng *eggplant / aubergine*
tálì *string*
támà *right / correct*
tandáng *rooster*
tangháli *midday*
tanghalían *lunch*
táo pò *anyone at home*
tápa *sliced fried beef*
tapós *afterwards / then*
tatlóng béses isáng áraw *three times a day*
tátay *father*
tátayô *will stand*
téka *just a moment / wait a minute*
telépono *telephone*
tenyénte *captain*
téna *let's go*
térnong sáya *a lady's long gown (of Spanish origin)*
tíket *ticket*
tíket ninyó *your ticket*
tig/ tiga *each*
tigatlóng píso *three pesos each*
timbángan *scales*
tinanggáp *received*
tinanóng *was asked*
tinápay *bread*
tinatáwag *calling*
tindáhan *store*
tindáhan ng laruán *toy store*
tindá(ng) damít *clothes for sale*
tindéra/ tindéro *vendor / sales assistant*
tingnán *look*
tingnan ko ngâ *let me see / examine*
tingnan ninyó / mo *you have a look*
tinulúngan *helped*
títingnan ko *let me see*
tiráhan *residence / address*
tíya *aunt*

tiyán ko *my stomach*
totoó *true*
tíyo *uncle*
tóyo *soy sauce*
tradisyón(g) *tradition*
tsá *tea*
tséke *cheque*
tsubíbo *ferris wheel*
tsupér *(boat) driver*
túbig *water*
tugtúgin *music*
tulóy *as a result / as well*
tumátakbo *running*
tumáwag *call*
tumawíd ka *you cross*
tumígil *stopped*
tumingín *look*
tumugtóg *played*
tumúlong *helped*
tumútunóg *making a sound*
tungkól sa *about*
tutulúngan *will help*
tuwáng-tuwâ *happy*
tuwíng Linggó *every Sunday*
ubos ná *ran out / consumed / finished*
ulán *rain*
úlo niyá *his / her head*
umakyát *climb up*
umága *morning*
umalís *departed*
umarkilá ng bangkâ *to hire a boat*
uminóm *to drink*
umiklî *to become short*
umórder *to order*
umórder pa táyo *let's order some more*
umulán *rained*
úna *first*
úpang *in order to / so that*
útang na loób *debt of gratitude*
uulítin *will repeat*
walâ *no/ none*
waláng asáwa *not married / unmarried*
wala báng táwad *any chance of a discount?*
wala póng anumán *you're welcome*
yárì sa *made of*
yátà *I think*
yelo *ice*

ENGLISH–TAGALOG GLOSSARY

All verbs in this glossary are in the root form unless otherwise indicated.

about *tungkol sa*
accompanied *isinama*
according to *sang-ayon sa*
add *magdagdag*
afternoon *hapon*
afterwards/ then *pagkatapos / tapos*
again/ once more *muli*
agree *sang-ayon*
agree, I *oo nga*
airport *paliparan*
alight/ get off *baba*
all in all/ altogether *lahat-lahat*
all right/ OK/ so long *o, sige*
alone *nag-iisa*
already *na*
also *saka; rin / din*
always *lagi*
America *America*
and *at*
animal *hayop*
anywhere *kahit saan*
apparently *daw / raw*
apritada *apritada (a kind of main dish, fried)*
arm *bisig*
around *paligid*
arrive *dating*
arrival *dating*
as a result/ as well *tuloy*
ask (for something) *hingi*
ask (a question) *tanong*
assorted *sarisari(ng)*
at *nasa (**prefix**)*
at *sa*
attractive *kaakit-akit*
attach *kabit*
aunt *tiya*
(I'm) available *puwede ako*

(newborn) baby *sanggol*
bachelor *binata*
bamboo *kawayan*

banana *saging*
band *banda*
baptism *binyagan*
barrio *baryo*
bathroom *paliguan/ banyo*
beautiful *maganda*
because *kasi/ dahil sa/ sapagka't*
bed *kama*
bedroom *silid-tulugan*
behind/ at the back *likuran*
big *malaki*
(quite) big *malaki-laki*
bigger *mas malaki*
bitter melon *ampalaya*
black *itim*
blackboard *pisara*
bland/ flat in taste *matabang*
blouse *blusa*
boat (canoe) *bangka*
(to go) boating *mamangka*
body *katawan*
boiled rice *kanin*
book *aklat*
borrow *hiram*
borrow money *nangungutang*
bother *abala*
(I) bought *may binili ako(ng)*
box *kahon*
bread *tinapay*
breakfast *almusal*
(to have) breakfast *mag-almusal*
brother *kapatid*
brother (older) *kuya*
brother-in-law *bayaw*
bucket *balde*
buntal (Philippine fibre) *buntal*
bunting *palawit*
but *pero/ subali't*
buy *bili*
(to) buy for *ibili*

cabbage *repolyo*
call *tawag*
camera *kamera*
can/ possible *maaari/ puwede*
capital *puhunan*
captain *kapitan/ tenyente*
car *kotse*
cart *karosa*
carved *inukit*
Catholic *katoliko*
chair *silya*
chaos *kaguluhan*
(to) change *magpalit*
cheap *mura*
cheque *tseke*
chicken *manok*
chicken soup *sopas manok*
child *bata/anak*
choose *pili*
(to) choose from *mapagpipilian*
church *simbahan*
classmates *kaklase*
clean *malinis*
clever/ good at *magaling/ marunong*
climb *akyat*
climb up *umakyat*
clothes *damit*
cockfight *sabong*
cockpit *sabungan*
coconut, young *murang niyog*
cold *malamig*
colour *kulay*
colourful *makulay*
come on *halikayo*
(to) come with/ go with *sumama*
companion *kasama*
concern *pag-alaala*
consort *abay*
consume *ubos*
contest *labanan / paligsahan*
cook *luto*
cook (noun) *tagapagluto*
corner *kanto*
count *bilang*
cross *tawid*
crowded *siksikan*
crown *korona*
curtain *kurtina*
custom *kaugalian*

dance *sayaw*
dancing *pagsayaw*

darken *dumidilim*
daughter *anak*
day/ sun *araw*
decoration *dekorasyon*
(a) delicacy *kutsinta/dila-dila*
delicious *masarap*
depart *alis*
departure *alis*
destination *punta*
diarrhoea *pagtatae*
difficult/ poor *mahirap*
dirty *marumi*
disturbance *pang-aabala/abala*
disappear *mawala*
do *gawa*
don't *huwag*
double *pandalawahan*
dozen *dosena*
dressmaker *modista*
(to) drink *uminom*
drinking glass *baso*
drinks *inumin*
drive *ligid*
(boat) driver *tsuper*
during *noon*

each *tig/tiga*
early *nang maaga*
earnestly *lubusan(g)*
easily *madali(ng)*
eat *kain*
eggplant/ aubergine *talong*
embarrassed *nahihiya*
embarrassing *nakakahiya*
embroidered *burdado(ng)*
England *Inglaterra*
(to) enjoy *mag-enjoy*
enquire *magtanong*
envelope *sobre*
environment *kapaligiran*
everybody *lahat*
every day *araw-araw*
exchange *(ang) palit*
expensive *mahal*
eyes *mata*

family *pamilya*
fan *pamaypay*
far *malayo*
fare *pamasahe*
fast *mabilis*
father *tatay/ ama/ itay*
favourite *paborito*

feast day *pista(ng)*
feed *pinakakain*
female/ woman *babae*
ferris wheel *tsubibo*
fiesta *pista*
fifteen *labinlima*
(to) find *humanap*
fine/pretty *maganda*
(I'm) fine *mabuti rin naman*
finger food to go with drinks *pulutan*
finished/ consumed *naubos*
fireworks *paputok*
first *una*
fish *isda*
fisherman *mangingisda*
fishing *nangingisda*
fish pond *palaisdaan*
fixed/ arranged *inayos*
flag *bandera/ bandila*
flood *baha*
flower *bulaklak*
food/ eating *pagkain*
food preparation *handa*
follow *sunod*
for *para sa*
forget *kalimutan*
fragrant *mabango*
frame *kuwadro*
fresh *sariwa(ng)*
friend *kaibigan*
from *buhat sa/ galing sa*
from (origin) *taga*
fruit *prutas*
fruit trees *punong kahoy*

games *palaro*
gardenia *rosal*
gifts *pasalubong/ regalo*
(to) be given *ibigay*
get/fetch *kuha*
give *bigay*
(to) give around *pamigay*
go *punta*
godchild *inaanak*
godfather *ninong*
godmother *ninang*
going to *papunta sa*
good *mabuti*
good afternoon *magandang hapon*
goodbye *paalam*
good evening (formal) *magandang gabi po*
good morning *magandang umaga*

gore *suwagin*
grandchild *apo*
grandfather *lolo*
grandmother *lola*
grass *damo*
grilled *inihaw*
guava *bayabas*
guest/ visitor *bisita/ panauhin*
guyabano (soursap) *guyabano*

haircut *gupit*
(to have a) haircut *magpagupit*
hair *buhok*
hand *kamay*
hand over *abot*
handkerchiefs *panyolito*
happy *maligaya(ng)/ masaya tuwang-tuwa*
has/ have *may/ mayroon*
help *tulong*
hat *sombrero*
hen *inahin*
her *kaniya(ng)*
here *dito*
here is *heto*
hesitate *mag-aatubili*
high *mataas*
hire *arkila*
(to) hire a boat *umarkila ng bangka*
his/ her *niya*
hold *hawak*
home *bahay*
honeymoon *pulot-gata*
hook with a pole *sungkit*
(I) hope *sana*
horse *kabayo*
hot *mainit*
hour *oras*
house *bahay*
how are you (formal singular) *kumusta kayo*
how many/ a few *ilan(g)*
how much *magkano*
how much is it? *magkano naman* (informal plural)
(to) hurry *daliin*
hurting/ painful *masakit*
husband *asawa*

ice cream *sorbetes*
idea *ideya*
if/ when *kapag/ kung*
ilangilang *ilangilang flower*

immediately *kaagad*
improve *bumuti*
in *nasa/sa*
(to) include *isama*
including *kasama*
in order to/ so that *upang*
isn't it? *hindi ba*
inside *sa loob (ng)*
instead of *sa halip na*
instead *kundi*
invited *imbitado/ kumbidado*

job *gawain*

kind *mabait*
kinds *uri*
kissing the hand *nagmamano*
knife *kutsilyo*
know *alam*

lanzones (fruit similar to lychees) *lansones*
last night *kagabi*
last week *noong isang linggo*
later *mamaya*
learn *matuto*
leave *alis*
left *kaliwa*
letter *sulat*
life *buhay*
(I) like *gusto ko*
like (comparison) *katulad ng*
like that *ganiyan/ ganoon*
living/ residence *nakatira*
long *mahaba*
look after *bahala*
look *tingnan/ tumingin*
looks/ appears/ seems *mukhang*
loose *maluwag/maluwang*
loosely *nang maluwag*
lose *malulugi*
love *gusto*
lunch *tanghalian*
lying down *nakahiga*

made of *yari sa*
(to) make *gumawa*
man/ male *lalaki*
mango *mangga*
many/ plenty *marami(ng)*
many of *karamihan*
map *mapa*
margarine *mantikilya*
market *palengke*
married *ikinasal*

massage *masahe*
matches *posporo*
measurement *sukat*
medicine *gamot*
midday *tanghali*
might/ cow *baka*
milk *gatas*
milkfish *bangus*
money *pera/ kuwarta*
more *higit/ mas lalo*
morning *umaga*
mother *nanay/ inay/ ina*
mouth *bibig*
Mrs *ginang*
music *tugtugin*
must/should *dapat*
my *ko*

name *pangalan*
nape *batok*
near *malapit, sa may*
nearest *pinakamalapit*
need *kailangan*
neighbours *kapitbahay*
nephew *pamangkin*
new *bago*
next/ beside *sa tabi*
next time *sa susunod*
next week *sa isang linggo*
nice *masarap*
niece *pamangkin*
night *gabi*
no *hindi*
no/ none *wala*
noodles cooked in the Filipino way *pansit*
noticed *napansin*
now *na / ngayon*
number *numero*

of/ of the *ng*
of course *aba oo/ aba oo naman*
offering *paghahain/pag-aalay*
officemates *kaopisina*
officiating *nagseseremonya*
often *kadalasan*
on *nasa/sa*
one *isa*
only/just *lang*
opened *ibinuka*
opinion *palagay*
or *o kaya'y*
oranges *dalanghita*
(to) order *umorder*

other *iba*
our *namin*

pak choi *pechay*
parade *parada*
parcel *pakete*
parents *magulang*
park *parke*
party *salu-salo*
pass *abot*
passenger *pasahero*
passport *pasaporte*
pawpaw *papaya*
payment *bayad*
(to) pay with *ipambayad*
peace *katahimikan*
pen *bolpen*
pencil *lapis*
pepper *paminta/ sili*
perhaps *siguro*
petrol *gasolina*
photograph/ picture *larawan*
photographer *retratista*
picture *retrato*
pineapple *pinya*
place *lugar*
planting *pagtanim*
plants *halaman*
(a) plate of *isang plato (ng)*
plate *plato/ pinggan*
play *laro*
playground *palaruan*
pleased to meet you (formal) *ikinagagalak ko kayong makilala*
pleased *nasiyahan*
(to) post *ihulog*
prawns *hipon*
prepare *handa*
prepared food *naghanda*
prescriptions *reseta*
pretty *maganda*
price *halaga*
priest *pari*
problem *problema*
put *lagay*

queen *reyna*
quiet *tahimik*

rain *ulan*
reach *abot*
read *basa*
really *talaga*
reception *handaan*

receipt *resibo*
receive *tanggap*
recommend *rekomenda*
refreshment *pampalamig*
reins *renda*
repeat *ulit*
replace *palitan*
residence/ address *tirahan*
return *balik*
rice cakes *kakanin*
rice field *palayan*
rich *mayaman*
rid *sakay*
ride *sumakay*
right (direction) *kanan*
right/ correct *tama*
ring bearer *tagapagdala ng singsing*
ripe *hinog*
road/ way/ path *daan*
room *kuwarto/ quarter/ one fourth*
rooster *tandang*
rubbish *basura*
run *takbo*

sack *sako*
salt *asin*
Saturday *Sabado*
sauce/ dressing *sarsa*
saucer *platito*
sauteed vegetable *ginisang gulay*
(the) savings *inimpok/ inipon*
saving money *nag-iipon ng pera*
say *sabi*
scales *timbangan*
(a) scarf *ng bandana*
sea *dagat*
see *kita*
seems like/ as if *parang*
sell *tinda*
(to) serve/ feed *pakainin*
serving *pagsisilbi*
shame *mahiya /hiya*
shine *sikat*
ship *barko*
shopping *pamimili*
short *maikli*
shortcomings *pagkukulang*
(to) shorten *paikliin / umikli*
single *pang-isahan*
sister (older) *ate*
sister *kapatid*
sister-in-law *hipag*

sit down *upo*
size *sukat*
skirt *palda*
sky *langit/ himpapawid*
sleep *tulog*
slightly *medyo*
small *maliit*
smelly *mabaho*
smile *ngiti*
so *pala*
sometimes *kung minsan*
son *anak*
so that/ in order to *para*
soy sauce *toyo*
spade *pala*
spend *gastos*
spouse *asawa*
spring rolls *lumpia*
sprinkle with *sabog*
squash *kalabasa*
squid adobo *adobong pusit*
stable *sabsaban*
stalls *puwesto*
stamp *selyo*
stand *tayo*
standing *nakatayo*
stewed milkfish (with vinegar or tamarind
    and garlic) *sinigang na bangus*
still *pa*
stomach *tiyan*
stomach ache *sakit ng tiyan*
stop *para / tigil / hinto*
store *tindahan*
straight *diretso/ tuwid*
street *kalye/ kalsada/ road*
street guide *street guide*
stretch *banat*
string *tali*
(to take a) stroll *mamasyal*
student *estudyante*
study *nag-aaral*
suckling pig *litson*
suddenly *bigla*
suffice/ that will do *puwede na*
suit *bagay*
suitcase *maleta*
Sunday *Linggo*
surprised *nagulat*
swallow *inom / lunok*
(to) swim *lumangoy*

table *mesa*
take *kuha*

(to) take from *kunan*
talk to *kausapin*
taxi *taksi*
tea *tsaa*
teacher *guro*
telephone *telepono*
tell *sabi*
terno (a long gown of Spanish origin)
    ternong saya
than *kaysa/ kaysa sa*
thank you *salamat*
thank you very much *maraming salamat*
that *iyan*
that (over there) *iyon*
that's all (just those) *iyan lang*
that's why *kaya*
the *ang*
then/ before *noon*
there *doon*
there is/ there are *may/mayroon*
throw *tapon*
these *ang mga ito*
thick *makapal*
thing *bagay*
think *mag-isip*
(I) think *yata*
this *ito / nito*
those *ang mga iyan*
ticket *tiket*
time *oras*
tired *pagod*
tire oneself, to *magpagod*
to *sa*
today *ngayong*
toilet *kubeta*
tomatoes *kamatis*
tomorrow *bukas*
tongue *dila*
tonight *mamayang gabi*
town *kabayanan*
toy *laruan(g)*
toy store *tindahan ng laruan*
tradition *tradisyon(g)*
travel *biyahe*
trip *paglalakbay*
true *totoo*
try *isukat*
two *dalawa*
typhoon *bagyo*

umbrella *payong*
uncle *tiyo*
understand *naiintindihan*

unmarried *walang asawa*
until *hanggang sa*

vacancy *bakante*
vacation *bakasyon*
vegetables *gulay*
vehicle *sasakyan*
vendor/ sales assistant *tindera/ tindero*
very/ too/ quite/ extremely *masyado(ng)*
village *baryo*
visit/ stop by *punta*

walk/ move, to *lumakad*
(to) walk straight ahead *dumiretso*
wallet *pitaka*
want *gusto / nais*
wash *hugas*
(to) watch *manood*
water *tubig*
water/ liquid *sabaw*
water buffalo *kalabaw*
we *tayo/ kami*
weather *panahon*
wedding *kasal/ kasalan*
wedding assistant(s) *(mga) abay sa kasal*
wedding dress *damit pangkasal*
week *linggo*
welcome *maligayang pagdating*
(you're) welcome *wala pong anuman / ano(ng)*
what *ano (ng), anu-ano (formal)*
what time *anong oras*
when *kailan*
when/ during *noong*
where (location) *nasaan*

where (direction) *saan*
which *alin*
while *habang*
whispering *bumubulong*
who *sino*
whole *buo*
whose *kanino*
why *bakit/ kung bakit*
wife *asawa*
window *bintana*
windy *humangin*
with *kasama*
wooden *kahoy*
(to) win *manalo*
wonder *taka*
work *trabaho*
(to) worry *mag-alala/ mag-isip*
worsen *sumasama*
woven *nilala(ng)*
wrapped *nakabalot*
wrapping paper *pambalot*
write *sulat*

year *taon*
yellow *dilaw*
yes (formal) *opo*
yesterday *kahapon*
yet *pa*
you (singular) *ka*
you (plural informal/ formal singular) *kayo*
youngest *pinakabunso*
your *ninyo/ inyong*